ADVANCE PRAISE FOR
YOUR MULTIMILLION DOLLAR EXIT

"*Your Multimillion-Dollar Exit* is a must-read. It spells out what a businessperson needs to think about in terms of a successful business exit and life exit. The end goal being to pay the least taxes, to transfer the most wealth, and to continue the business the way you envision it."

—**BOB MARGOLIS**, entrepreneur,
Chief Executive Officer at TM Development

"Wayne Zell has been an invaluable advisor to me personally and to my business partners. I've watched him work closely with other successful entrepreneurs as well. He has an unparalleled grasp of complex legal issues, an ability to explain those issues clearly, and a genuine desire to provide bespoke legal advice that takes into account each of his clients' unique needs and aspirations. In this book, he turns his considerable skills to providing concise, practical, and detailed advice to entrepreneurs that are either considering an exit from their business or, if they are not, should be planning *now* for one in the future. Reading this book is the next best thing to sitting down with Wayne one on one. Truthfully, every entrepreneur should do both."

—**ELI COHEN**, Managing Director at GenTrust Wealth
Management and Catenary Alternatives Asset Management LLC

"The tools and real-life stories in *Your Multimillion-Dollar Exit* are essential ingredients in an entrepreneur's tool kit for designing a comprehensive exit plan, whether the exit is anticipated or unanticipated."

—**MARIO DELUCA**, CPA, JD, LLM, Partner at Crowe LLP

"Wayne's new book, *Your Multimillion-Dollar Exit*, is a must-read. I personally wouldn't have been able to position my IT services business for a successful sale without Wayne's knowledge, multidisciplinary experience, and practical advice."

—**DAVID EISNER**, Founder, former CEO, and Chairman at Dataprise, Inc.

"I was delighted to learn Wayne was writing a book for entrepreneurs—and frankly, any businessperson—about transitions and exits. I know that it's far too easy to focus on growing your business and defer these critical issues. I've known Wayne for decades and worked with him on several company exits, and now as a long-term client in estate and tax issues. I can't think of anyone who could be more valuable and insightful in helping entrepreneurs to optimize results while protecting their families and legacies. He's the type of attorney I appreciate: a trusted advisor who says you "should" do this, not you "could" do this. This book should be at the top of your stack—it presents immediately applicable knowledge to numerous important aspects of your business and personal life."

—**JOHN BURTON**, entrepreneur, Co-Founder at Updata Ventures

"This is a book for every stage of entrepreneurship. Ideally, read it as you begin, but it serves at any stage. Wayne takes complex subjects and makes them simple. He takes emotionally fraught subjects and makes them easier to address. He takes your hard work and love and shows you how to turn it into value for you and your family."

—**KATRINA VANHUSS**, CEO at Turnkey for Good

"As an entrepreneur, founder, and CEO of multiple businesses, I understand the challenges and worries of how to protect one's wealth built through a business. *Your Multimillion-Dollar Exit* is an essential tool for all who want to craft a thoughtful plan to maximize the value they have created."

—**JOHN BECKER**, entrepreneur and CEO

"Too often, I find business owners who don't begin thinking about the consequences of selling their business until they are ready to exit. As Wayne illustrates in this book, that is extremely late in the game and puts the owner at a handicap trying to deal with structures and considerations that could've been codified years earlier while at the same time trying to be responsive to the pressures of transaction deadlines. Given Wayne's extensive experience, you should read *Your Multimillion-Dollar Exit*. It will provide you with the means to design a successful business exit that will greatly relieve your stress when that day comes."

—**PHIL NOLAN**, former CEO at Stanley, Inc.

"Whether you plan to exit your business in months or not for many years, Wayne Zell's *Your Multimillion-Dollar Exit* is the book for you. Zell has written an essential planning guide for the business owner. It is chock-full of the strategies, techniques, and tools Zell has developed and honed over decades of leadership as a CPA, a tax/business attorney, and an entrepreneur."

—**CATHI COHEN**, LCSW, CGP, Clinical Director and Founder at In Step

"Having coached, trained, and lived the life of an entrepreneur for over 30 years, I certainly understand the challenges and fears that go with it. This book is a critical tool in every business owner's planning arsenal. You can learn the legal, practical, and real-world advice that is necessary for success through this book…or you can learn the hard way!"

—**ROB JOLLES**, speaker, author, consultant, coach, and President at Jolles Associates, Inc.

"Your Multimillion-Dollar Exit contains a ton of rich and deep content for entrepreneurs and business owners, based upon Wayne Zell's 42 years' experience as a CPA and 37 years as a tax, business, and estate attorney. I know him well and have seen him in action. You need to read this book!"

—**STEVE GLADIS**, PhD, author, speaker, and CEO of Steve Gladis Leadership Partners

"Wayne Zell's newest book is a must-read for entrepreneurs and anyone who wants to be much more financially successful. I have known and worked with Wayne on financial matters for years and know firsthand that he is incredibly knowledgeable and skilled at what he does, with proven results. Entrepreneurs who care about their financial future should pick up this book without hesitation and follow his expert advice."

—**ARNOLD PUNARO**, Major General, USMC (Ret.), and CEO at The Punaro Group

"Wayne Zell has written a book for entrepreneurs about entrepreneurs who want to craft a thoughtful plan to exit their businesses and leave their legacies intact."

—**PETER D. AQUINO**, Chairman and CEO at SeaChange International

YOUR MULTIMILLION-DOLLAR EXIT

THE ENTREPRENEUR'S BUSINESS SUCCESS(ION) PLANNER

A BLUEPRINT FOR WEALTH GUIDE

WAYNE M. ZELL, JD, CPA

HOUNDSTOOTH
PRESS

COPYRIGHT © 2023 WAYNE M. ZELL, JD, CPA
All rights reserved.

No part of this book may be reproduced in any form or by any electronic or mechanical means, including information storage and retrieval systems, without written permission from the author, except for the use of brief quotations in a book review.

YOUR MULTI-MILLION DOLLAR EXIT
The Entrepreneur's Business Success(ion) Planner: A Blueprint for Wealth Guide
First Edition

ISBN 978-1-5445-3991-1   *Hardcover*
        978-1-5445-3990-4   *Paperback*
        978-1-5445-3989-8   *Ebook*

DISCLAIMER

While he is both an attorney and a certified public accountant, the author is not providing legal, tax, investment, or financial advice or any specific recommendations beyond planning what's best for your own individual situation. The reader should consult with his or her own financial, legal, tax, and other professional advisors to determine what is appropriate for his or her own situation.

CONTENTS

Foreword *by Eric Castro*   xiii

Introduction   xv

Executive Summary: Tying Together the Lessons Learned   xxiii

1. The Ideal Business Success(ion) Planning Framework   1
2. My Best Business Success(ion) Exit Strategies   43
3. What Is My Business Worth?   89
4. What Success(ion) Exit Strategy Works Best for Me?   119
5. What's the Exit Process?   199
6. Now That I've Exited, What's Next?   299

Acknowledgments   315

Glossary   321

Notes   335

Index   345

FOREWORD

by ERIC CASTRO

Co-Founder, BHG Money, a multibillion-dollar source
of financing for professionals and businesses

When my brother Bobby and I started Bankers Healthcare Group with our partner, Al, in 2001, we had an ambitious vision of where we wanted to go. More than two decades later, we have realized that vision, but after many starts and stops and after overcoming many bumps and bruises. Today, BHG Money serves as a trusted partner to hundreds of thousands of clients, helping them achieve their business and personal goals.

Wayne Zell has been an incredibly important part of our journey. His legal advice, coupled with a great growth and business mindset, has made our lives more secure. It's helped us focus on our personal and business matters and stop worrying about the unexpected, unanticipated events we all fear—disability and death. In addition, his rare combination of tax, legal, and business knowledge sets him apart from most other advisers.

Your Multimillion-Dollar Exit captures Wayne's decades of experience in a way that makes the complex clear and the daunting tasks understandable and manageable. He brings together his knowledge of tax, estate, and business planning in a no-nonsense manner that is useful for entrepreneurs just starting out and others who are well on their way to a successful exit.

I wish I had had the benefit of Wayne's expertise in the early days of BHG. We might've avoided some of the mistakes that entrepreneurs inevitably make as we experimented and grew our business. As you venture on your entrepreneurial journey, don't forget that you need good advisers by your side and tools to help you navigate rough waters that may lie ahead.

I heartily endorse this book as an entrepreneur's essential tool kit, full of stories and examples, one that you should keep on your desk and refer to constantly as you have questions through your entrepreneurial journey.

INTRODUCTION

One Saturday afternoon several years ago, I received a call from a friend of one of my kids. He was frantic. His father had just died suddenly and unexpectedly. He was frozen with fear and anxiety. I had begun working with his dad on estate planning and Business Success(ion)™ planning,[1] but we hadn't even started the process when I received the dismal news.

The father had started a government contracting business and had received a small investment from two close friends with experience in the space. He was a "service-disabled veteran," which qualified his business for special treatment under the Small Business Administration rules. Most of his contracts were "service-disabled veteran organization" small business contracts, meaning that a business had to be owned 51% or more by a service-disabled veteran to be able to bid on a government contract.

Like many entrepreneurs, the father did not have a will or any other documents to plan for his death or disability. Fortunately, I had experience in both estate planning and business planning and went to work with the family on formulating a framework to protect the founder's investment in his business.

We leaped into action. We formed a board of directors consisting of the two outside investors who had extensive experience in government contracting, two family members, and me. We studied and analyzed the financial performance of the business, mobilized an accounting firm to give us current financial information, and, with the help of the experienced investors, recruited managers to try to replace the dynamic founder.

The founder had been building a successful business that essentially did government contract work for the US Department of State and other agencies in the cybersecurity space. The founder had developed a uniquely successful internal proposal-generating engine that identified contracts on which to bid that fell within the company's expertise. The managers stepped in and continued to respond to government proposals for work, created a significant pipeline of new business, and serviced existing business successfully.

Meanwhile, the board met monthly to ensure the continued growth of the business and evaluate its operations and performance. Once the business stabilized and continued growing, I introduced several investment bankers who were experienced in the government contracting field. The board's goal was to determine whether the company could be sold and, if so, at what price and when.

INTRODUCTION

Most of the investment bankers felt that because of the company's focus on small business set-aside work, it would have a difficult time being sold and that, even if it could be sold, the business would fetch no more than $10–$11 million.

One investment banker was much more positive. He felt that the company could be sold, and at a much higher price than the others projected. We signed an engagement letter with the investment banker and proceeded into an auction process to sell the business. Several months later, after negotiating definitive agreements with the chosen purchaser—a private equity (PE) fund just entering the government contracting business—we closed the transaction, yielding the family and other investors over $29 million!

> **DEEPER DIVE**
> To help provide a level playing field for small businesses, the US government limits competition for certain contracts to small businesses. Those contracts are called small business set-asides, and they help small businesses compete for and win federal contracts.

Fortunately, this story had a successful ending that arose from the founder's unexpected exit. Not all these stories end positively or happily.

What if you die or become permanently disabled unexpectedly? Do you have a will or trust in place to determine who receives your business and other assets? When will they have access to the business and other assets?

Who will run the business if you are unable to?

How will you replace the income lost from the business to support your family if you can't work?

Even if you have done some basic estate planning (i.e., you have a will or trust) and have maybe even purchased some life insurance to provide cash to support your family, have you thought about the death tax that may need to be paid to the federal government and the states on the value of your business after you are gone?

If you want to sell your business, what have you done to prepare for the sale?

How much do you want for your business—that is, what do you think it is worth? What do others think the business is worth? If there is a difference between what you want and what someone might pay you for the business, what are the gaps causing the difference in value, and how do you identify and fill these value gaps? Who can help you answer these questions?

If you want your family to keep the business, is anyone in the family able to run it? Or will you have to hire outside managers to run the business if the family can't? Can the business afford to hire these folks?

The key lesson learned from this first story is that planning for your exit should start at the very beginning of the business. I know you've seen and heard this before from others. But having lived through the business evolution and exits of hundreds of entrepreneurs, I am writing this book to provide you with the essential tools so you can start planning now

INTRODUCTION

and benefit from my 37+ years of experience as a transactional tax, estate planning, and corporate attorney and 42+ years as a tax accountant.

I use many examples throughout the book based upon real-life events but have changed the names and facts to protect the identities of my clients. So if you see your first name associated with a transaction you don't recognize or another's name linked to what appears to be your transaction, it's intentional.

If you are an action-oriented entrepreneur who wants to do the best you can for your family and yourself and maximize the value you have created through years of hard work, then you want to read this book and refer to portions of it from time to time as your business evolves or as you start new ventures. It will provide you with resources and a framework to successfully plan for your chosen exit. To help you navigate the core concepts of this book, I've included a glossary of key terms. These terms are denoted throughout the text by italics.

This book contains an executive summary and six main chapters as illustrated in the diagram following this introduction.

- The Executive Summary outlines the Lessons Learned included at the end of each section in every chapter. It summarizes the entire book at the beginning so you can focus your reading and planning.

- Chapter 1, "The Ideal Business Success(ion) Planning Framework," emphasizes that the time to begin planning is now and provides three basic frameworks to follow depending on the status of your business. It also presents the story of the hypothetical father–daughter team of George and Hannah and their thriving business, 3DP.

- Chapter 2, "My Best Business Success(ion) Exit Strategies," focuses on how to plan for unexpected exits and how to build a well-planned exit.

- Chapter 3, "What Is My Business Worth?" asks you to determine what your business is worth to you and others who might be interested in purchasing it.

- Chapter 4, "What Success(ion) Exit Strategy Works Best for Me?" invites you to concentrate on what exit strategy works best for you, your employees, and your family.

- Chapter 5, "What's the Exit Process?" dives deep into the process of preparing your company for sale and shows you how to successfully sell your business.

- Chapter 6, "Now That I've Exited, What's Next?" delves into your post-exit planning and helps you focus on what matters most in your life.

Each Chapter contains:

- **Deeper Dives** that explain and provide background on some of the technical details described in the book

INTRODUCTION

- **Ideas in Action** that present real-world examples of the concepts included in each chapter

- **Lessons Learned** at the end of each section that capture the key points

- **The Story of George and Hannah** that follows the journey of two fictional entrepreneurs, George and his daughter Hannah, as they navigate George's successful exit from his business

You have also seen references to Business Success(ion) planning on the cover and throughout the book. I created this stylized term (which is in the process of being registered with the US Patent and Trademark Office) to intentionally tie your Business Success(ion) planning to the success of your business. Every owner should have a Business Success(ion) plan, and having one will contribute to the ultimate success of your business!

I hope you receive as much enjoyment from this book as I did in creating it, and, more importantly, that you rely on it as a key resource in your entrepreneurial journey.

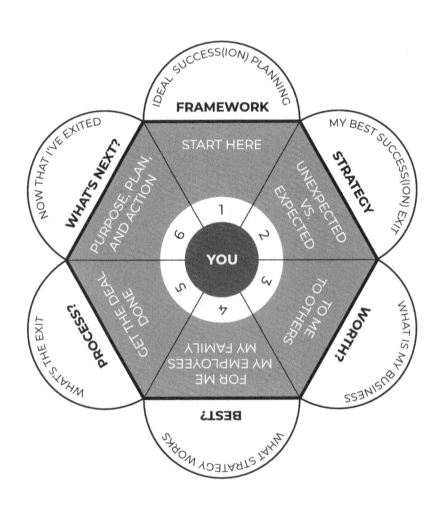

EXECUTIVE SUMMARY

TYING TOGETHER THE LESSONS LEARNED

> "Success is not final; failure is not fatal:
> it is the courage to continue that counts."
> —WINSTON CHURCHILL

CHAPTER 1

THE IDEAL BUSINESS SUCCESS(ION) PLANNING FRAMEWORK

I know it's hard for you to take time out from growing your business. It may also be hard to focus on what happens to your business if you die or become disabled; it's not something you want to dwell on or discuss with anyone. However, you can alleviate your fear and reduce your anxiety by creating an exit plan now.

If you are just starting out, you should begin planning your exit at the outset of your entrepreneurial journey.

- It's not too late if you are late to the game.

- Failure to plan exposes you and your loved ones to unnecessary economic and psychological risks.

- Planning for the unexpected and a well-planned exit will give you peace of mind and allow you to sleep, work, and function better.

First, you need to identify the framework that fits your business: the Rocket Ship, the Legacy/Stall-Out, or the Free Fall/End Game framework. Focus on what you can control today. If you haven't done so already, you should try to build your business around the *Entrepreneurial Operating System*® (EOS) described in Gino Wickman's book *Traction* so you can be the Rocket Ship!

Then you should identify and prepare for your ultimate exit plan by planning for the unexpected today: use a *revocable trust* to own your business and a *management succession plan* (MSP) to keep it running. In designing and implementing an exit plan that suits your business, consider the following:

- The revocable trust will allow you and your family to avoid the delays and costs of going to court to gain access to your assets and control your business.

- The MSP, if properly linked to your *estate planning*, will allow you to anticipate the unexpected by constructing a short-term plan to run your business if you die or become disabled and a long-term plan that will ease the burden on your family and employees by giving them a road map of what to do and who should implement the plan if you are out of pocket.

- The ultimate Business Success(ion) exit plan should combine short-term and long-term plans if the unexpected happens to you, with a thoughtful long-term exit plan suited to your business and desires.

CHAPTER 2

MY BEST BUSINESS SUCCESS(ION) EXIT STRATEGIES

Planning for the unexpected starts with the creation of a revocable trust to own your business interest. By transferring your business to your trust, you will save your heirs time and money they would otherwise expend by having to go to court to transfer your business in the event of your incapacity or death. You should do the following:

- Appoint someone capable of serving as your successor *trustee* who can stand in your shoes to run the business; think about naming a successor co-trustee or trustees if you are concerned about the ability of the named successor to serve alone. After all, it's a big, important job to serve as a trustee.

- Think carefully about who should serve in this critical role and whether you want them to have sole and exclusive power over what happens to your business if you are not around. They are *fiduciaries* with the highest level of responsibility to manage your assets prudently and competently for the benefit of your loved ones.

You should also build an MSP that is linked to your revocable trust. This means that your trustee will be bound to follow the terms of your MSP, which will name and empower individuals who will oversee daily business operations, how they will be paid, and whether they will be entitled to receive incentives in the form of cash or *equity* bonuses if they perform exceptionally well.

The MSP should also name a board of directors or managers who will be responsible and accountable for managing the employees you name to run the business and managing the business itself. Your MSP should

- leave the long-term decisions to the board if you have not yet formulated your ultimate exit plan;
- include your trustees, family members, and professionals who have experience and knowledge of your business and industry; and
- be updated periodically as you develop and refine your long-term objectives.

If you want to try to sell your business in a *merger or an acquisition* with an unrelated third party, you could sell all your business to a strategic buyer, or part or all of your business to a *private equity* (PE) firm or *family office*. Before you identify the buyer, try to determine what you want from the transaction on an after-tax basis and understand what your business is worth before you jump in. Consider the following in structuring your transaction:

- If you take back stock in the transaction, you will need to consider tax, securities law, and other legal issues and restrictions relating

EXECUTIVE SUMMARY

to your receipt of stock or other securities in another company so you are not caught off guard in completing the transaction.

- For example, are the shares you are receiving taxable to you on receipt without your having the ability to sell them right away to pay the taxes on what you receive?

- Even if you aren't required to pay tax immediately on the securities you receive, you need to understand whether you will ever be able to sell the securities to receive the value of your business and additional upside.

You will also want to investigate who the potential buyer is, their track record with prior acquisitions, and what to expect after the transaction is closed by talking with other sellers, investment bankers, accountants, attorneys, and advisors who have dealt with the potential buyer.

Additionally, if you take *rollover equity* in the ongoing business, make sure you do so in the most tax-efficient manner possible.

Alternatively, you may want to sell your business to your management team.

- They will need to procure financing to buy you out, which may not be easy to obtain. If your business generates enough cash flow to finance the sale and continue growing the company, a private or commercial lender may be willing to finance the deal and your management team may be inclined to engage in a buyout transaction.

- If the business is not generating enough cash to pay off the purchase price, grow the company, and provide incentives to the continuing managers, then you could finance the deal, but you would be assuming the risk of nonpayment.
    - In that case, you could try to protect yourself by taking a *security interest* in the stock or *membership interests* you are selling as well as the assets of the business.
    - You could further protect yourself by having the managers and their spouses guarantee the obligation to pay you back. With adequate protections, a seller-financed sale may work, but your anxiety could be significant if the economy turns sour or the managers do not perform.

Another exit alternative may involve using an *employee stock ownership plan* (ESOP) to transfer your shares to your employees. If you choose an ESOP, consider the following:

- You must be willing to spend significant funds to establish an ESOP and comply with ongoing, complex Internal Revenue Service (IRS) and Department of Labor (DOL) regulations.

- The business must generate sufficient cash flow to service any leverage used to purchase your stock or company stock. More importantly, an ESOP only works if your employees are motivated to share in the risks and rewards of owning a business.

You could also attempt to take your company public, either through an *initial public offering* (IPO) or a *special purpose acquisition company* (SPAC), neither of which is an easy task in a volatile stock market.

EXECUTIVE SUMMARY

- These techniques also require significant professional assistance from experienced and expensive securities and corporate attorneys and accounting firms to comply quarterly and annually with complex securities laws.

- While IPOs work best with Rocket Ships on the way off the launchpad, SPACs can provide fuel from an IPO to incumbent businesses that need financing and have a growth plan to succeed.

CHAPTER 3

WHAT IS MY BUSINESS WORTH?

You should work with a *Certified Financial Planner* (CFP) or an accountant to evaluate all your assets, including the value of your business, to help you determine how much you will need to retire or otherwise stop working (if you need to) and live comfortably for the rest of your life. This exercise should do the following:

- Address your "wants" as well as your "needs" to ensure you are not being too conservative with your planning.

- Project how much you are currently taking home from the business after taxes and whether you should continue holding on to the business vs. selling it.

- Base your conclusions regarding the value of your business on assumptions that are supported by facts. What you think the business is worth may not reconcile with what others think.

To start the process of understanding the value of your business, you may want to talk with other business owners and industry experts.

- You could hire a business appraiser to give you an informal valuation for your business before putting it on the market.

- You don't need a formal report unless you need the valuation to support pretransaction estate planning or gifting strategies, and those valuations are invariably lower than a valuation to determine your strategic value to an interested buyer.

You should identify and fill the *value gaps* in your business before putting it up for sale.

- Hire a consultant to help you identify the value gaps.

- Understand that going concern value and *goodwill* represent the most significant portion of the value of your business.

- Structure your sale to include selling *personal goodwill* where appropriate to minimize the overall tax impact.

Appraisers and corporate development officers typically use *discounted cash flow* analysis to value your business. In performing this analysis, appraisers should consider the following:

- They must use a *discount rate* that measures your *cost of capital* to predict the present value of your cash flows.

EXECUTIVE SUMMARY

- This involves a mixture of math and art, and great subjectivity may reveal a discount rate that, if too high, will devalue your business.

- If the discount rate is low, the risk of operating your business may be low, leading to a higher overall value.

In most cases, buyers and investment bankers will typically use multiples of *earnings before interest, taxes, depreciation, and amortization* (EBITDA) to value your business. Remember to complete these steps:

- Adjust your EBITDA for personal expenses and nonrecurring items that may have artificially depressed (or increased) earnings.

- Use cash flow to determine the value of a business, but don't ignore intangible assets (e.g., technology) that might increase the multiple and value.

Ultimately, the value of your business is what a willing buyer will pay you and what you will be willing to accept.

CHAPTER 4

WHAT SUCCESS(ION) EXIT STRATEGY WORKS BEST FOR ME?

Your exit strategy should compare the after-tax proceeds you will receive if you sell your business with what you would earn, after taxes, if you held on to the business.

- If you will earn more over a short period of time than you would if you sell the business, then keep working and transition the business in a different way.

- Of course, if the net proceeds from a sale eclipse your after-tax earnings; if you have reached the point of exhaustion and must get out of the business; or if you believe technology, economic, or other changes are coming that will inhibit your ability to continue earning at the level you have in the past, then selling now may make the most sense.

If you decide to sell, structure the sale in the most tax-efficient manner.

- The buyer will try to write off the value of your assets by treating the sale as an asset purchase.

- The structure of the transaction will impact the net after-tax result greatly.

- If the buyer wins out and you are compelled to structure the deal as an asset purchase for tax purposes, you should try to negotiate an increase in your purchase price to offset the increase in taxes you will incur because of the buyer's attempts to deduct the value of your goodwill and other tangible assets.

Many of you will try to reduce state income taxes by changing your *residency* to a low- or no-income tax state before the sale occurs. Be careful!

EXECUTIVE SUMMARY

- Your resident state's auditors will closely examine a variety of factors to determine whether you really intended to establish *domicile*/residency in another state.

- Maintaining a permanent home in your original home state, among other things, may defeat your attempts at avoiding home-state income tax on the sale.

Earnouts may be an important component in the overall purchase price for your business. That is, the buyer may be unwilling to pay 100% cash at closing and may demand that a portion of the price be held back until you achieve certain revenue or *profit* targets. In that case, consider these important factors:

- You will want to control your ability to earn the earnout and to receive a portion of the targeted payment if you come close to the targets.

- This may include keeping your team together during the earnout period, such that if the buyer terminates key team members without cause or switches them to other parts of the buyer's company, the earnout should be accelerated.

- Try to prohibit the buyer from loading up your business with new costs and overhead that would prevent you from meeting profit or EBITDA targets.

In any case, you must be ready to relinquish control of your business once you sell or transfer it. It's hard leaving your passion, but with proper planning, you can do so methodically and in style. To be comfortable in leaving your legacy, consider these factors:

- You will want to identify buyers who will perpetuate the vision and values you have spent so much time and effort developing and implementing. This includes treating your employees and customers with the greatest of care.

- The purchase agreement should include provisions about continuing your employees as part of the acquiring company's workforce and providing them with equal or better pay and benefits than they currently enjoy.

You may want to provide change-in-control bonuses to individuals who have been particularly helpful to you in building the business, preparing the business for sale, and consummating the transaction. These bonuses are paid only if the deal closes and could be based on a dollar amount or a percentage of the net proceeds received in the transaction.

To incentivize key employees to stay with the company after closing, you may want to offer them retention bonuses payable over the time they remain with the company.

- These bonuses may be part of the transaction proceeds, be paid by the buyer, or be split between you and the buyer.

- They should be accelerated if the buyer terminates the employee without cause or the employee leaves with good reason.

EXECUTIVE SUMMARY

In your *due diligence* of the buyer and in understanding how your firm will integrate into the buyer's operations, make sure you know what your employees will be paid, the benefits they will receive, and any obligations they will have (i.e., *noncompetes*) after the closing, to ensure they will remain with the company.

In addition to structuring and timing your estate planning well in advance of the sale of or exit from your business, you should consider different approaches to minimizing *gift and estate tax* upon your death, yet try to retain control over the assets as much as possible.

- These techniques may include combinations of *grantor retained annuity trusts* (GRATs), *intentionally defective grantor trusts* (IDGTs), *spousal lifetime access trusts* (SLATs), family holding companies, and *dynasty trusts*.

- Their utility will depend on whether the proceeds you expect to receive in the transaction will cause your overall estate to significantly exceed your lifetime exemptions from gift and estate taxes.

If you are charitably inclined, you should consider giving a portion of your wealth to charity either outright or in a manner that allows you or your heirs to receive benefits from a *charitable trust* during your lifetime or after you are gone.

- Every dollar donated to charity reduces your estate and the estate tax that could be triggered upon your death.

In summary, you can use *advanced estate planning* techniques that apply to your specific situation rather than a cookie-cutter approach that solves someone else's issues.

CHAPTER 5

WHAT'S THE EXIT PROCESS?

You should get your corporate house in order before approaching prospective sellers.

- This includes updating and completing your corporate minute book and stock ledger and approving of important prior transactions.

- You should also make sure that the ownership of your business is settled and that there are no outlier owners to whom you may have inadvertently promised equity.

You should have your attorney make sure the business is properly qualified and registered in all states and jurisdictions in which you operate. She should do the following:

- Review your contracts with customers and suppliers to make sure you don't have any noncompete, change-in-control, or other obligations that would impede or prevent the sale from occurring.

- Conduct a legal audit to ensure you are in compliance with all applicable laws and the provisions of your contracts, leases, and other agreements; no litigation or other claims are pending or

EXECUTIVE SUMMARY

threatened; you own or possess valid licenses to your intellectual property; and you have no environmental or other problems that will haunt you in the due diligence process or that can be corrected before starting due diligence.

Your chief financial officer and accounting firm should ensure your financial statements comply with *generally accepted accounting principles* (GAAP) and contain footnote disclosures about your accounting policies and positions. They should verify that all income tax, sales tax, payroll tax, and other tax returns have been timely filed and taxes have been timely paid. You must be ready to disclose any current or past audits and the results.

You will also need to verify that your employees have completed all necessary paperwork, including Form I-9, Form W-4, and *nondisclosure agreements* (NDAs) that protect your confidential information.

Moreover, it wouldn't hurt to check in with your customers and vendors regularly to ensure your strong relationships with them before the buyer starts snooping around.

Your team should include attorneys of various disciplines, a *certified public accountant* (CPA), a financial planner, an investment banker or a business broker (depending upon your situation), and a business appraiser if you need an indication of value in advance or if you engage in pretransaction estate planning.

Your Rock Star team will help you get ready for the acquisition.

- In addition to your regular attorney, you may want to expand your team to include a corporate attorney to lead the transaction, supported by specialists in tax, employee benefits, real estate, technology, and securities law, among other disciplines.

- Your CPA needs to have experience in preparing clients for acquisitions, a deep understanding of tax laws, and the capability to prepare GAAP-compliant financial statements.

The choice of whether to use an investment banker or a business broker may depend on the size of the transaction and whether you intend to engage many or few potential buyers.

- The investment banker may be most qualified to lead an auction process among potential buyers.

- The business broker may specialize in smaller deals with specific industry focus.

A financial planner will help you understand how a transaction will impact your financial future.

Once the team is assembled, you will need a strong nondisclosure agreement to prevent prospective buyers from disclosing or using your confidential information and from soliciting or engaging your employees, contractors, and clients. If you conduct an auction process:

- your investment banker (with the help of your attorney) will get the NDAs circulated and signed; and

- they will solicit *indications of interest* (IOIs) from various parties that will provide you with a sense of who may be interested in buying your business and the range of values they might be willing to pay for it.

Once you narrow down the list of potential buyers, you will seek *letters of intent* (LOIs) from your top choices.

You, together with your attorneys and your investment banker or business broker, will negotiate an LOI with a prospective buyer.

- The LOI will contain nonbinding provisions relating to the purchase price, the deal structure, key employee compensation and restrictions (e.g., noncompete provisions), escrows, holdbacks and earnouts, working capital targets, and other deal-specific matters.

- It will also include binding provisions that give the prospective buyer exclusive rights for a limited period of time to conduct due diligence and move toward a definitive purchase agreement, ensure confidentiality of the LOI terms, and guarantee other important provisions relating to fees and dispute resolution, among other things.

Once the LOI is negotiated and signed, your attorneys will begin the process of negotiating the definitive agreement, which is the focal point of the transaction.

- The definitive agreement includes details on the purchase price, how and when it will be paid, and whether any purchase-price adjustments must be made.

- It also contains extensive representations and warranties you and the buyer will need to give each other about your respective businesses (with the seller's being much more extensive); covenants (i.e., promises) such as noncompetition, confidentiality, and tax filing covenants; and indemnification and liability limitations.

You may want to consider having the buyer obtain representation and warranty (R&W) insurance to limit your liability for breaches of nonfundamental representations and warranties. Usually, you will need to share the cost of the insurance, but the benefits may well be worth the cost.

Regardless of whether you obtain R&W insurance coverage, you will be required to prepare detailed disclosure schedules that back up the purchase agreement and that map closely to the due diligence process.

- Preparing disclosure schedules is often the most tedious and time-consuming task in the purchase process.

- This step will be much easier if you have done your corporate housecleaning and built your data room in advance.

In addition to the definitive purchase agreement, you may need to negotiate and enter into escrow agreements, where a portion of the purchase price is held back to protect the buyer from breaches of representations and warranties and to ensure there is adequate working capital left in the business.

EXECUTIVE SUMMARY

The buyer may also need to enter into employment agreements with you and your key employees, retention agreements, option cancellation agreements, operating agreements for rollover equity, and other agreements that are ancillary but important to the overall transaction.

CHAPTER 6

NOW THAT I'VE EXITED, WHAT'S NEXT?

Once you have exited your business, your life isn't over:

- In some cases, you may begin to pursue dreams you've postponed or put on the back burner to build your business.

- You should take time to reflect on your life and the abundance you have created for yourself and others.

- More importantly, you should design or revive your ultimate purpose (if you haven't already) and your vision for your remaining years.

You may still have additional business aspirations—pursue them with the same passion and dedication you used to build your business.

You may want to improve your physical or mental health through exercise, diet, and new, healthy habits. Map out what you want to achieve and do it!

You may want to help others by volunteering your time with nonprofits; teaching or coaching in the local community or primary, secondary, or advanced degree institutions; or helping other entrepreneurs just starting their journey. Giving back is the greatest gift and reaps the greatest rewards. Plan out your days to include time to give back.

You may want to spend more time with your family, focusing on your kids and grandkids, nieces and nephews, siblings, and parents. Allocate all or part of your time and energy to your family. They need you and want you with them!

Whatever you want to pursue, document your purpose, create your vision, identify your core values, and set specific, measurable, achievable, relevant, and time-based (SMART) goals for each activity.

- Then create an action plan outlining how and when you will achieve those goals.

- Just because you've had a successful exit doesn't mean that you stop planning. In fact, planning never stops.

Go after your dreams, fill your bucket list, plan on how and when you will cross off the items on that list, and do it with all the passion and energy you possess! PMA![2]

YOUR MULTIMILLION-DOLLAR EXIT

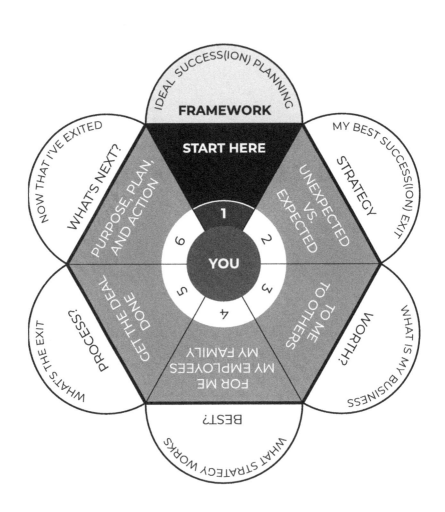

CHAPTER 1

THE IDEAL BUSINESS SUCCESS(ION) PLANNING FRAMEWORK

> "Someone's sitting in the shade today because someone planted a tree a long time ago."
> —WARREN BUFFETT

THE TIME TO PLAN IS AT THE BEGINNING— NOW! (AVOID UNEXPECTED EXITS)

I was 18 years old when I landed in Miami with 20 bucks in my pocket and clothes that fell out of my suitcase as they were coming off a conveyor belt because my brother and I had stuffed the only suitcase we had with duct tape. And so it's one of those stories of welcome to America and make the best of it.
—Ben Edson, entrepreneur, Founder and CEO of VariQ, a Capgemini Government Solutions Partner

Scan the QR code to watch the entire interview

youtube.com/ @ZellLaw/videos

Q*ue será, será,* or what will be, will be. Doris Day made the song by that name famous in the 1950s, and it still applies to most of us today.[3] Hoping for the best and doing nothing equates to no planning at all. And no planning can lead to ultimate disaster. If you're forced, due to unexpected events, to sell your business and *liquidate* your assets at a deep discount, then it may be too late to plan. However, if you are a motivated, forward-thinking entrepreneur, you still have time to plan, so read on.

You can do something to plan for the unexpected. You can anticipate the unknown. You just need to think ahead a little bit, instead of ignoring the possibility of failure, death, or *disability.*

If you are a growth-minded[4] entrepreneur who has infused "ninja innovation"[5] with a "founder's mentality"[6] into your business and employees, you have probably built your business with a clear mission, vision, values, and identity, based upon a well-conceived, dynamic, and properly executed business plan. Even if you are just starting out, this book contains resources and a road map that will help you in planning for the future. In either case, this book will help you create an effective Business Success(ion) exit plan with a well-defined conclusion to your entrepreneurial journey.

DEEPER DIVE

Ninja Innovation, by Gary Shapiro, equates the successful entrepreneur to a ninja warrior, based upon observations from his and his family's journeys to obtain their black belts in tae kwon do and his 30 years of experience in leading the Consumer Electronics Association. His bottom line: "to be successful, one must set goals; to achieve these goals, one must form a strategy; and to fully execute that strategy, one must never let failures get in the way." Rather, you must use your failures to get better. As a ninja entrepreneur, you won't win every battle; in fact, you may lose more than you win. Keep in mind that the status quo is only for the short term.

DEEPER DIVE

Businesses with a founder's mentality (Chris Zook and James Allen first wrote *The Founder's Mentality*) exude three basic traits:

1. The business has an insurgent mission; the company benefits underserved customers, redefines the rules of the industry, or creates new markets.
2. The founders have a frontline obsession; the founders obsess with customers, employees, and all details of the business, and typically drive sales, product development, or both.
3. Everyone in the company must have an owner's mindset; all employees at every level feel and act like the owner of the business, focusing on controlling costs, having a bias toward acting, and avoiding bureaucracy.

EXIT PLANNING MEANS DIFFERENT THINGS TO DIFFERENT PEOPLE

Business exit planning focuses on identifying and filling the *value gaps* in your business and leads you through the process of designing an exit plan or continuing to the next level by growing the business. To you as a business owner, it generally means selling the business or quitting and liquidating it. You may not realize that it also includes planning for unexpected, unanticipated exits caused by disability or death.

If you want to continue growing your business or retaining an ownership interest while someone else grows it for you, you may not have to exit the business; planning for your retirement or transitioning the business to someone else is a viable exit strategy. You've either decided to continue running the business as an absentee owner or take the business to the next level.

Some of you haven't even thought about what happens at the natural end of your business or even your life. Many of you don't want to talk (or even think) about having the business taken away from you or your family because of disability or death. In part, it's your laser focus on the business that makes you a successful entrepreneur; you have the uncanny ability to block out the negative what-ifs and capitalize on the "go for it," risk-embracing attitude to grow and operate your business.

You also may not want to anticipate negative events like death, disability, technology or product obsolescence, economic downturns, and the like.

Here are some common responses I get when I implore my clients to seriously consider exit planning:

I'm too busy pursuing my passion—building and growing my business.

The topics of death and disability scare me. They are too morbid and depressing to discuss. I'm a positive person and can't go there.

Nothing's going to happen to me. I'm in good physical and mental shape, I take care of myself, and my life expectancy is way longer than my business runway. I'll sell it before anything happens.

Think of the founder in the story I told in the Introduction. He was on the road to greatness when the unthinkable and unexpected happened.

You must plan for the inevitable from the beginning; otherwise, you will be leaving your family with potentially nothing or a heck of a lot less than what they could have received. In other words, it's better to plan for different outcomes than to do nothing at all. It's like dying without a will or *trust*—you can either leave the fate of your business to creditors and the state or leave your family in a comfortable position because you have planned for various contingencies. So you should plan to sell or give away your business, plan for what happens if you can't sell it, plan on how to keep the business in the family, and plan for unexpected events that may happen to you before you execute plan A, B, or C.

TODAY AND TOMORROW

As the *baby-boomer* generation ages, hundreds of thousands of businesses have become available for sale. *Mergers and acquisitions* may be hot today, but it may not be that way tomorrow, particularly if another recession or downturn in the economy occurs. Businesses function in cycles. There are economic highs and lows in every generation.

You must plan for both and take advantage of the highs when opportunities abound. **Hundreds of thousands of business owners may not be able to sell their businesses because there won't be buyers for every business that is available for sale.** Understanding this basic fact is critical to doing your Business Success(ion) planning.

For family-owned businesses, the prospects are even scarier. According to PwC's 2021 US Family Business Survey, only 24% of all family businesses successfully transition to the next generation. Moreover, while 58% of those businesses surveyed have succession plans, most of the plans are informal; only 24% report that they have a "robust, documented and communicated succession plan in place."[7] This means that more than 75% of every family business will not survive beyond the founder's generation. Of those surveyed, nearly 67% lack a cohesive Business Success(ion) plan. Pretty scary, huh?

You can do something to plan for the unexpected. You can anticipate the unknown. You just need to think ahead a little bit. Instead of ignoring the possibility of failure, death, disability, or market downturns, focus on what you need to do now to protect what you have built and are building. Protect your family. Don't wait—do it now.

DESIGN YOUR BUSINESS SUCCESS(ION) PLAN

Your Business Success(ion) planning process involves determining where your business is today and where it's headed.

- **Your Business Success(ion) plan will include a *management succession plan* (MSP) that focuses on unexpected events and a long-term exit plan you intend to follow if everything goes as expected.**

- You can design a plan customized to your specific situation. Whether you are in the very early stages of growing your business or operating a mature business, now is the time to prepare your Business Success(ion) plan.

Every Business Success(ion) plan looks different. The plan depends on

- your personal goals;
- how much you want to take out of the business;
- when you want to exit; and
- whether and how you want to leave a legacy for your family, employees, and customers.

It also anticipates the unexpected, in the form of an MSP.

MANAGEMENT SUCCESSION PLAN

Your MSP should contain a short-term component that outlines what would happen if you died or became disabled tomorrow. It also should include your longer-term strategy if the unexpected happens, which will vary depending on where your business falls within the three frameworks described in the next section. In addition to your MSP, your Business Success(ion) plan will include a long-term exit plan anticipating that everything goes according to your business plan.

You should address the following matters in the short-term portion of your MSP.

Name a Board of Directors or Board of Managers

This board would consist of the *trustee(s)* of your *revocable trust* who will hold and control your ownership interest in the business following your death or disability, one or more family members (who may or may not be your trustee), and two or three of your trusted advisors (who may be your attorney, *certified public accountant* (CPA), and/or a business advisor with familiarity of your business or industry).

1. If you are comfortable with your choice of trustee, then the trustee should have veto power over decisions made by the board.

2. If you are not entirely comfortable with your trustee controlling all decisions relating to the business or you need someone else to balance the decision-making of your chosen trustee, you could expand the list of trustees of your revocable trust to include some of the same people serving on the board or another person who is not serving on the board who has good business judgment, or give the trustee 1 vote out of many votes on the board.

3. In any case, your trust should require the trustee to be bound by the MSP, which would include voting in favor of the directors and officers you name in the plan.

4. Make sure you legally bind the board to follow your short-term plan. This may be for a short period, such as 3 to 6 months, until the board has had time to determine the best course of action for the company. Each board member should be required individually to accept the plan before being formally appointed to serve.

5. Establish whether and how board members will be compensated for their service:
    a. Professionals, such as attorneys and CPAs, may charge their hourly rates to serve.
    b. Other board members could charge an hourly rate as well, but you may need to establish compensation guidelines to avoid paying too much for the advisors in comparison to the value you receive.
    c. Consider giving the outside directors the right to receive a percentage of the profits from operations or from the sale of the business. This would incentivize them to keep their eyes on the business and ensure that the business remains profitable. Arguably, the aggregate percentage allocated to the board members should not exceed 5–10% of total net profits or net proceeds.

DEEPER DIVE

A "trust" simply refers to a legal relationship between you and your property. If you create a trust, you are called the "grantor," "settlor," or "trustor." You transfer legal title in the property to someone called a "trustee," who must hold the property for the benefit of someone known as the *beneficiary*. In a typical revocable trust, you can be the grantor, trustee, and beneficiary of your trust, retaining total control over the property you put in the trust. You also can appoint one or more trustees to manage your affairs if you become disabled/incapacitated or die. A "revocable" trust means you can change the trust at any time, add assets to it, or withdraw assets and funds from it without anyone else's involvement or permission.

THE IDEAL BUSINESS SUCCESS(ION) PLANNING FRAMEWORK

Instead of (or in addition to) appointing a *board of directors*—or board of managers in a *limited liability company* (LLC)—you could create and appoint a board of advisors as part of your MSP.

- A board of advisors may consist of some of the same individuals who might serve on your board of directors (or board of managers), but it is much less formal than a board of directors.

- The primary difference is that members of a board of advisors typically do not act in a *fiduciary capacity*, whereas a board of directors owes fiduciary duties to the corporation and its shareholders.

- These duties include the duty of care in managing the corporation, the duty of loyalty to do what is in the best interests of the shareholders and the corporation, and the duty to administer the business of the corporation prudently.

- By contrast, advisors act more like consultants to your business.

DEEPER DIVE

You've seen TV ads by financial firms touting that they are fiduciaries because they are required to "act in their client's best interest." In the world of trusts and businesses, it means much more. A fiduciary owes legal duties to the person whose interests they represent. In a trust or corporation, the trustee or director owes duties of care, loyalty, prudence, confidentiality, good faith, and disclosure. They not only must act in the best interest of the trust beneficiary or shareholders, but they also must take extra care to gather all material information relating to a decision before making it, act without conflicts of interest, make wise and prudent decisions regarding investments based upon the beneficiary's or shareholder's individual situation, keep confidential information secret, and provide full disclosure to the beneficiary or shareholder of everything under the trustee's or director's control. Failure to do this may result in a breach of fiduciary duty lawsuit and damages that could be awarded to the beneficiaries or shareholders. Clearly, a trustee or director cannot take assets belonging to the trust unless it provides the beneficiary or shareholder with adequate consideration or an advantage and results in no harm.

Advisors may be compensated in a manner like the board of directors or managers, but their participation in the business's net profits or net proceeds is typically much less than what a formal board of directors/managers receives, simply because the directors and managers bear greater responsibility and risk.

In either case, your MSP should outline the terms on which directors or advisors will participate in business activities and be compensated for their efforts. It is also a good idea to have a written contract with your directors/managers and advisors to specifically state the terms of their engagement, compensation, and *nondisclosure* provisions protecting your business secrets.

Name Who Will Serve (or Continue Serving) as Officers or Managers of Your Company

These officers or managers (i.e., president, chief operating officer, manager, chief financial officer, controller, and vice presidents or directors of sales, marketing, and manufacturing) will take over if you die or become disabled before the company is sold. If you have the right people serving in the right positions, consider whether the chair of the board of directors or managers should negotiate employment agreements with these folks to give them security and incentives to stay with the company.

1. You will need to periodically evaluate whether any or all of the critical positions at the company can be filled by the existing employees and whether they would be willing to continue working for the company if something happens to you.

2. You will need to allow existing employees to continue running the business until the board or trustee(s) find suitable replacement(s) or pursue a sale.

The long-term portion of the MSP emphasizes what should be done beyond the 3 to 6 months after you die or become disabled but before you have had a chance to execute your long-term expected exit plan. It can instruct and empower your board or management committee to take long-term actions, such as interviewing and hiring an investment banker, a business broker, and other team members to help manage the sale of the business or its assets, or recruiting and hiring a replacement executive team to keep the business running and profitable if a sale isn't feasible.

IDEAS IN ACTION

Ralph insisted on keeping his retail music business running indefinitely following his death. In fact, he included provisions in his trust to require that the business be continued after his death. His wife and sons had worked in the business extensively, and he believed they would want to continue the business long after he was gone. Unfortunately, his wife passed away and his sons decided they did not want to continue the business. Ralph's plan did not anticipate this important turn of events. Fortunately, his trust gave his trustees enough leeway so they could sell or shut down the business if necessary, but it provided no guidance on how to proceed.

What could Ralph have done differently? He could have created a road map of steps to take (in an MSP) if the family did not want to continue the business, including the following:

- Assembling a board of directors or board of advisors, with family and nonfamily members participating. The nonfamily members could include independent professionals or people knowledgeable in the retail music business.

- Instructing the board on whom to interview and hire as potential team members to assist with a sale process.

- Preparing projections for the business if he were no longer working.

- Ascertaining and filling the value gaps and determining the estimated value of the business while he was still alive.

- Creating a contingency plan in the event that the other plans did not come to fruition.

- Purchasing life and disability insurance in sufficient amounts to protect his family and the employees in the event of his untimely demise.

LONG-TERM EXPECTED EXIT PLAN

Once you have your MSP in place, you can continue dreaming and building your ultimate long-term exit plan. Chapter 2 outlines the typical strategies most owners use to exit their businesses and how they work, and Chapters 3–5 lay out the steps you should take to achieve a successful, intentional exit from your business.

MY PLAN VS. YOUR PLAN

Given my experience, my clients ask me every day what will happen when I die or if I become disabled. I assure them that I have created my own Business Success(ion) plan. We have an MSP in place that dictates who will run the business in the short run in the event of my sudden incapacity or death. It also contemplates how to pay for the short-term and long-term operation of the business in my absence and identifies outside attorneys to whom the practice can be transitioned with minimal disruption to our clients.

For our long-term expected plan, we have hired and are training younger generations of attorneys who will run the practice when I can't practice any longer. We have built an *Entrepreneurial Operating System* (EOS) with processes; the right people in the right spots; a 3-year, 5-year, and 10-year plan; data measuring our performance against the plan; and more.[8] We have also implemented a marketing plan to attract clients beyond my tenure.

My plan will be different from yours. My plan is designed for an entrepreneurial law firm, anticipating projected growth and infrastructure investments over the next several years, reduced time spent on the law practice after a sustained level of growth is achieved, and ultimately full retirement from the practice of law. If I die or become disabled before then, I have insurance and a detailed MSP and estate plan in place to protect my family, my employees, and my clients.

You should design an MSP with a short-term and longer-term contingency plan in case things end unexpectedly. You should also have a long-term exit plan that anticipates your personal exit at some point in the future, even if the exit is not by a sale of the company but by retirement and turning over the reins to the next group of managers. Just remember to incorporate a customized MSP into your Business Success(ion) strategy. I have provided you with an example of an MSP for a closely held business on my website at *www.waynezell.com/resources*.

The next section outlines 3 frameworks for Business Success(ion) planning. Which framework you use depends on the stage of your business (insurgency, incumbency, or Free Fall/End Game) and how you prefer to exit from your business.

LESSONS LEARNED
- Business Success(ion) exit planning should begin when you form your business.
- Your Business Success(ion) exit plan should anticipate the unexpected in the form of an MSP linked to your estate *planning* documents, and a long-term expected exit plan.

- The short-term component of your MSP should name a board of directors or managers who are responsible for carrying on the business or selling it. It should also name the individuals responsible for running the day-to-day operations. The MSP should include details on everyone's compensation structure and the terms of their employment or engagement.
- The long-term component of your MSP should provide a road map to your successors as to what you want to accomplish in your absence and the steps they should take to get there.
- The long-term expected exit plan encompasses your business plan and long-term strategy for the business to achieve its ultimate success and is dealt with extensively in the chapters that follow.
- Selling your business may become more difficult as *baby boomers* age and the supply of available businesses far exceeds the demand.
- Family-owned businesses have little chance of success beyond the founder's generation unless detailed Business Success(ion) plans are made and implemented.

THREE FRAMEWORKS FOR BUSINESS SUCCESS(ION) PLANNING

I'll never forget the day I left school at the end of 9th grade. I was 14 years old. I don't think I was a difficult kid, but I always had a lot of curiosity, a lot of questions. And I would always raise my hand in class. A lot of teachers were just frustrated by it, but I didn't catch on to the question, so I had to ask it again and again. I think that's what happened with the teachers. I just wanted to leave school because I felt like

I wasn't worthy. So, I told my mom, and she gave me no heartburn. She said, 'Bob, you could be anything you want to be.'

—Bobby Castro, entrepreneur and Co-Founder of a multibillion-dollar corporation

Scan the QR code to watch the entire interview

youtube.com/
@ZellLaw/videos

I suggest three frameworks for your Business Success(ion) plan: one for the business that is growing exponentially (also referred to as the Rocket Ship or insurgent); one for the stalled-out or Legacy business (the Legacy, Lifestyle, or Stall-Out, or the incumbent); and one for businesses in free fall or where you are at the end of the entrepreneurial game (Free Fall or End Game), where the business has hit a sudden downturn, you die or become disabled unexpectedly before you have completed your journey, or otherwise you are so tired of the business that you need to get out now.

THE ROCKET SHIP FRAMEWORK

1. Be a Ninja Innovator, Be Shockproof, and Have an EOS

You may already know this, but every business that is a true Rocket Ship has the following characteristics of ninja innovation:

- They want to be better than the competition.
- They have the right team that operates cohesively as a team.

- They recognize that taking risks is unavoidable.
- They are disciplined and if they fail, they fail spectacularly.
- They have a dynamic strategy that allows for quick tactical changes.
- They are ethical.
- They hire the best people and pursue the most innovative road to success.
- They are creative and daring in how they approach business and solve problems.
- They are part of something that is more than an individual effort.
- They are stealthy and virtually invisible in how they get things done.[9]

True Rocket Ships are also "shockproof"; their leaders align strategy, organization, and talent to create lasting success:

- They have a strategy on how they intend to reach their stated objectives, creating value by differentiating themselves from competitors and focusing on the right markets and customers.

- They have an organization that designs work at the individual, team, and organizational levels. It addresses the processes performed to execute the strategy.

- They have talented individuals or teams who have unique and valued capabilities.

- Their leaders are focused on how they and those they lead can grow and learn every day to improve strategy execution and results.[10]

Your Rocket Ship may have all these characteristics, and you may run your business with discipline that coordinates the various moving parts like a well-oiled machine. If you are not there yet, **you may want to implement an EOS that will allow you to strengthen the 6 key components of operating your business.** If you are just starting out or trying to gain control of your soaring Rocket Ship, you should take the following actions:

- You must have a mission (your ultimate purpose) and a vision that propel the business forward and are embraced by your workforce.

- You need to recruit, hire, and keep the right people in the right roles in your business.

- You must set attainable goals over specified periods and collect financial and performance data to measure your performance against your goals.

- You need to construct, document, and refine the processes you use in your business.

- You must make sure you meet frequently with your management team to measure your progress against your plan.

An EOS requires that you construct a 10-year business plan. I know what you're saying: "Any plan that projects the future of the business 10 years from now is total b—s—t." It's not that you can predict where your business will be in 10 years; rather, you are projecting

THE IDEAL BUSINESS SUCCESS(ION) PLANNING FRAMEWORK

where you want to be. The beauty of this approach is that your exit plan may end before the 10-year term expires. You may want to sell the business or take it public in that time frame. Rocket Ships usually take off and are acquired by third parties, sell securities to the public, or flame out.

In any case, stay focused on your vision and goals and implement a dynamic strategic plan to achieve them. Assemble the right people in the right seats, and get everyone flying in the same direction. Taking your eye off the ball and pursuing multiple disjointed goals will divert your attention and dilute your efforts to achieve your ultimate exit.

2. Identify and Prepare for Your Business Success(ion) Plan

Since the Rocket Ship is built to fly and succeed wildly, you probably envision selling your business to the highest bidder or taking the business public and reaping the benefits of providing liquidity (i.e., cash, spending money) for you and your investors. Here's how to get there:

- Get your corporate house in order and build a data room with your business history, financial and tax information, employee details, contracts, leases and agreements, benefit plan filings and documents, and other information about your business that is readily accessible to you, your advisors, and potential buyers.

- Assemble a team of professionals to help you achieve your successful launch and ultimate exit. The team will grow over time as you add key advisors in various disciplines at the appropriate times. These advisors should include attorneys,

CPAs, financial planners, investment bankers and business brokers, investment advisors, insurance experts, and others who can ensure your growth and success.

- Engage advisors who can help you identify the value gaps in your business before you offer your business for sale.

The plan also involves thinking about your family by hiring a financial planner to ensure your resources are sufficient to carry you through your life, constructing a smart and effective estate plan to provide ongoing resources in the form of life insurance and liquid assets, and executing trusts, wills, and ancillary documents to ensure everyone's safety and comfort.

It may also involve *advanced estate planning* if the expected proceeds from the sale of your Rocket Ship are expected to cause your wealth to exceed the death and inheritance tax exemption thresholds. Advanced estate planning techniques will help reduce the amount of federal and state death and inheritance taxes that could be levied upon your death or the death of your surviving partner or spouse.

If you plan to allow your employees to participate in the growth of your business, you may want to provide them with *equity-based incentives*. These incentives may include actual stock or ownership interests in the business, stock options or LLC equity options or warrants, *phantom stock/equity* or stock/equity appreciation rights, or simply an agreement to pay a portion of the net proceeds of the business to the employees when the business is sold.

THE IDEAL BUSINESS SUCCESS(ION) PLANNING FRAMEWORK

Whether you employ advanced estate planning techniques or provide equity-based incentives to employees, directors, managers, or contractors, you should hire an appraiser to value your business and the equity interests being transferred. An appraisal report will be required if you gift or sell ownership interests to family members or trusts for their benefit. A report may also be required if you issue equity to employees or contractors to comply with federal tax law.

These topics are discussed in detail in Chapters 3–5.

3. Expect the Unexpected

In addition to suggesting ways to plan for the ultimate exit in the form of a sale or public offering, you need to plan for the unexpected, even if you have a fast-moving Rocket Ship.

> **IDEAS IN ACTION**
>
> Caroline, age 35, was building a fast-moving Rocket Ship that was developing a disruptive technology. Her company had just signed on new customers and was growing exponentially. Then lightning struck—she was diagnosed with stage 4 ovarian cancer and died suddenly three months later. As the dynamic founder of her company, she was deeply involved in controlling all aspects of the business. She didn't have an MSP, a will, or any other estate planning documents in place.

Unlike Caroline, you will need to create a sound, basic estate plan and an MSP to anticipate and counter the short-run and longer-term effects of an early, unanticipated exit. Your plan may involve appointing specific individuals to continue operating the business in the event of your untimely death or disability. It may also require that you appoint a committee or board to oversee the business operators and ensure the family is protected. **Your basic estate plan should be synchronized with the MSP regardless of what stage your business is in.**

THE LEGACY OR LIFESTYLE FRAMEWORK

You may be building a business that is designed to generate consistent *income* for you until you are ready to retire and perhaps continue during retirement. In this scenario, you are not convinced the business can be sold at enough of a *profit* to make it worth selling, or you may be generating consistent cash flow from the business to meet your and your family's needs. I refer to this type of business as a Legacy business.

IDEAS IN ACTION

Let's say your wholly owned business consistently generates $500,000 of profit per year without you having to work more than 20 hours per week. You have 10 employees who make good salaries and bonuses and receive good benefits from your company. If the business passes the profits through to you (as an *S corporation* or LLC taxed as a partnership), you might take home $300,000 after taxes. If you could sell the business for $2 million, would you be interested in the sale? After taxes, you might be able to pocket $1.4 million in a sale. Still interested? If you kept working in the business for an additional 5 years, you could net more after taxes. Is the sale still worth pursuing? Factoring in the present value of a dollar, the business may or may not be worth selling now.

- What if you must work 40- to 60-hour weeks to generate the same amount of cash flow?

THE IDEAL BUSINESS SUCCESS(ION) PLANNING FRAMEWORK

- What if you've reached burnout status and just can't spend any more time or effort on the business?

- What if you could delegate the 20 hours you were spending to someone else and still pocket the profits from the business?

You need to ask yourself these and other questions to decide whether to sell your business or keep it running.

Another scenario may involve a business that has hit "stall-out" status.[11] When a business experiences a sudden slowdown in growth, it is in stall-out mode. Your Rocket Ship or other formerly growing business loses the momentum it needs to continue growing, burdened by increased organizational complexity, loss or dilution of its mission or your passion, a significant economic downturn, or technological obsolescence of your products or services.

In either the Legacy or Stall-Out business model, the Business Success(ion) planning framework looks different from the Rocket Ship framework, in that the management of growth is no longer top of mind to you as the founder. Instead, you must focus on maintaining the status quo and generating consistent cash flow for you and your family. Selling your business may not be a viable option.

IDEAS IN ACTION

Chris, age 60, owns 100% of his electrical supply business. The business did well while Chris was running the day-to-day operations. When Chris was forced to leave the business in the charge of a "trusted" employee, he came back after several months to find that profits had become losses and revenues had declined as well. On further investigation into the causes of these changes, Chris's accountant discovered that the trusted employee should not have been trusted at all because the employee had diverted projects to a side business the employee was running and had absconded with contracts worth hundreds of thousands of dollars to the business.

IDEAS IN ACTION

Marlene, age 36, entrusted her chief financial officer (CFO) with running the business when she had unscheduled surgery. She granted the CFO complete power (under a broadly drafted financial power of attorney) to handle all aspects of the business without any oversight. When Marlene recovered and returned to work, she discovered that the CFO had increased his salary and stolen assets from the business, leaving the business on the verge of bankruptcy.

IDEAS IN ACTION

Angie, age 42, passed away after a bout with cancer and left the business to her partner to run. Unfortunately, Angie's partner had no experience in running a business and had not managed the finances for the family. In addition, Angie had failed to purchase any life insurance that would have provided liquidity to the family in the event of her untimely death. The business declined rapidly under the stewardship of Angie's partner, leaving nothing left to salvage in the end.

Each of these cases illustrates the absolute necessity of having a comprehensive, short-term MSP. The plans could look something like this:

THE IDEAL BUSINESS SUCCESS(ION) PLANNING FRAMEWORK

- In Chris's case, he could have named the trusted employee as the individual in charge of operations, but he could have also named additional individuals who would be responsible for different aspects of the business, providing for separation of duties and responsibilities to protect the business from fraud, misappropriation, or theft. Chris's plan could have been as follows:
    - Name the trusted employee as chief of operations (COO) and appoint another individual not subject to the COO's control to separately manage the financial aspects of the business, such as a CFO or controller who reports directly to the board of directors.
    - Require the COO and CFO/controller to sign checks together, or have a family member or another trusted employee or board member to countersign checks, approve contracts, and take certain actions that require oversight.
    - Engage an independent accountant to review the internally prepared books and records monthly to ensure that nothing unusual was occurring.
    - Appoint a board of directors or managers to further oversee operations in Chris's absence.

- Marlene should have been more careful in appointing 1 person with total power over her business operations.
    - Like Chris, she could have named a second individual to serve as a co-agent with the CFO to ensure that two sets of eyes were always on every transaction and more than one signature was on checks over a certain amount.
    - Obviously, this decision boils down to a matter of trust in the individuals who are working with you. However,

temptations can be great in these types of situations, and even people with the greatest integrity may pursue alternative, nefarious ends.
- Stated differently, having a second set of eyes on your business if you're not around is a really good idea. Marlene's short-term MSP could have included that important requirement.

- Angie should have built her estate plan to include a revocable trust to hold her ownership interest in the business to avoid *probate*.
  - She should have also named a trustee other than (or in addition to) her partner to serve as business trustee in charge of managing the business and ensuring that profits are distributed to the trust and made available to the family.
  - If the individual named as business trustee serves with others who are involved in operating the business, then there is a check and balance on the business trustee to ensure that everything is being operated smoothly and with integrity.

These are all components of a successful short-term MSP. What distinguishes the Stalled-Out or Legacy business from the Rocket Ship is a greater emphasis and urgency on short-term planning. In addition to planning for the unexpected, a Legacy business may establish a glide path for the founder to exit gracefully, particularly if the business cannot be sold to a third party for an acceptable price.

Your MSP could empower inside managers to continue operating the business or recruit outsiders to take over your responsibilities, with oversight from an independent board of directors or committee consisting of your business trustee, outside advisors, and family members.

Recruiting your replacement is not as easy as it sounds. It may take months of seeking the right candidate, interviewing, and offering the candidate enough in the form of compensation, upside, and security to make it worthwhile to the replacement. It may also require that the company hire more than 1 individual to fill your shoes. Because of potential delays in hiring a replacement, the immediate, short-term plan should permit existing employees to continue running the business with oversight from a board or committee appointed in the MSP.

The long-term plan for a Legacy business with stable or even declining revenues and profits may include an exit strategy where you can sell percentages of the business over time to those who continue to operate the business if the family or existing employees cannot manage the business successfully. It may also permit the family to continue owning a share of the business after the management structure has changed, but it should contain significant protections for the family so that the ongoing managers cannot abuse their position and manipulate the business to favor the managers to the detriment of the family.

IDEAS IN ACTION

Recently, Frank, age 55, passed away and left his business interest to his spouse without properly planning for the transition. He was a trusting soul who decided to transition his wealth advisory practice to an individual he had recently met. The parties brought in an outside attorney to draft an operating agreement for the business. The operating

> agreement did not prevent the new partner—who had not built the business and had no preexisting relationship with Frank's clients—from manipulating the business in his favor and tripling his compensation after Frank died. The family was devastated by the wanton actions of the successor partner. There were no constraints on his coming in and changing the overall economics of the business to his benefit and to the family's detriment.

How can you protect your family against unscrupulous investors, business partners, or employees who may take action that adversely impacts your family? Have your attorney construct an operating agreement or shareholders' agreement at the beginning that clearly anticipates what happens if you die or become disabled, and either plans for continued ownership of all or part of the business by the family or requires a buyout of the family using the proceeds of life insurance purchased specifically for this purpose. Some business exit planners refer to this as a *buy-sell agreement*, but it is more than just providing insurance proceeds to your family if you die or become permanently disabled.

The buy-sell agreement may include a provision that requires the business or interested employees to purchase your interest upon your death or disability. Your company or partners could purchase life insurance, the proceeds of which could be used to purchase your ownership interest in the company and provide liquidity to your family.

If the insurance proceeds are insufficient, you can require the company to secure outside financing to purchase the interest or self-finance the buyout with a *promissory note* secured by your ownership interest. The remaining owners could personally guarantee any financing used to buy your business interest. Your financing documents could also require the company and the continuing shareholders to provide transparency in the business's financial reporting and operations and other covenants to prevent manipulation of earnings and cash flow (e.g., precluding unwarranted increases in managers' salaries and bonuses unless mutually agreed-upon performance targets are met).

If you want to protect your family by purchasing enough life insurance to replace all or a portion of the value of the business upon your death, then use a life insurance trust or an LLC taxed as a partnership to receive the insurance proceeds and purchase your ownership interest in the business.

If there are no remaining owners (i.e., you are the sole owner), your plan can transition ownership to others provided that sufficient insurance proceeds and additional financing are made available to the family to transfer the interest. For example, I have used an LLC to purchase the founder's ownership interest, where the LLC was owned by those employees who were willing and able to continue operating the business after the founder's death. The LLC used the insurance proceeds to purchase the sole owner's interest in the business.

In brief, the framework for a family Legacy or Lifestyle business or a Stalled-Out business really emphasizes short-term protections for the founder and the founder's family. Long-term protection can be achieved simply by building out the MSP with protections in the form of advanced estate planning, a system of checks and balances, and a functional board or committee that oversees the operators of the business.

THE FREE FALL OR END GAME FRAMEWORK

If your business is in a free fall or if you just discovered that you are suffering from a terminal illness, you still need an MSP, but the urgency of implementing it accelerates dramatically.[12] Time becomes scarce in this framework, so you must carefully focus on maximizing the value of what you have and transitioning what's left in the best way possible.

In addition to basic estate planning techniques discussed above, if the value of your business and estate is large enough, you should consider applying advanced estate planning techniques, such as a *private annuity* or *self-canceling installment note*, where your life expectancy is shortened due to terminal illness or severe incapacity and you want the business to continue after you are gone. These techniques (discussed in detail in Chapter 4) make sense where your business and your remaining assets are worth more than the federal and state *estate tax* exemptions and you have no immediate plans to sell the business to an unrelated third party. You are basically transferring the business to a family member or a trust for their benefit in exchange for an annuity or installment debt payments that terminate upon your death. In that case, the value of the business interest is excluded from your gross estate, and the annuity and note are not included in your estate either.

Other planning techniques (described in Chapter 4) may apply where you do not want to include the value of the business in your estate because the total estate exceeds the available lifetime exemptions from estate tax. Even if your taxable estate includes the value of your business, your executor or trustee may be able to defer payment of any federal estate tax for as long as 15 years at a very low interest rate if you die owning at least 35% of the business and certain other requirements are met. If the value of your business and other assets is less than the estate tax exemptions, you could just hold on to the business until your death, in which case your heirs will receive an increase in the income tax basis of your ownership interest (also referred to as a "step-up" in basis) without adverse death-tax consequences.

If a free fall appears imminent, you need to stabilize the business before it's too late. The Business Success(ion) plan morphs into more of a *liquidation* strategy to reap the benefits of any valuable assets the business may continue to hold. In other words, if the *liquidation value* of your business (i.e., you can only sell the business for the current separate value of the tangible assets, such as *accounts receivable*, inventory, and furniture, fixtures, and equipment) is greater than its value as a going concern, it may be best to sell off the assets piecemeal and generate as much profit as possible.[13] Again, your CPA and attorney, as well as a business appraiser and business broker, may be very useful in managing this process, depending on the stage of the free fall and the amount of money involved. Your advisors working together on your behalf may be able to generate more than salvage value.

Why not establish relationships with these professionals now instead of waiting for the inevitable to happen? Who knows? They may be able to sell the business as a going concern and reap greater benefits for your family.

IDEAS IN ACTION

I represented Ed (age 60), who owned a property and casualty insurance agency. He was in poor health and hired me to take immediate action to ensure the assets in his business would be transitioned properly and efficiently rather than in a distressed sale. First, we built his basic estate plan so the business interest would pass to his heirs outside the probate process. Second, we developed a short-term strategy in an MSP to facilitate the sale of the business, even if he was no longer alive, leaving his daughter in charge of the transition. We were able to sell the business successfully following Ed's death, providing cash flow to his family while balancing the buyer's need to minimize his risk in the acquisition.

Finally, in either a free fall or an unanticipated illness situation, you can minimize the disruption to your family by ensuring that your business interest is held by a revocable living trust linked to a clearly drafted MSP. By taking this extra step, your executor or *personal representative* will not be forced to shepherd the business interest through probate, which is a court-driven process that may cause unnecessary delays and costs.

SUMMARY OF THE THREE FRAMEWORKS

All three Business Success(ion) planning frameworks employ the same components, but they emphasize different aspects depending on the stage the business is in. In every case, you need to follow these steps:

1. **Identify the stage of your business, and plan from there.**
    a. If you are an insurgent running a Rocket Ship, you hopefully have plenty of time to plan for a successful exit and engage in short-term planning for unexpected events.
    b. If you are an incumbent running a Legacy, Lifestyle, or Stalled-Out business, the business is stable but not growing. You will need to decide how you want to

transition the business so that either the family remains in charge, or inside or outside managers continue operating the business if the business cannot be sold.

c. If you're in a Free Fall or at the End Game, estate planning becomes paramount because time is of the essence before it is too late to plan. You will also need the help of your advisors to maximize what you have left.

2. **Develop an MSP with short-term and long-term components.**
    a. The short-term part of the plan identifies specific individuals who will operate the business in your absence.
        i. It appoints a committee or board of trusted advisors and family members to oversee the operators and ensure that the business is being operated in the best interests of your family.
        ii. The plan will also incorporate estate planning to minimize delays and disruptions caused by the probate process, avoid unnecessary taxes and costs, and provide protection for your family following death or disability.
    b. The long-term portion of the MSP will focus on an exit strategy for you from the business or for the business if you are no longer there.
        i. Ideally, if the business can be sold, your appointed board will court investment bankers or business brokers to assist in the transition of the business so proceeds can be generated for the family.
        ii. If the business is too small or unattractive to investment bankers or business brokers, there may

still be interested buyers; your team can assist in finding them and transitioning ownership to a third party.

iii. Apart from selling or liquidating your business, you can develop a strategy to transition the business to family members or managers who may be willing to continue operating the business for the benefit of the family.

Let's focus on a comprehensive example in the next section to get you thinking about which framework to apply in your business and the details of your Business Success(ion) exit plan.

LESSONS LEARNED

- Identify the framework that fits your business—the Rocket Ship, the Legacy/Stall-Out, or the Free Fall/End Game framework—and focus on what you can control today.
- If you haven't done so already, build your business as a ninja innovator that is shockproof, with an EOS, so you can be the Rocket Ship!
- Identify and prepare for your ultimate Business Success(ion) exit plan by planning for the unexpected today, using a revocable trust to own your business and an MSP to keep it running, and then designing an exit plan that suits your business.

THE STORY OF GEORGE AND HANNAH
A COMPREHENSIVE EXAMPLE

The following comprehensive example covers topics discussed throughout this book. I've indicated where in the book to find further reading on each topic as it relates to the example.

George is an entrepreneur. He just turned 65 and learned that he has stage 4 prostate cancer. But that's not stopping him.

George and his daughter Hannah run a 3D printing specialty business called 3DP. George started the business about 10 years ago. In addition to manufacturing and selling 3D printers and parts, 3DP also does rapid prototyping and additive manufacturing for certain select clients. An engineer by training, George developed new techniques of building 3D printers and software programming that further enable the production of 3D printers. These techniques have not been patented but are proprietary and vitally important to George's business. The business has plenty of competition, and profit margins in some areas are starting to decline because of aggressive marketing strategies by 3DP's competitors, whereas other areas of the business have become extremely lucrative.

Hannah, age 35, also a computer science engineer and married with two kids, joined George in the business about 6 years ago. She's now running the research and technology side of the business and makes around $150,000 per year, plus annual performance bonuses of up to 40% of her salary. Hannah has become adept in taking George's brilliant ideas and using her own ingenuity to create and commercialize new ways of building, manufacturing, and utilizing 3D printers. She's also quite concerned about the worldwide housing crisis and is interested in taking the technologies to manufacture 3D-printed housing rapidly and safely for those in need.

Besides Hannah, George has two other key employees who are indispensable to the business. One of them runs sales and marketing (her salary is $250,000, plus annual performance bonuses of up to 30% of her salary), and the other runs manufacturing (his salary is $200,000, plus bonuses of up to 25% of his salary). George is paid $350,000 per year in salary and does not receive a bonus (but receives 100% of profits distributed after salaries, bonuses, and other expenses). The business is currently generating around $30 million in revenue per year, has about 100 employees, and is profitable, generating about $5 million in profit per year. It has been growing at a rate of about 10% per year on average.

Further, 3DP is an LLC that has elected to be taxed as an S corporation. George owns 100% of the *membership interests* of the LLC. See Chapter 4.

Moreover, 3DP leases its facilities from another LLC that George owns in his own name. The facility is worth about $1.5 million, and George owns 100% of the LLC. 3DP pays the LLC just enough to cover the mortgage, taxes, utilities, and insurance on the property. There is an outstanding mortgage of $500,000 on the property.

George has two other children: Ian and Jessica. Neither is involved with the business, and both have their own careers. Both Ian and Jessica are married, and Jessica has one child.

George has no idea what his business is worth but is currently evaluating all his options. He believes that he has about $1 million in retirement assets and around $2 million in liquid assets. He also owns a home that is worth about $1 million. He has no life insurance currently.

George wants to know what to do with his business.

- Should George just give his ownership in 3DP to Hannah because she is deeply involved in the business? Should he leave any part of the business to the other kids, Ian and Jessica? Should he wait until he dies or do it during his lifetime? See Chapters 2–4 for more insight on ideas George should consider.

- George has no idea what the business is worth to a potential buyer. What should he do to determine the value of 3DP? See Chapter 3.

- What are George's possible Business Success(ion) strategies?

- If George wants to sell the business, what should he do next? See Chapter 5.

- George is conflicted. If he sells the business, Hannah may be out of a job. How can he protect Hannah and his other key employees if he exits completely from the business post-sale? See Chapters 4 and 5.

- If George does not want to sell the business to an outsider, what are his options to enable him to monetize the value of what he has built? See Chapter 4.

- Once George figures out his exit strategy, what should he do next? See Chapter 5.

- If George successfully exits from his business, what's left for him? See Chapter 6.

Have fun reading the rest of the book and applying George's and your facts to the various topics discussed. Let's focus next on the various succession strategies available to you.

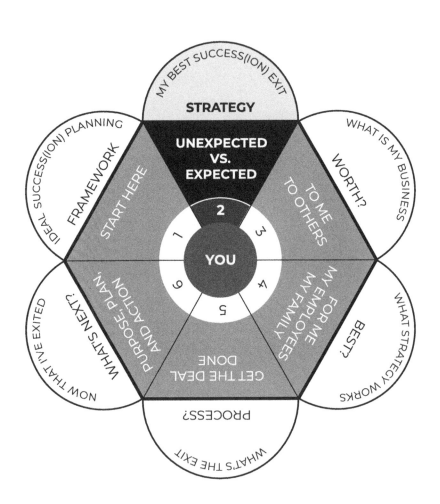

CHAPTER 2

MY BEST BUSINESS SUCCESS(ION) EXIT STRATEGIES

> "Always plan ahead. It wasn't raining when Noah built the ark."
> —RICHARD CUSHING

UNEXPECTED AND UNPLANNED EXITS

I think you have to work hard and never give up and focus 100% on your customer, the person who's paying you, and make sure you don't ever sacrifice on quality. I think that's why we've grown. We've never looked at the bottom line. We never looked at the money. We just focused on quality. Our goal was always to be the best-run company of its size in the world.

—Tien Wong, entrepreneur, successful business owner, and networker extraordinaire

Scan the QR code to watch the entire interview

youtube.com/ @ZellLaw/videos

Y ou now know you need a cohesive *management succession plan* (MSP) for your business that incorporates your short-term and long-term strategies mandating how the business will navigate rough waters if something happens to you unexpectedly or how it will survive and succeed if you plan for it. Next, let's focus on what to do to anticipate the unexpected events of *disability* or death.

THE STORY OF GEORGE AND HANNAH
BASIC ESTATE PLANNING WITH AN MSP

Let's assume the worst for George in our case study from Chapter 1. What happens to this amazing business if George dies suddenly and has done nothing to plan for his demise? His kids will scramble to plan a funeral for George, not knowing whether he wanted to be cremated or buried or even if he wanted a religious or memorial service. He never discussed it with the kids. So the kids must make some tough decisions, arrange for a funeral, and pay for it with their own funds until they can be reimbursed from George's assets.

Your first reaction might be to ask, "Why doesn't George just create a joint bank account with one of his kids and tell them that the money is to be used in the event something happens to him?" Well, that's not a bad idea, but it's not the best idea. If the money passes directly to the child because it's titled as joint tenants with rights of survivorship, the child has complete ownership and control of the account at George's death and total discretion over whether to use the money for the requested purpose. Or the child could just take the money and run. It also creates a gift to the account recipient if the money is accessed before death, which may create *estate and gift tax* complications depending on the size of George's estate. As we will see later, George's business may be worth a lot more than the federal estate tax exemption, which may result in gift tax having to be paid on the joint account unnecessarily.

So we know we need to plan for George's potential demise soon. What else should George be concerned with? Well, in most jurisdictions, someone will have to be appointed as the administrator of George's estate, and the estate—which consists of the *membership interests* in 3DP and the real estate *limited liability company* (LLC) and George's other assets—will have to go through the court-driven process known as *probate* for the assets to be available to pay expenses and distributable to the heirs. The court-appointed administrator will have to prepare and file an inventory within a certain period after being appointed. The administrator also must file accountings to report every asset that flows in and out of the estate until the estate is ultimately closed. This process can cause significant delays in winding up George's affairs and may cost upward of 2–5% or more of the assets in George's estate.

"OK," you say, "I get it. Apparently, you want George to avoid going through the probate process, which means that we need to get George a will and other *estate planning* documents, right?" Not exactly, because even if George had a will, his named *executor* would be required to take the estate through the probate process anyway.

My solution—used in all 50 states and the District of Columbia—is to create a *revocable living trust* for George, along with a will and other estate planning documents, and put his assets, including the 3DP and real estate LLC membership interests,[14] into the *revocable trust* now so that his named successor *trustee* can step in and manage his affairs if he becomes incapacitated or following his death without going to court!

Putting your assets into a trust of which you are the sole trustee does not change anything in the way you own or enjoy your assets. **If you are the sole trustee (i.e., the person in charge) as well as the grantor (a.k.a. settlor or creator) of the trust, you can contribute assets, withdraw assets, terminate the trust, or amend it at any time for any reason, without asking anyone for approval.** The main benefit of using this type of trust is to avoid probate upon your death and avoid "living probate" that could occur upon your incapacity.

Now we're getting somewhere! Next, as part of his planning, **George may consider naming Hannah to serve as his successor trustee who, at the very least, will be in control of the business and anything else covered by the trust.** Hannah may make the most sense as successor trustee under these facts, simply because she knows 3DP's business. If George thinks that Hannah cannot handle this responsibility alone for any reason, or that appointing Hannah may cause discord among other family members, he could name someone to serve as a co-trustee with her or not name her at all. **He could also name a special business trustee just to run the business and have the other kids involved as co-trustees with Hannah.**

Invariably, you may first turn to other family members to serve in the role of trustee. But you're not limited to family members serving as trustees, and for various reasons, you may not want to name family members in that critical role.

George has the option of naming other professionals (and so do you, with respect to your business), such as a *certified public accountant* (CPA), an attorney, or a corporate *fiduciary*, to assist Hannah in the daunting, serious role of managing 3DP and George's other assets. These professionals understand what it means to be a trustee, who is a fiduciary held to the highest standard in terms of protecting assets for the benefit of the trust's *beneficiaries*, which would include all of George's children, not just Hannah.[15] George or you could also name a friend or an associate with business knowledge and good judgment to serve in that role.

If George does not transfer his membership interests into his revocable trust before becoming incapacitated, he will want to execute a power of attorney that appoints someone as his agent with the power to do so before George dies. Failure to transfer the membership interests or stock of a closely held business (or even a publicly traded corporation) into the trust before death will result in probate, again resulting in delays in accessing the assets and extra costs.

The agent under the power of attorney will also have the power to manage George's financial affairs that are outside of the trust. This might include controlling bank and securities accounts outside of the trust, overseeing safe deposit boxes, managing his pets, handling litigation, settling disputes, and negotiating, executing, and terminating contracts with third parties. The agent will also have access to George's benefit plans at work and will ensure that George's retirement benefits and other assets that allow for *beneficiary* designations flow to the proper recipients based on his wishes.

"But then," you ask, "what about the business? Is Hannah or another trustee going to be running the business by themselves? Do they even know how to do it?"

The MSP is designed to address these issues. George can design a short-term plan that designates Hannah as the chief operating officer of the company immediately after George becomes incapacitated or dies. He can also appoint the other two key employees to remain in their roles and serve until a long-term plan can be constructed. The MSP should be sufficiently granular to provide for the salaries and bonuses of the key employees. Bonuses may involve creating a performance plan to which the employees will be held accountable and measured against. The bonuses could be in the form of cash or ownership in 3DP, depending on what George wants.

If he doesn't want to spend a lot of time structuring a performance plan to include as part of the MSP, he doesn't have to. He can simply refer to the performance plan in the MSP and take that up later with his key employees and his attorney. If no plan is ever constructed before George's incapacity or death, the board can work with the key employees to develop a plan that ensures they remain focused on and incentivized to stay with the business.

Even if George is uncertain as to which path to take regarding the ultimate Business Success(ion) plan for 3DP, **he should still proceed in creating the MSP.** He can always specify certain individuals and their roles now and change it later if he has time. **He can also leave the decision-making process in the hands of a board of managers that he appoints in the MSP now.**[16] As noted, the board might consist of his CPA, his corporate attorney, another business colleague familiar with the industry in which 3DP competes, and possibly one or two members of the family to balance out decision-making and voting. The MSP may also vest voting control in the family members who are on the board. (Note: this may require an amendment to 3DP's operating agreement.)

Importantly, George's revocable trust must incorporate the MSP into the terms of the trust, and the MSP needs to cross-reference the trust. The trust agreement should make clear that the trustees must follow the MSP, and the MSP governs in the event of any conflict or confusion with the trust agreement. George should adopt member resolutions and amend and restate his operating agreement to create the board of managers and adopt the MSP and any other provisions that are required to implement this new structure. The MSP and LLC operating agreement can be amended and updated by George at any time in the future, just as his estate planning documents can and should be updated periodically.[17]

Now that you have planned for the unexpected, let's turn to some of the strategies you (and George) can consider in your Business Success(ion) plan to achieve a well-planned exit.

DEEPER DIVE

Joint tenants with rights of survivorship, or JTWROS for short, is a form of property ownership. If you own a bank account with someone as JTWROS, then you are treated as an equal owner, and upon your death, your co-owner acquires total ownership of the account, even if your will or *trust* says otherwise. Creditors can sever the joint tenancy and access half the account. If the co-owner withdraws money from the account that you deposited, you are treated as making a gift to the co-owner and may have to report the gift on a gift tax return.

LESSONS LEARNED

- Create a revocable trust to own your business interest and transfer the interest into the trust to avoid court involvement.
- Putting your assets into a trust of which you are the sole trustee does not change anything in the way you own or enjoy your assets. If you are the sole trustee and you are the grantor of the trust, you can contribute assets, withdraw assets, terminate the trust, or amend it at any time for any reason, without asking anyone for approval.
- Name someone capable of serving as your successor trustee who can stand in your shoes to run the business, and think about naming a successor co-trustee if you are concerned about the ability of your named successor to serve alone. Think carefully about who should serve in this critical role and whether you want them to have sole and exclusive power over what happens to your business if you are not around.
- Link your MSP and operating/shareholders' agreement to your revocable trust.
- Your MSP plans for the short term by naming individuals who will run the daily business operations, how they will be paid, and whether they will be entitled to receive incentives in the form of cash or *equity* bonuses if they perform exceptionally well.
- Name a *board of directors* or managers in your MSP who will be responsible and accountable for managing the employees you name to run the business.

- Leave the long-term decisions to the board if you have not yet formulated your exit plan and be sure to amend the MSP after you solidify your long-term plan.
- Don't delay in creating your short-term MSP!

WELL-PLANNED EXIT STRATEGIES

I had a small, tight-knit group of managers that were with me for most, if not all, the journey, over 25 years, and 1 partner who was with me almost from the beginning. He and I were the yin and yang managing the business, where I focused primarily on strategy, financial aspects, and technical aspects, and he focused on sales and human resources.

—David Eisner, entrepreneur, former CEO and Founder of Dataprise, Inc.

Scan the QR code to watch the entire interview

youtube.com/@ZellLaw/videos

MERGER AND ACQUISITION/SALE TO AN OUTSIDER

One alternative for you to achieve a successful, well-planned exit is to sell your business. The sale of your business is also commonly referred to as a *merger and acquisition* (M&A), depending upon the structure of the deal and the type of consideration you may receive for your business. The sale may also be referred to as a stock/equity sale or an *asset sale*, again depending on the structure.

If you sell your small business to another small business or an individual, you may be willing to take back financing (i.e., lend them money to purchase your business) in addition to receiving some cash so the buyer has an easier time affording the purchase. Conversely, if your business is significant in size, with millions of dollars of revenue and *profits* and many employees, a buyer is going to need to have significant financing to ensure your purchase price ultimately gets paid. **Regardless of the size of the deal, your universe of prospective buyers usually consists of strategic buyers,** *private equity* **(PE) buyers, and** *family offices.*

DEEPER DIVE

The buyer usually wants to treat the acquisition of your business as a purchase of assets for tax purposes, even though they may only acquire stock or LLC interests. This is particularly true if your business is operated as an LLC taxed as a partnership or as an *S corporation*. Conversely, you would rather just sell your stock or LLC interests directly to the buyer and get 100% *capital gains* treatment on the sale of your equity.

- Treating the stock/equity sale as an asset sale for *income* tax purposes permits the buyer to write off the cost of your business, which may consist primarily of *goodwill* that can be amortized for tax purposes over 15 years on a straight-line basis. You won't mind selling your goodwill if it can be taxed at lower long-term capital gains rates. But if the transaction is treated as a sale of assets, some of the purchase price may need to be allocated to assets that generate *ordinary income* taxed at a higher rate, such as *accounts receivable* and equipment that you previously depreciated.

- If your business is treated as an S corporation, the buyer may want you to make elections under Internal Revenue Code (IRC) Section 338(h)(10) or Section 336(e) to treat the stock sale as a sale of assets, or they may want to reorganize your business in an F *reorganization* to create the same results for the buyer and allow any *rollover equity* you receive to avoid current taxation on the sale.
- These complexities are beyond the scope of this book, but simply put, **the tax nuances of the deal will affect your ultimate decision on whether to sell, how much to sell, the purchase price, and how to structure the sale to minimize adverse income tax consequences.**
- In some cases, you may need to pay tax on the rollover equity you receive without the ability to sell the equity to recoup the taxes you just paid. In other cases, you will want to receive the rollover equity on a tax-deferred basis.
- If the buyer insists on treating the deal as an asset sale for tax purposes, you should try to negotiate an increase in your purchase price due to the higher ordinary income tax generated by the buyer's desired treatment.

Strategic Buyers

Strategic buyers look at your business as a way of enhancing products or services they already sell, but you may give them a geographic or strategic advantage by allowing them to open in new markets or access new customers. You may also add value to their business in the form of new products or services they don't currently offer. In other words, there's something you have that they don't, and they want to add your business to theirs to increase long-term profits. Because you have something they want as part of their platform, strategic buyers may pay you a higher purchase price for your business. Other strategic buyers may be individuals who want to buy your business.

You may be looking for a strategic buyer for whom you can fill a *value gap* and enhance their business model.[18] For example, if you have technology that the strategic buyer already relies on to deliver their products or services or includes as part of their product offerings, adding you to the buyer's platform makes the buyer more valuable.

You may already know another company that could be a good candidate to buy your business. You may have worked on projects or joint ventures with them that, if you were part of their business, would increase their value. These strategic buyers may be ideal buyers for your business, but if you limit your choices to the businesses you know, you may be selling yourself short. An investment banker, a business broker, a corporate attorney, a CPA, or your board of advisors or directors may all help you expand your universe of potential strategic buyers through their extensive contacts and relationships.

IDEAS IN ACTION

Juan owned a small government contracting firm that was working with one of the behemoths in the industry on a highly specialized service for a specific government agency. They had teamed together for a year on various projects. One day, the government contractor asked Juan whether he wanted to sell his business to the contractor. He responded, "How much are you willing to pay?" bypassing the processes outlined in this book. The contractor offered Juan enough to satisfy his personal goal of selling the business for a significant sum of money. Juan accepted the offer, and they closed the deal in record time because the buyer knew Juan and his business very well, and both parties were comfortable with each other.

Private Equity Buyers

PE buyers focus on investments that will yield significant financial returns to their investors over a specific time. They usually want to ensure your business will succeed on its own without continued involvement or additional investment beyond the initial purchase. At the same time, the best PE buyers have experience in investing in other similarly sized businesses in your industry. They know the risks inherent in your business, and they hopefully understand what a successful business looks like when they are evaluating you as a target.

PE buyers come in so many shapes and sizes that it's hard to describe a "typical" PE firm. Trillions of dollars have been invested in PE funds, and the trend continues to increase, even as stock market returns ebb and flow.[19] As investment dollars come in, the PE firm must deploy these dollars to acquire portfolio companies or build platforms within an industry to achieve their investment strategies, which are myriad and diverse. Undoubtedly, if you are a Rocket Ship, there is an investment strategy and a PE investor out there for your business if it is growing and has the right components.

Even with increased volatility in the public markets, PE investments have expanded dramatically in the 21st century. Some PE buyers will be focused on your customer list, contracts, or technologies that may yield additional synergies with other portfolio companies they manage. In that case, the PE buyer may be less interested in retaining your workforce and more interested in capitalizing on expanding existing product and service offerings to the customer base of their portfolio companies.

In other cases, PE investors insert their own managers and board members to run the target's business. Even if you have been successful in running and growing your business over time, the PE firm may think they can do it better. There seems to be a bias among some PE fund managers as to how to properly run a business they acquire. If they've been successful in taking portfolio companies to the next level, they may know what they're talking about. However, if they're getting into a new industry or purchasing your company as the cornerstone of a new platform into which they will combine other similar companies, their focus on your assets and lack of focus on your people may not yield the best results.

IDEAS IN ACTION

I recently sold a company in the construction business to a PE–backed, multibillion-dollar company that had already acquired other similar companies in different parts of the country. My client carefully interviewed other sellers to this PE-backed business and discovered, much to his delight, that the sellers were all ecstatic about how they were treated by the buyer and the way in which management allows the acquired companies to continue to operate as part of a greater whole but independently in the way they customarily do business. The PE-backed management simply tries to add value based on experience with the acquired companies and provides information and guidance to their acquired companies, gleaned from operating similar successful businesses. That's an ideal PE buyer.

In another case, Don raised PE capital to fund his retail consumer products business. The PE firm wanted to be deeply involved in the management of a business they just funded. By contrast, Don had operated this business successfully for many years in his own way but did not necessarily follow the rules the PE firm wanted to impose. It only took 1 year of struggling to work together before Don demanded that the PE firm be bought out. That experience cost Don significant time, money, and, most of all, energy in dealing with a PE investor who really did not meet his needs.

PE deals often involve a 2-step process. In the first step, the PE firm acquires 20–90% of your company. You are expected to "roll over" some of your purchase price into equity of the acquiring company. The structures of these transactions can be quite complex, but the outcome is generally the same.

If you're going to accept a stake in the buyer's business, you need to ask whether and when you will be able to sell that stake to reap the benefits of the rollover equity portion of the transaction. PE buyers want to hold on to your business and grow it until it achieves a certain return on investment they've promised their investors.

IDEAS IN ACTION

Recently, Jack sold his business to a PE firm and, less than a year later, the PE firm found a buyer for the business (along with several other similarly situated businesses) that allowed Jack to quadruple his investment in the rollover equity he received in the original transaction. Either the original sale price was too low, and Jack should have been more careful in deciding on the original sale price, or the

PE firm was able to unleash or reveal additional value to a potential buyer that resulted in benefits not only to the PE firm but to the rollover investors, including Jack.

Not all deals end this way; try to negotiate protections in your rollover investment documents to allow you to realize the benefits of the rollover equity.

IDEAS IN ACTION

Bill, a regional leader in the managed services industry, sold his business to a PE firm right before COVID-19 hit. Bill retained a 20% stake in the continuing business. Following the closing, sales were not as robust as originally projected. The PE buyer reacted by bringing in its own managers to replace Bill and the rest of his management team. Because of the unanticipated effects of the pandemic, it may take quite a while before Bill will reap any benefit from the rollover equity he retained in the transaction. Bill was not required to sell his rollover equity at a price below its original value, so he could not be penalized for the PE firm's failure to achieve its investment goals after closing. Bill also retained an option to sell his rollover equity at a specific time in the future.

Ask your attorney to negotiate special rights that will enable you to require the PE firm to repurchase your stock after some minimum period has passed at a purchase price at least equal to the value of the rollover equity you received in the original transaction. This is known as a "put" right (i.e., the right to force the other party to buy your ownership interest), and it may provide some downside protection for you. PE firms will resist being forced to buy your interest, but there may be negotiating room depending on the value and importance of your company to the PE buyer. If you cannot get a "put" right, at least try to get a minimum price for your rollover equity. Remember, PE firms are most concerned about maximizing the return on investment for their investors, so anything that diminishes the return will meet strong resistance.

PE buyers will demand control of your board of directors or board of managers following the acquisition if they've acquired more than a majority stake in your business. You may not want this result. If things don't go well after the investment, you don't want the PE firm penalizing you for nonperformance by forcing you or your management team out or even worse.

IDEAS IN ACTION

Four founders were able to sell a 40% stake in their company to a PE firm for an attractive multiple without relinquishing control. The founders included a provision that reduces the PE firm's ownership interest if certain performance targets are hit. For example, if revenues increase by more than 15% per year, the PE investor's ownership interest decreases to as low as half of their original percentage ownership if the revenue increase continues for 5 years.

There's plenty of PE funding available to fuel acquisitions and investments. If the economy turns down dramatically, as it did in 2008 and 2009, then multiples will drop and the availability of businesses to be sold at high multiples will decline. Nonetheless, sellers may still be willing to sell their businesses, even at lower values. The question will be whether the PE buyer or investor is the right exit for you.

Family Offices

Another exit strategy is to sell to a "family office." A family office is a private wealth management advisory firm that is established by an ultra-high-net-worth individual to manage their family's private wealth.[20] Any firm that provides investment advice only to family members, is wholly owned and controlled by family members, and does not hold itself out to the public as an investment advisor is considered a family office. Family offices have skyrocketed in number both globally and in the United States. In 2017, Capgemini estimated the number of single-family offices had grown to over 3,000 in the United States alone, and that number is continuously growing.[21]

Well-run family offices have professionals who assist the family in managing their wealth and investing it in portfolio companies that fit within the family office's values and strategy. In many cases, the family office has a long-term view of operating the businesses it acquires. This may result in a significant cash payout to you if you sell your business to a family office or may result in an ongoing ownership interest in a business that generates cash flow not only for the family office but also for you if you retain a piece of the equity.

Some family offices prefer to buy out 100% of the business; others will invest anywhere from 20–90% to acquire an ownership stake in the business. Even if the family office acquires more than a majority stake, it may be willing to let you and your managers or key employees continue operating your business under the tutelage and oversight of the family office's managers.

The family office may provide you with a unique investment or sale opportunity. Many family offices focus on long-term investing strategies, as compared to the shorter-term focus of PE investors. They may also specialize in your industry and may have experienced personal success in selling their businesses. In addition, a family office, while having substantial economic clout, may not want to be involved in the day-to-day functioning of your business. They will be looking for well-managed and sustainable companies like yours.

If you don't already have connections to family offices, an investment banker may be essential to introduce you to the universe of family offices, strategic buyers, and PE investors that may want to purchase your business. Also, the Family Office Exchange is an excellent source of information.[22]

IDEAS IN ACTION

A large *registered investment advisor* (RIA) was recently merged into a family office that also had an RIA subsidiary. Both RIAs were of comparable size and had been courting each other for several years, but the obstacle in completing the transaction was that the buyer's former CEO did not really exemplify the culture my client, Kathy, had created. The family office replaced the CEO with a new CEO who had experience in the industry and created a culture like Kathy's. When Kathy discovered the change in management, conversations renewed between the parties. It was a very thoughtful and intense series of negotiations that ultimately led to the successful merger into a family office–controlled entity. This was the "right way" to do an acquisition because the parties were like-minded not only in how to operate their businesses but also in their cultures, philosophies, and values.

A family office may want to invest and take a minority stake in your business or may want to acquire a controlling interest but allow you and your managers to continue operating it. The primary difference between a family office and a PE firm is that the family office usually resulted from the successful operation, growth, and sale or other liquidity event of a family-owned or other business that generated significant wealth that is concentrated and controlled by family members. Some of these family offices may be over a century old, and some of them may be brand-new, resulting from recent transactions. PE firms often seek outside investors, which may include family offices.

Like many PE firms, a family office will want a member of its management team or family to participate on your board after you sell all or a piece of your business to the family office. In my experience, family offices are less concerned about controlling day-to-day operations than PE investors. They only get involved if there are real problems after the acquisition.

INSIDER SALES: MANAGEMENT BUYOUTS

As an alternative to an M&A transaction with a strategic buyer, PE firm, or family office, you could try to sell your business to your management team. Fueled by the *leveraged buyout* (LBO) craze in the 1980s, *management buyouts* (MBOs) proliferated in the 1980s and early 1990s. LBOs and MBOs are still popular.

An LBO is one company's acquisition of another company (target) using a significant amount of borrowed money (debt or leverage) to pay the purchase price. The assets of the target are often used as collateral for the loans, along with the assets of the acquiring company. Using debt, which normally costs less than equity, can reduce the overall cost of financing the acquisition. The *cost of debt* is lower in part because interest payments are deductible for income tax purposes, whereas dividend payments normally are not. (Getting a tax deduction for interest on the debt reduces the cost by the tax rate imposed on the borrower, times the interest incurred.) This reduced cost of financing allows greater gains to accrue to the equity in the business, and, as a result, the debt serves as a lever to increase the returns to the equity owners.[23]

In an MBO that uses debt to finance the acquisition, the management team borrows from merchant bankers, private lenders, commercial banks, or PE funds to purchase your business. To convince the lender to fund the purchase, the management team must show that the business can produce enough cash flow—not only to pay off the debt but also to sustain and grow the business.

Financing for LBOs and MBOs is not as easy to come by as it was in the world of junk bonds during the 1980s. **Today, a business that generates excellent cash flow may enable managers to assemble the necessary financing to buy the business.** The lenders, however, will require the managers to undertake significant risks in doing so, by forcing them to provide personal guarantees for the debt that is being provided to purchase the business. If private or commercial lending sources are not available, you may not be willing to finance all or any portion of the purchase price that the managers are paying you, simply because of the risk that they may not be able to pay the purchase price from the cash flow of the business.

If your situation is dire but you are confident in your management team, you may be willing to let the managers borrow from you to

pay the purchase price in the hope that they generate enough cash to pay you for the value of your business. Savvy sellers like you will want to retain certain protections against default by the managers. This might include keeping a *security interest* in the stock or membership interests that you're selling to the managers. It might also include a security interest in the overall assets of the business, simply because you are acting as the bank in the transaction. In addition, you may insist on the managers and their spouses personally guaranteeing the debt used to purchase your interest.

The managers, on the other hand, aren't going to want to be cash poor in buying you out, particularly if the debt is so large and burdensome that they cannot afford to pay themselves or other employees adequate salaries or utilize excess funds being generated by the business to grow it. It becomes a delicate balancing act between your need to receive the value of your business and the managers' personal risk in buying your business.

MBOs are often the most difficult transactions to negotiate and close. The results depend heavily on the availability of capital to the management team/buyers. If the management team is properly motivated to acquire your business, they should engage separate counsel and separate advisors to help them structure a deal that will allow them to acquire your ownership interest. You should be represented by separate counsel and advisors as well. Because your interest is averse to the managers, negotiations can be quite complex and tricky. Each of you should pay for your own expenses.

IDEAS IN ACTION

Tia wanted to engineer a management buyout of an RIA. The seller was not actively involved in the day-to-day management, and she and her partner (a huge financial services company) were interested in spinning off the investment advisory business to focus on other things. Tia was the president of the company and had been successful in growing the RIA business from scratch (with the seller's help). Her biggest challenge was finding financing for the acquisition, which she overcame when she found a local bank that was willing to finance the deal. Tia negotiated a successful MBO, and, after raising additional funds in a later transaction with a PE firm to support the growth of the company, she ultimately grew the company and resold it a decade later. She and the other equity investors kept a rollover equity stake in the ongoing entity and were able to sell their interests for an increased multiple over what they paid for the business originally. All in all, it was a very successful MBO story.

The strength of selling your business to your managers is that they know the business, suppliers, vendors, and clients/customers. They may also have creative thoughts on how to grow the business. If they have "skin in the game" in the form of their own invested capital, they'll be more motivated to make the business profitable. You could retain a minority stake in the business as well, yielding full responsibility for running the company to the managers and keeping open access to the financial performance and plans of the company.

A weakness of the MBO strategy is that the managers usually lack sufficient capital to purchase the business, indicating the need for seller financing or no deal at all. In addition, the managers may lack your force of personality, which could jeopardize prospects for the company, particularly if your charisma fueled the growth and success of the business.

You should not risk selling your business to your managers unless you are certain they will remain dedicated to its ongoing success and will be able to pay the purchase price you are seeking. As noted, you can take back seller financing, where you receive a *promissory note* from each of the managers who are buying your ownership interest or the company or both. The longer it takes to pay off the purchase price, the greater the risk to you as the seller. To compensate for the increased risk, you may require a significant initial deposit, a higher interest rate in the notes, greater security in the form of pledges of the ownership interests you are selling and company assets, and personal guarantees of the managers and their spouses, so you can recover the benefit of your bargain.

If a manager defaults on the note, you can recover a portion of the equity that has been sold but remains unpaid. You will want to retain additional protections in the promissory note and purchase agreement in the event you end up holding a minority interest after the sale. If that unpaid portion leaves you as a minority owner without adequate protections from the original deal documents, you may be holding a minority interest in your own company without the ability to control the business or repayment of your note.

FAMILY-OWNED BUSINESSES

Family-owned businesses raise so many questions and unique issues that myriad books have been written on how to build, sustain, and transition the business to the next generation. With all this guidance, you would think family-business owners would have greater success than the data indicates in leaving their businesses to the next generation. Yet, a family-owned business is rife with challenges such as the following:

- Death of the charismatic founder or family member who works in the business

- New, inexperienced, and unknowledgeable family members and their spouses entering into the business

- Inequality in treatment between generations and within the same generation

- Family strife and psychological and behavioral challenges that lead to tensions within the family

If you have a family-owned business, most experts agree that you must develop a transition plan to allow you to gracefully reduce your role in the business. Ah, the MSP surfaces again! You will need to follow these steps:

- Build a governance model that will work for the family going forward.

- Articulate your goals in how you are going to transition the business to future generations and define the value you have created and hope to receive for your years of toil.

- Develop your own personal exit strategy that the remaining family members adopt and help implement.

- Determine who will remain employed, their compensation, and how long (if at all) they will be guaranteed employment going forward.
  - Arguably, you should exclude those family members with a sense of entitlement (but without the work ethic of other family members) from running or having a significant say in the business.
  - There should also be a family employment policy infused into the MSP for a family-owned business.

Your plan needs to be communicated to your family members with great sensitivity and care. Communicating these ideas among family members can be an extremely difficult, emotional exercise. Bringing in a family governance expert will help you and your family set the stage for operating the business during your active lifetime and preparing for the transition. There are even apps built to help family-owned businesses organize documents, manage meetings, make decisions, and share information with family members, shareholders, and directors.

Once you get past these important details, you can then delve into the mechanics and structuring of the long-term portion of the MSP and the overall long-term exit plan. The exit may include a sale to a strategic buyer, PE firm, or family office, or it may anticipate keeping the family business operating in your absence. Income and transfer (gift and estate) taxes play a significant role in the planning, particularly if the business is valuable and you have considerable assets outside the business.

Your planning team will play a critical role in this part of the planning process. In addition to family governance experts, CPAs, estate planning and business attorneys, financial planners, insurance agents, and appraisers will help you and your family get to the desired exit. Having an experienced quarterback run the process is critically important to the overall success of the plan.

There are many great resources available for you to use in understanding some of the nuances family-owned businesses face. In *Secrets to Succession*, author Gerard Gust lays out a process for ensuring success in transitioning a family-owned business. He emphasizes that the parent should hire his child for an existing job rather than creating one for the child. If that means the child must start working in the mailroom or as a janitor, then so be it. Being relegated to a life of menial tasks while the founder continues to lord over the company may cause the child to lose interest and seek employment elsewhere. However, if the child has the ability and the drive, giving the child the opportunity to work in many aspects of the business will create a well-rounded manager.

The presence of a charismatic founder may inhibit the family's participation in the business. I've seen this in many cases with my clients and have experienced it personally within my family.

From the time I was 17 until I graduated from college, I worked in my family's retail jewelry business. I learned and handled every aspect of the business. I took inventory; cleaned and organized jewelry within display cases; assisted in preparing and reviewing financial statements and tax returns; learned the nuances of diamonds and other precious stones, watches, gold, platinum, and silver; mastered selling the merchandise; and experienced the highs and lows of a retail business with my parents and sometimes my siblings. It fascinated me. For my first finance class at the McIntire School of Commerce at the University of Virginia, I analyzed business ratios of the family business and made recommendations on how to improve the company's performance. As an accounting major, I applied some of the concepts I was learning in college to a real business.

But when I tried to infuse my enthusiasm and newly found knowledge into the family business, my parents put a damper on that excitement. My ability to exercise independent judgment would be delayed significantly and subordinated to their control, perhaps until my parents were ready to retire, which was many years later. At that point, I made a conscious decision to continue my education and instead became a CPA and a lawyer. However, the skills I gained as a young entrepreneur working for my parents were invaluable. They taught me how to be an entrepreneur, which is why I enjoy running my own law firm.

If you are a charismatic founder, giving your children the ability to fully participate in the business from a young age and educating them along the way in all aspects of the business, including providing them with professional education if they're so inclined, is a wonderful gift. As a charismatic founder, you had the vision and the drive to create and make a successful business. Your children may be intimidated or overpowered by you. They may want to pursue a different career path, or they may not have your skills and talents. Even if your kids want to be involved in the business, the best solution is to develop and implement a Business Success(ion) plan where professional managers can be hired to help the family run the business after you retire or if you experience an unexpected exit.

MY BEST BUSINESS SUCCESS(ION) EXIT STRATEGIES

If your Rocket Ship continues to thrive and grow, it can continue beyond your lifetime. If you run a Legacy or Lifestyle business, you should structure an MSP with short-term operating plans and long-term exit plans. If you experience an unexpected exit or decide to retire permanently, finding competent and properly incentivized managers who adopt and promote the company's vision and values will be a difficult task. In addition, managers may be reluctant to work for families that control the business, unless there's some upside for the management team in the form of equity incentives, bonuses, or other incentive compensation, and downside protection (e.g., severance plans) if the arrangement doesn't work out. There should also be a structure to insulate the management team from the whims of unplanned family decision-making.

In a family-owned business, in addition to selling the business as an alternative to providing financial safety for the family, you can gift ownership interests during your lifetime to a child who is interested in running the business. There may be other children who are not participating or as involved as the child who receives voting shares or majority control of the business. In that instance, you may want to consider "equalizing" the gift made to the "involved child" with a gift of other assets to the less-involved children, or having a portion of your ownership interest placed in a trust for all the children and managed by a trustworthy team of your family and outside advisors for the benefit of the family. The plan may give voting control of most decisions to the "involved" child but reserve key decisions for all those involved.

Finally, to provide access to wealth outside the business, obtaining additional life insurance on the founder or allocating other nonbusiness assets can help equalize the impact of giving shares of the business to the "involved" children. Techniques for transfers to family members are discussed in greater detail in Chapter 4.

EMPLOYEE STOCK OWNERSHIP PLANS

Many companies utilize *employee stock ownership plans* (ESOPs) to transition business ownership to the next generation of employees and managers. This device is typically not used in a family-owned business where control is transferred to future generations of the family. As the name implies, it's used where the employees want to stay involved in the business after you exit.

An ESOP is a form of qualified retirement plan that provides special benefits under the IRC to the company that sponsors the ESOP, the shareholders of the company who sell shares to the ESOP, and the employees of the sponsoring company. Basically, an ESOP gives employees an ownership interest in the company through a qualified trust that owns the stock in the company directly.

ESOPs can be "leveraged" or "unleveraged." A leveraged ESOP refers to an ESOP that borrows money from a bank or other lender to purchase a selling shareholder's stock in the sponsoring company. The ESOP-owned company stock serves as the loan collateral. In effect, the sponsoring company guarantees the loan.

The ESOP borrows money from a bank and uses the proceeds to purchase stock from the sponsoring company or its shareholders. The sponsoring company makes tax-deductible contributions to the ESOP so the ESOP can repay the bank loan and purchase additional stock in the future. When the ESOP pays back the loan, the bank/lender releases the shares held as collateral to the ESOP, which then allocates the shares to the ESOP participants' (i.e., employees) accounts.

In addition, an ESOP sponsor may deduct cash dividends paid on company stock held by an ESOP to the extent the dividends are used to pay principal and interest on the ESOP loan incurred to buy the company stock. Dividends used in this manner are not counted toward the 25% contribution limit for leveraged ESOPs.[24]

Not all ESOPs are leveraged. In an unleveraged ESOP, the ESOP does not borrow to purchase company shares, whether from you at the initial ESOP transaction or when repurchasing from employees. Annually, the sponsoring company simply contributes cash or shares to the ESOP. The ESOP uses the contributed cash to purchase shares from you and other shareholders or from the company directly. The company pays you for your shares directly at the time of the initial sale transaction. The ESOP trust repurchases employee stock from vested employees without borrowing money from a lender using cash that has been contributed to the plan.

The most obvious reason to use an unleveraged ESOP is when your company has cash available to contribute to the ESOP, which can then purchase shares from you or the employees. Why incur debt if it is unnecessary to do so to finance the transaction?

You can finance the sale of your shares to an ESOP as well by accepting a promissory note from the ESOP in exchange for your shares. Your financing must be on commercially reasonable terms;

you cannot charge the ESOP an interest rate above market rates or have terms that are more favorable than a commercial lender would provide.

Whether or not the ESOP is leveraged, an ESOP should have a separate, independent trustee acting on behalf of the ESOP trust and its participants. An independent trustee should be experienced with ESOPs and not related or subordinate to you. You, as the founder, typically will not participate in the ESOP.

S Corporation Benefits

The primary benefit of using an *S corporation* to sponsor an ESOP is that the ESOP-owned shares are exempt from income taxation.

IDEAS IN ACTION

Let's say you sell 75% of your company's outstanding shares to an ESOP for your employees, and the following year, the company generates $1 million in taxable income. In that case, only $250,000 of the income will be taxable to you as a 25% shareholder; the remaining $750,000 will not be subject to income tax!

C Corporation Benefits

A *C corporation* ESOP sponsor is entitled to deduct the following amounts each tax year:[25]

- Contributions used to repay the ESOP loan principal up to 25% of covered payroll
- 100% of contributions used to repay ESOP loan interest

- Certain "nonelective" contributions up to an additional 25% of covered payroll

Pros and Cons of Using an ESOP

Pros:

- You get a tax deduction for contributions to the ESOP used to purchase your company's stock.

- You can shelter growth from income taxes until stock is sold and proceeds are distributed to the participants.

- You can shelter S corporation earnings from income tax to the extent shares are held by the ESOP. If the ESOP owns 100% of the shares of an S corporation, the S corporation's earnings are completely tax-exempt.

- If you own a C corporation, you may get to defer income tax on sales of your stock to an ESOP if you reinvest the proceeds into qualified publicly traded securities. Ultimately, you can completely avoid income tax on the qualified securities if you hold the securities until your death.

- Your C corporation can deduct dividends used to pay dividends to employee-participants in the plan.

The ESOP participants usually pay ordinary income tax when the shares are sold out of the ESOP and proceeds are distributed or when the participant terminates service with the sponsoring company, triggering a repurchase of the departing employee's ESOP shares.[26]

Cons:

- ESOPs can be very expensive to implement and maintain. For example, one prominent ESOP provider charges at least $20,000 to establish the ESOP. You must hire an experienced ESOP/ *ERISA* attorney and plan administrator with ESOP expertise to assist in the annual maintenance of the ESOP. (ERISA is the Employee Retirement Income Security Act of 1974, as amended.) You must also pay an appraiser annually to value the stock of the sponsoring company. Annual *appraisal* and administration fees typically run around $25,000 or more.

- You should hire an independent trustee to act as fiduciary for the ESOP, which will increase costs and may create obstacles for you in operating the company.

- The presence of an ESOP makes it harder to sell the company if an ESOP owns shares.

DEEPER DIVE

An ESOP can be a major impediment to the sale of a company, particularly if the ESOP owns preferred stock as well as common stock of the company. Separate law firms must represent the ESOP trustees, the company, the buyer, the founders, and the lender providing financing for the acquisition. In every aspect, the transaction must be fair to the

ESOP. The appraisers must revalue the company and render a fairness opinion at the time of the sale. If there are perceived structural defects in the transaction, counsel for the trustees will continuously raise objections until the defects are cured. Executives (including continuing managers other than the founders) will be precluded from receiving extra compensation or bonuses in the transaction if the ESOP is perceived as suffering a detriment caused by the extra compensation. In addition, any favorable financing or terms that would be given to the common stockholders that are not available to the ESOP holders on equal or better terms will be disallowed.

Conclusion on ESOPs

ESOPs may offer you a viable exit planning alternative if you are willing to pay the cost of establishing and maintaining the ESOP, your employees are motivated to participate in the ESOP, and your company generates sufficient cash flow to fund the ESOP or repay any leverage incurred to provide funding for the purchase of shares and distribution of proceeds to departing employees.

GOING PUBLIC

Initial Public Offerings

Finally, you can exit a business if you take it public in an *initial public offering* (IPO)—that is, register the stock you are offering for sale with the Securities and Exchange Commission (SEC) and in states where the company will issue securities. The public purchases stock from the company in an IPO, and cash is infused in the business to allow it to grow. In many cases, you can sell some or all of your shares as part of the public offering. This is negotiated with the underwriter who manages the offering. Even if you can register your shares, the underwriter will demand that you "lock up" your shares (i.e., not sell them) for some period after the IPO is completed and the market has stabilized. The lockup period is usually at least 6 months after the IPO goes "effective" (i.e., after the SEC has approved of the registration of the stock and allows the stock to be sold on a stock exchange), although the underwriter may release the shares from lockup if the newly issued shares are being traded regularly and the stock price is stable or increasing steadily.

The IPO process is not for the weakhearted. It is a complex process driven by attorneys, investment bankers, and accountants who exert Herculean efforts (and receive Zeus-like compensation) to bring the company to the public markets and one that requires extraordinary attention to detail.

After the IPO has been registered and the company is public, the real fun begins. Being a publicly traded company requires incredibly detailed quarterly reporting on Form 10-Q, transactional disclosures on Form 8-K, and annual reporting and audits on Form 10-K. It also requires preparing and filing proxy statements with extensive disclosures on voting procedures, nominated candidates for the board of directors, and compensation of directors and key executives. Following the IPO, top executives must report their purchases and sales of securities, and the list goes on. Being publicly traded is a high-pressure, high-risk, but potentially high-reward undertaking.

Special Purpose Acquisition Companies (SPACs)

As an alternative to the traditional IPO, one of the more creative techniques that has gained increasing popularity in recent years is the utilization of the *special purpose acquisition company* (SPAC). A SPAC is a company that has no commercial operations and is formed strictly to raise capital through an IPO to acquire or merge with an existing privately owned operating company for a specific purpose or in a specific industry.

In 2020, 247 SPACs were created with $80 billion invested, and in 2021, there were a record 613 SPAC IPOs. By comparison, only 59 SPACs came to market in 2019.[27]

SPACs have very specific rules regarding how they can raise the money, when they must deploy the money (i.e., generally within 2 years after the capital raise), and what happens if they do not deploy the money in the way that they promised within the required time period (i.e., they must return the money to investors). In the wake of increasing inflation and stock market volatility in 2022, SPAC offerings have declined precipitously.

The numbers behind SPACs are mind-boggling. You typically see the sponsor (i.e., the pre-IPO SPAC investor) trying to raise at least $250 million in capital, of which $6–$8 million is invested to cover administrative costs that include underwriting, attorney, and *due diligence* fees. With the structure and concept in place, the SPAC then sells millions of shares to investors at a set price. Before offering the shares to the public, the sponsor purchases about 20% of the shares at a steep discount from the public offering price. If the sponsors succeed in executing a merger with an operating target company within 2 years, their founders' shares become vested at the higher public offering price, potentially making the sponsors a fortune. If your business is big enough to attract a SPAC, you may want to seek this alternative exit strategy.

If you have the stomach for it, you can take your company public either through an IPO or by being acquired by a SPAC. Either strategy may offer you a lucrative exit.

A FEW MORE NOTES OF CAUTION ON M&A AND REORGANIZATION TRANSACTIONS

In some cases, a prospective buyer may want to merge with you and give you a continuing equity interest in the buyer's business without giving you significant cash in the deal. Unless you have a great business relationship and trust with the buyer, you need to be cautious here.

- First, if you receive publicly traded stock and have the ability to trade that stock over a relatively short period after the deal closes (i.e., because the buyer has promised to register your stock with the SEC or issues previously registered stock to you) or if there is a planned liquidity event (i.e., subsequent sale of the buyer) that will occur soon after the merger, then your risk of holding illiquid securities is significantly reduced.

- However, if you receive stock in a closely held business that has no definite exit plan or no specific time frame for the exit, you may get nothing for your efforts in the long run. Instead, you might be better off selling your business through an IPO either to the public or to a SPAC.

In addition, you should make sure the stock you get in the transaction is not taxable to you on receipt.

- If the stock is taxed on receipt, you may not have enough cash to pay the tax on the transaction.

- Conversely, if the transaction is treated as a tax-free reorganization, then the stock you get will not be taxed upon receipt; only cash or other "boot" (e.g., buyer's assumption of your liabilities) will be taxable to you.

Another key concern in any transaction is the legality of the purchase.

- In other words, does the combination of your company with another business raise any antitrust issues under federal laws?

- Does the transaction require *Hart–Scott–Rodino* (HSR) approval from the Federal Trade Commission (FTC) because the transaction is over a certain size? If so, the companies must notify federal antitrust authorities under the Hart–Scott–Rodino Antitrust Improvements Act of 1976, as amended, and its rules and regulations (HSR Act) before consummating a transaction.

DEEPER DIVE

The HSR Act requires companies of a certain size involved in a transaction exceeding reportability thresholds to file a premerger notification with the FTC and Department of Justice (DOJ) and observe a 30-day waiting period unless an exemption applies. In 2021, the FTC decreased the HSR

filing thresholds due to the economic recession caused by the COVID-19 pandemic. For transactions closing after February 23, 2022, the FTC increased the size-of-transaction threshold to $101 million; this is adjusted annually.

- The revised $101 million size-of-transaction threshold applies to transactions in which the buyer will hold voting securities, noncorporate interests, or assets valued at or above $101 million. These transactions may require a premerger notification to the FTC if the size-of-parties test is also satisfied and no HSR Act exemptions are applicable.
- The HSR size-of-parties threshold generally requires that one party to the transaction have annual net sales or total assets of $202 million or more in 2022, and that the other party have annual net sales or total assets of at least $20.2 million in 2022.
- For transactions valued at more than $101 million but not more than $403.9 million, no premerger notification is required if the ultimate parent entities of one or both parties to the transaction do not satisfy the size-of-parties threshold. Transactions valued at more than $403.9 million in 2022 will be subject to premerger notification requirements regardless of the size of the parties, unless an HSR Act exemption applies.

Here's an example:

IDEAS IN ACTION

Let's say you receive rollover equity in a PE transaction, or you get stock of a strategic partner in a merger.

- You want to be sure that you can diversify your holdings into other assets, including cash, after the transaction.

- You could require the buyer to purchase your stock in a transaction known as a redemption after a certain period if the buyer has not sold or registered your stock in a public offering before then.
- The buyer may restrict your ability to demand this special treatment, unless you are terminated from continued employment with the company without cause (to be defined in the agreement) or you leave employment with good reason (also a defined term).
- These are all negotiating points in your deal as a founder. Your goal is to achieve maximum liquidity and flexibility in the stock that you receive in the deal.

Also, if you receive a significant percentage of the purchase price in the form of securities of a strategic buyer in a merger or other reorganization transaction, you will want to obtain as much information about the buyer as you are required to give the buyer about your business.

- If the buyer is publicly traded, there should be significant information available on the buyer.
- However, if the buyer is privately held, you will want to know the buyer's financial condition by requesting copies of audited financial statements; details on the buyer's capital structure; the stock you will receive and whether restrictions on transfer will be imposed; the condition of the buyer's business; the state of the buyer's relationships and the status of contracts with customers, suppliers, and employees; and all other information pertinent to the operation of the buyer's business.
- In other words, you should conduct significant due diligence on the buyer and its business if you are receiving the buyer's stock, just as the buyer must conduct due diligence on your business.

You need to consider tax, your ability to sell securities, and other issues if you're going to take back a large portion of the value of your business in somebody else's stock or ownership interests.

> ### THE STORY OF GEORGE AND HANNAH
> # DETERMINE GEORGE'S NEEDS
>
> As for George, it's too early for us to advise him on what to do here other than to outline the various alternatives available for his exit. He has a lot of choices if he wants to sell the business. As you'll see in Chapters 3 and 4, he needs to
>
> - determine what he needs and wants to take out of the business and what the business is worth and
> - determine what will be left for him and his employees after taxes and fees.
>
> Making these determinations will help George reach a decision on his best exit strategy. But clearly, with his business involved in cutting-edge technology, George may have many interested buyers.
>
> Let's help George next by helping him figure out what his business is worth.

LESSONS LEARNED

- There are many ways to sell your company. In a merger or an acquisition, you may be selling all of your business to a strategic buyer, or part or all of your business to a PE firm or family office.
    - Know what you want and what the business is worth before you jump in.

- Know who your buyer is, their track record with prior acquisitions, and what to expect post-transaction.
- Finally, if you take rollover equity, make sure you do so in the most tax-efficient manner possible.

- In an MBO, you may be able to sell your business to your management team. They will need to procure financing to buy you out, which may not be easy to obtain.
    - If the business generates enough cash flow to pay down management's debt and grow the company, a private or commercial lender may be willing to finance the deal.
    - If not, you could finance the deal, but you would be assuming the risk of nonpayment.
    - Protect yourself by taking a security interest in the stock or membership interests you are selling as well as the assets of the business.
    - Have the managers and their spouses personally guarantee the obligation to pay you back. With adequate protections, a seller-financed sale may work.

- Consider using an ESOP in certain cases.
    - You must be willing to invest significant capital in establishing the ESOP and continuously complying with complex IRS and DOL regulations.
    - With an ESOP, the business must generate sufficient cash flow to service any leverage used to purchase your stock or company stock.
    - More importantly, an ESOP only works if your employees are motivated to share in the risks and rewards of owning a business.

- Going public, either in a traditional IPO or SPAC, is not an easy task and requires significant professional backup and expertise to comply with complex securities laws.
    - IPOs work best with Rocket Ships blasting off the launchpad.
    - SPACs can provide fuel from an IPO to incumbent businesses or Rocket Ships that need a shot in the arm (capital) and have a new direction (a growth plan to make the investors wealthy).

- In all scenarios, be sure to understand the tax, securities law, and other legal issues relating to your receipt of stock or other securities in another company so you are not caught off guard in completing the transaction or when it's time to pay your taxes.

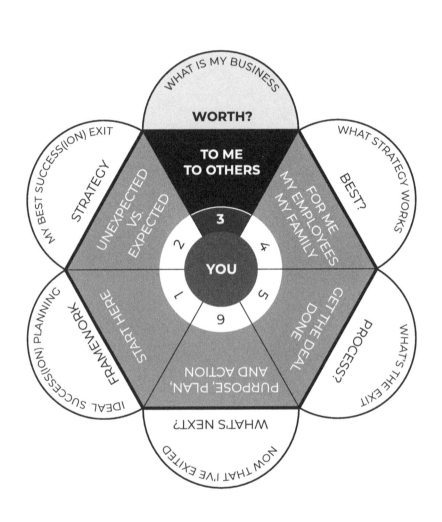

CHAPTER 3

WHAT IS MY BUSINESS WORTH?

"The fair market value is the price at which the property would change hands between a willing buyer and a willing seller, neither being under any compulsion to buy or to sell and both having reasonable knowledge of relevant facts."
—US V. CARTWRIGHT

HOW MUCH IS THE BUSINESS WORTH TO ME?

The idea of...having individuals that worked for us have the opportunity to buy in and become shareholders was really, really important to [creating an] ownership mindset. And my view is there's no better way to create an ownership mindset than to actually make them owners. There's no doubt it made it more complicated to sell with 24 shareholders—we had to get 24 signatures on a lot of different documents at a lot of different times.

—Matthew Dean, entrepreneur,
President and CEO, Markon Solutions

Scan the QR code to watch the entire interview

youtube.com/ @ZellLaw/videos

To answer this important question, first ask yourself and answer the following question: *How much do I need/want from the sale of my business?*

I would start by determining how much you need first. Your financial planner and *certified public accountant* **(CPA) should be involved in this decision process.** It would be useful if they help you prepare projections based on your current and projected growth in *income* and assets, along with expected expenditures. You want to be certain that you have enough to live on comfortably for the rest of your life and that you can support your family in the way you've become accustomed to living.

A CPA with the right tools will be able to assist you in performing projections based on your investment portfolio, your retirement assets, and other assets you own, including your business. There is no rule of thumb as to how much you need to live on for the rest of your life. The correct answer depends on how you currently live, your obligations, and special circumstances that may apply only to you. Your financial plan should also consider income taxes, transaction fees, and other expenses you will incur—whether you decide to sell your business or hold on to it. You should factor in the costs of healthcare, long-term care insurance, life insurance, children's education, home repairs and maintenance, vehicle replacement and upkeep, recreation and travel, and myriad other items.

The next step is to determine what you want from the business. Your "wants" may not equate with your "needs." In other words, you may need more money from the business than you may necessarily want, or you may want more from the business than you need. This adds significant subjectivity in calculating what you really need out of the business when it's time to exit. By back-planning your exit, you have a better understanding of what will make you comfortable and content at the end of your entrepreneurial journey.

Then compare what you would get if you kept the business running for a set period of years vs. selling the business now. In some cases, it may make sense to keep the business and wind it down gradually instead of trying to sell it to somebody.

Let's use George as an example of how this might work.

THE STORY OF GEORGE AND HANNAH
SELL VS. HOLD

Assume George can sell 3DP for $50 million cash today. Further assume that transaction fees and income taxes on the sale will equal around 33%, so his net from the transaction would be $33.33 million ($50 million × (1 − 33.33%)). If George currently generates $10 million of net income and cash flow annually, he could work for 6 more years and accomplish the same result. I get this by multiplying $10 million by 55%, which assumes an ordinary federal and state income tax rate of 45% that would be imposed on income distributable from an *S corporation*, multiplied by 6, or $33 million.

Of course, if George can get the entire purchase price in cash today, then it may be worth it for him to sell now and avoid the pain of having to continue to run the business for another 6 years and generate cash flow from operations for that period, particularly given his stage 4 prostate cancer and the possibility he may not survive the 6-year time frame.

On the other hand, if George is generating $5 million in cash flow per year from the business, it may make sense to sell now at the price being offered above. This depends on what George can generate from the business over a specific period, with confidence that he can continue to generate the cash flow needed to replace the net purchase price that he could get in the sale. If the purchase price is substantially less, George may evaluate his situation quite differently. George's illness also will greatly influence his decision to sell.

IDEAS IN ACTION

Here's another example. Pete decided to consider selling his retail business that he had built over the last 50 years. He engaged an investment banker, but he only wanted a small universe of potential buyers to bid on his business because he was concerned about word getting out about the potential sale. One potential buyer came in with an offer of $250 million. Pete thought the bid was low but decided to proceed anyway, hoping that he could

> convince the potential buyer to increase the price. During *due diligence*, the potential buyer's accountants uncovered a potentially massive payroll tax liability that substantially increased the risk of buying the business. Even with significant protections in the purchase agreement, the potential buyer reduced the offer by the estimated tax liability that could accrue if the company were audited and lost on the tax issue. Pete continued to believe his company was worth much more and called off the deal. Four years later, Pete's company went bankrupt, partially because of the COVID-19 pandemic and partially as a result of miscalculations he made in reengineering the business. Instead of getting less than he wanted, Pete got nothing in the end.

Everyone perceives the value of their business differently. **The risks of waiting to exit include economic downturns in the industry or the world**—the COVID-19 pandemic put over 630 businesses into bankruptcy, a 10-year high. **Also, declines in the business itself after waiting too long could endanger a successful exit.** If market conditions and the tax environment are right and, based upon reliable intelligence, may be changing adversely in the future, it may be better to sell now.

When President Joe Biden was elected in 2020 and Congress went Democratic, everyone expected taxes to increase dramatically. However, Senators Joe Manchin from West Virginia and Kyrsten Sinema from Arizona put the kibosh on the Senate's ability to pass legislation that would have increased taxes, as compared to the massive tax cuts enacted during the Trump administration. In the summer of 2022, Congress passed a slimmed-down infrastructure bill that increased taxes on corporations with a new minimum tax and enacted other tax increases to pay for climate change and prescription drug reforms. So while it's likely that tax increases or tax cuts will continue to occur, it's hard to predict the timing or impact of such changes. It's always prudent to run models anticipating potential tax changes and rate increases over time to ensure you're thoughtfully planning your exit.

At the other end of the spectrum is analysis by paralysis, which means you're seeking so much data and so many opinions and having to evaluate so many factors that you can't make a decision without reviewing even more data and opinions and considering more factors. Eventually, time will have passed, and you may have lost your opportunity to sell at the best price.

If you and your financial planning team can determine the amount you need to safely retire and not have to continue working, then you know the minimum net amount you need from the transaction. If you haven't done this type of analysis, I urge you to do so. It will give you great comfort to move forward with your planning and in negotiating the sale of your business. With inflation rising and falling, and with economic and tax changes always occurring, it's hard to accurately predict what the future will look like. **But a thoughtful analysis using different assumptions will give you a best case, a middle case, and a worst case; you will want to land somewhere in the middle or on the best-case side in terms of your plan to model the rest of your life financially.**

Once you know how much you need and want from the sale of your business, you still need to check your assumptions and figure out what others think your business is worth. The next section will help you understand how others value your business.

LESSONS LEARNED

- Have a financial planner and CPA evaluate all your assets, including your business, to help you determine how much you will need to retire or otherwise stop working and live comfortably the rest of your life.
- Run your projections using different assumptions, from best case to worst case.
- Make sure you address your "wants" to ensure you are not being too conservative or rigid with your planning.
- Project how much you are currently taking home from the business and whether you should continue holding on to the business vs. selling it.
- Don't wait too long or base your conclusions on the value of your business on baseless assumptions. After all, what you think the business is worth may not reconcile with reality.

HOW MUCH IS YOUR BUSINESS WORTH TO OTHERS?

There's been a flood [of cash] into private capital and into alternative investments from institutional investors and from high-net-worth folks into private equity and hedge funds. So, you've seen private equity as an aggressive buyer in the middle market. As you continue to have low interest rates and a strong credit market and you put all those things together, you end up with a lot of buyers and a lot of sellers.

—Bob Kipps, investment banker

Scan the QR code to watch the entire interview

youtube.com/ @ZellLaw/videos

TALK WITH OTHERS IN YOUR SPACE

You clearly want to talk with others who have recently sold businesses of comparable size in the same industry to gather anecdotal information on what similar businesses are selling for and to set your expectations. This unscientific approach is nonetheless useful in setting some benchmarks against which you can compare your business.

Alternatively, because your business may be unique as compared with others, **it's also a good idea to gather information from people who have confidential information on companies they have helped sell.** By networking with experienced appraisers, investment bankers, and business brokers, as well as CPAs and deal attorneys, you may gather enough information to at least understand what the current market is for your business and set benchmarks to help evaluate what it may be worth.

A More Scientific Approach: Get an Informal Valuation

You could also hire an appraiser or a business broker to conduct a more formal evaluation of your business. *Certified Valuation Analysts* and other valuation experts may intentionally understate the value of your business to protect themselves from liability that could be associated with an overvaluation if they are asked to give a formal *appraisal report* (e.g., for *gift tax* purposes or for purposes of meeting the income tax requirements for valuing corporate interests).

Many appraisers may be willing to perform an informal valuation and provide you with a methodology for how they determined the value along with supporting information without putting it into a formal report. Not only will this exercise cost you less than a full-blown appraisal, but it may also allow the appraiser to be more lenient in expressing a range of values that you might be able to obtain for your business. You are simply asking them for an informal estimate of value to support you in a potential sale of your business. This effort may help you understand how others will value your business when the time comes.

If you are offering *equity* to your employees and your business advisors and consultants, you may have already hired an appraiser to conduct an annual valuation to comply with IRC Section 409A. This could be used as a benchmark of current value. More on that later.

A More Thoughtful Approach: Identify and Fill the Value Gaps

Business exit planners and consultants have tools that can assist you in identifying not only the value of your business but also the *value gaps.* There are different definitions of what a value gap is. It has been defined as being simply the difference between what a seller perceives his or her business to be worth and what the actual value of that business is in the marketplace.

For a product company, value gaps may be revealed by declining or insufficient sales, slow or stunted growth in market share and revenues, low or no *profits*, or other factors that, despite the excellence of the product, result in a lower value based on market experience. A product expert may be needed to help correct the positioning of the product, the marketing channels and messaging, or other deficiencies in the manufacture or marketing of the product.

For a services company, low profit margins, poor customer reviews, high concentration in 1 customer, and high churn of employees and customers may reveal obvious value gaps in the business.

A prospective buyer may also recognize value gaps in the price they offer for your business, particularly if they view you through a different lens focused on their needs. **Whatever the case, you need to have the courage to identify the value gaps in your business and try to fill them before offering the business for sale.** Value-added strengths that buyers seek (and value gaps you may identify and need to fill) include the following.

1. **A Strong Management Team.** Are the players at your company going to be successful post-transaction? Do you have the important disciplines the buyer needs to keep the business running smoothly and profitably? Are there any gaps in the key management roles necessary to operate the business successfully?

Initially, the buyer will need your administrative personnel to help integrate your business with the buyer's, but if the buyer has the same or better infrastructure in terms of human resources (HR) management, financial management and accounting, or other administrative functions, then your administrative staff may not be critical to the ongoing success of the business. Key management positions that usually survive the closing and stay involved in the business may include leaders in operations, sales, product development, manufacturing, technology, marketing, business development, business intelligence, and others who will drive overall value through increased revenues and profits.

2. **Well-Documented Internal Processes and Systems for Running the Business and Operations.** Buyers want to see quickly how well your business is run. Consistency allows your business to grow and scale, and building and documenting the core processes that comprise your unique business model adds value to your business. According to

Gino Wickman in *Traction*, there are 6 core processes that every business must have to be successful:

1. HR processes (how to search, find, hire, orient, manage, review, promote, retain, and terminate people)
2. Marketing processes (how to get your message to your target audience and generate interest in what you are selling)
3. Sales processes (converting leads and prospects into customers)
4. Operations processes (how you make and deliver your product or services to customers)
5. Accounting processes (flow, management, and reporting of all money in and out of your business)
6. Customer retention processes (how you take care of your customers after delivering your product or service and how you retain them)

You should build and document your core processes in preparing your company for sale and identify value gaps in your business.

3. Loyal Employees Who Are Enthusiastic about the Business and Productive in Their Roles. Savvy entrepreneurs know that attracting and retaining good employees makes the business more valuable. In *Drive*, author Daniel Pink posits that in addition to rewarding employees economically, giving employees extrinsic motivation—that is, autonomy, recognition of their mastery and competency, and a sense of purpose for what they are doing, such as allowing them an opportunity to help others—inspires them to be their best and generates loyalty. Clearly, if you couple financial incentives with extrinsic motivators, you are well on your way to filling a common value gap many entrepreneurs face with their workforce.

4. **Excellent Customer Reviews and Feedback.** High customer satisfaction and loyalty invariably increase the value of your business. There are many ways to measure it, including the *net promoter score* (NPS®) metric, which you can use to evaluate whether your clients are happy with your products or services and whether the clients would refer you to someone else they know.[28] Having data and metrics to measure your customer satisfaction and loyalty adds value to your business.

5. **Growing Sales and Profits Every Year.** Showing consistent increases in revenue and *profit* year over year demonstrates growth and increases the overall value of your business to prospective buyers. Buyers and their corporate development officers and investment bankers are looking for constant growth in revenues and earnings, not stagnation or volatility.

6. **Strong Sales and Marketing Support.** You could have the best product in the world or excellent service providers but not be able to reach the right customers. Having a good marketing team to provide qualified leads for the business is essential to growing your pipeline of prospects. This includes market research in the form of evaluating competitors and identifying market opportunities, a lead generation engine, and proposal writing capability that creates a strong backlog of orders for your company. A strong sales support system will also bolster your ability to connect with prospects, secure them as customers, and keep them satisfied and returning for more products and services.

7. **Strong Branding.** A strong brand helps customers know what to expect. Think of Coca-Cola or Google. Your brand represents you and your promise to your customer. It helps you create clarity, stay focused,

and connect with your customers emotionally.[29] It also sets you apart from your competition. Without a strong brand, you may not be able to generate recurring sales from existing customers or attract new customers.

8. Diversified and Good Sources of Supply of Raw Materials or Products. Let's say you're known for making the best chocolate cake in the region. People fly in from across the country just to taste your cake. The secret ingredient, a chocolate that's imported from Tanzania, comes from 1 supplier. Without that supplier, your cake is not as great. What if that supplier goes out of business? Having a diversified source of supply allows you to continue making great cake or delivering great products. Depending on what you're making, it may be difficult to diversify your suppliers, and a lack of diversity could lead to risks that devalue your company.

9. Optimized Financial Reporting and Record Keeping. I am often asked, "Is QuickBooks good enough for handling my financial accounting and reporting needs?" My answer: "It depends." If you have a very small business and the only records you have ever kept are on the cash basis of accounting using QuickBooks as the accounting system, then QuickBooks may be enough. But if you are a growing Rocket Ship with an ever-increasing number of employees and complexity in your business, QuickBooks is probably not enough from a financial reporting perspective. You might also require the following:

- First, you may need to convert cash-basis statements into accrual-basis statements that are based on *generally accepted accounting principles* (GAAP).

- Second, your accountant may need to perform a reconciliation between the cash-basis statements and new accrual-basis statements required under GAAP.

- Third, your financial statements, to be in accordance with GAAP, will need to contain footnote disclosures that explain various components of your financial statements, including your method of accounting, revenue recognition principles, lease terms, depreciation and amortization conventions, deferred compensation, and a great deal more.

- Fourth, you may need greater sophistication in your accounting system to allow you to properly recognize revenue and allocate overhead and indirect costs in accordance with government regulations or industry standards. Also, integrating your budgeting and customer pipeline systems with your financial reporting will lead to more accurate reporting and forecasting.

10. **HR Documentation.** You need to maintain detailed HR records for every employee. You should have a Form I-9 on file for every employee, indicating proof of US citizenship status. In one transaction, we were forced to bring in an employment lawyer to audit compliance with the I-9 reporting and record-keeping requirements and re-create Form I-9 for every employee because the seller did not maintain adequate records. Penalties for failing to obtain and retain Form I-9s for your employees can be heavy.

In addition, you must maintain appropriate tax withholding records for every employee, including IRS Form W-4, indicating the number of tax exemptions claimed, as well as all payroll and employment tax returns and evidence of filings and withholdings for every year of the company's existence. You must also maintain Form W-9 for your independent contractors. A buyer will ask for this as part of the due diligence process, and having adequate documentation and records will increase the buyer's comfort level.

You should also maintain a separate file for each employee that includes the employee's offer letter, performance evaluations, records of any disciplinary proceedings, evidence of any equity or synthetic equity grants (e.g., stock options, *phantom stock*), termination letters, settlement and severance agreements, and *nondisclosure* and noninterference agreements, in particular.

11. **Corporate Organizational Documentation.** You need to maintain complete and accurate records of the business's organizational documents, including signed stock/equity certificates, stock/equity ledgers, minutes and consents of the *board of directors*/managers and shareholders/members, articles of incorporation or organization, bylaws, operating agreements, shareholder agreements, and other documents pertaining to the formation and organization of the entity. For an S corporation, you need to make sure you have a copy of IRS Form 2553 that was filed to elect S corporation status originally and the IRS letter granting that status.

How Do I Determine My Value Gaps?

Do you have any value gaps in your business?

There are many tools and experts available to carry out value gap analysis. You can hire a facilitator or an expert to help you complete a *strengths, weaknesses, opportunities, and threats* (SWOT) analysis, which can also be useful in identifying value gaps.[30] Specifically, you would focus on identifying weaknesses and opportunities to make your business more valuable, as well as threats to the success of your business. Other tools to perform gap analysis include McKinsey 7S and Fishbone.[31] These tools can help you find deficiencies in your business and the effects caused by the value gaps. The goal is to fill the gaps before you offer the business for sale.

If you can't wait, you should be aware of the value gaps when beginning your discussions with prospective buyers. Frequently, it's hard for founders to admit there are any value gaps in their business. There is often a significant divergence between what the seller feels the business is worth and what he or she can obtain in the marketplace.

TYPES OF VALUATIONS
Going Concern Value vs. Liquidation Value

The value of a business that is a going concern should be measured against its *liquidation value*. "Going concern value" represents the potential future profits your business can generate. Buyers analyze going concern value when they believe a company has the potential to survive and grow in the future. The main factor to consider when calculating going concern value is the most recent 3 to 4 years of earnings data. Using past data to reveal recent trends, investors can set future income expectations. Valuation experts usually weight most recent years more heavily than earlier years.

Going concern value typically includes the value of intangible assets, such as *goodwill*, patents, trademarks and copyrights, know-how, trade secrets, and other assets that may not be shown on your company's balance sheet. "Goodwill" embodies your business's ability to generate revenues based upon the various components you have successfully woven together with quality employees, good management, high customer retention, and excellent products and services.

By contrast, "liquidation value" anticipates that the business is not growing and, in fact, is in decline and worth more dissolved than as a going concern. The difference is that if a business *liquidates*, you basically get the value of the assets inside the business. In a liquidation sale, the prices you may attract if you must sell inventory, equipment, or intangible assets separately may be significantly less than what you could sell the assets for in the open market as part of a going concern.

Goodwill

In many service businesses that are being sold today, goodwill is the dominant portion of the purchase price. Specifically, goodwill is the portion of the purchase price that is higher than the sum of the net fair value of all assets purchased and liabilities assumed by the buyer in the acquisition.[32] Goodwill usually relates to the ability of your business to generate revenues and profits into the future.

When goodwill is sold, it generates *capital gains* for the business or the owners, which are currently taxable at rates lower than *ordinary income* from wages and other sources.

In addition to business goodwill, there is a concept known as *personal goodwill* when selling a personal service business. In essence, personal goodwill is an asset that is identified with an individual, not the business itself. It is generated from the personal expertise or business relationships of an individual employee or shareholder. Several cases have approved of the use of personal goodwill in acquisitions if certain requirements are met.[33]

Personal goodwill can reduce the overall income tax for you in an acquisition (particularly if you operate your business as a *C corporation*) **and may allow you and possibly your key employees to participate in the sale of a business if they can establish the existence of personal goodwill apart from the business.** Like business goodwill, gain on the sale of personal goodwill is generally considered capital gain and usually receives a preferential capital gains tax rate (currently up to 20%), as opposed to the higher ordinary income tax rate for the receipt of compensation.[34] With ordinary income tax rates as high as 37%, a direct sale of personal goodwill can often generate significant tax benefits.[35] In addition, the buyer receives a step-up in asset basis upon acquiring personal goodwill, which can be amortized over 15 years and would not otherwise be deductible if all amounts paid were considered paid for the corporation's stock.

HOW DO APPRAISERS VALUE YOUR BUSINESS?

Overview

Appraisers are business valuation experts who use various standard metrics to value your business. **Most commonly, the appraiser uses your recent financial results to project cash flow from the business over a period of years and into the future indefinitely, and then calculates the present value of cash flows by using a** *discount rate* **that reflects the** *cost of capital* **to your business.** As you will see, this technique incorporates several subjective variables to reach a conclusion on the value of the business.

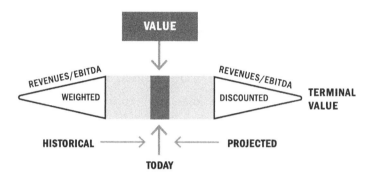

First, are recent financial results truly indicative of what will happen in the future? Perhaps not, but they are the only measures available that show what your business could produce.

Second, how can anyone safely project cash flow over a period longer than one year with any real sense of accuracy? Be honest—looking into the future beyond one year is quite speculative but necessary in terms of valuing the business's prospects.

Third, to calculate the discount rate, the appraiser must determine the *cost of debt and equity* to your business. Although the cost of debt may appear to be easily calculated if you have a clear borrowing history (i.e., it is based on the rate at which you can borrow funds in the marketplace), no one can predict the future of interest rates and how they will affect your business's cost of debt. In addition, the *cost of equity* involves a highly uncertain calculation; it increases as the riskiness of the business increases (decreasing the overall *discounted cash flow* and the value of your business). In other words, the discount rate reflects the business's ability to borrow and finance operations with equity. **The higher the discount rate, the lower the value because there's more risk inherent in the business.**

Historical Financial Statements

With this background, your first step in the valuation exercise is to provide the appraiser with your historical financial statements. You may need to make certain adjustments to the financial statements to omit nonrecurring items, such as the cost of litigation or extraordinary gains on the sale of a division or other assets, and personal expenses, such as personal use of vehicles, charitable contributions, and other personal expenses that you may have run through the business legally.

Forecasts

Because the value of your business is not based solely upon historical results, your next step is to have your CPA, your financial planner, or another person experienced in building complex cash flow projections help you create reasonable but accurate forecasts of your business if you haven't already done so as part of your business planning process. These projections will be crucial in developing a discounted cash flow analysis. The forecasts will evaluate your pipeline of potential customers, recurring revenues and expenses, and backlog of existing work as well as consider industry trends, inflation projections, and other macroeconomic factors affecting your business.

Comparable Companies

Appraisers also look at comparable companies that have engaged in sale or merger transactions over recent years. This comparable company analysis may or may not be relevant to your situation. For example, if you are a government contractor engaged in developing new, cutting-edge cybersecurity products or services, the appraiser may not have useful information to effectively utilize a comparable company analysis. They may only have generic information on other incomparable cybersecurity companies, and their database may be limited to deals in which they were involved or to publicly available information.

They also use public company data, which must usually be discounted heavily in order to be compared with your closely held, private company since a private company's equity is not readily tradable on a public exchange. In other words, there is a discount associated with a private company's equity that is not marketable and can't be sold easily to third parties as public company stock can.

As noted, you should adjust your discounted cash flow projections to add back expenses that are either personal or private in nature or are nonrecurring to the business. These expenses artificially reduce earnings and the calculation of *earnings before interest, taxes, depreciation, and amortization* **(EBITDA),**[36] **which is a common measure used in valuing a business.** EBITDA can also be converted into "free cash flow" with minor adjustments to reveal the baseline for calculating discounted cash flow.

DEEPER DIVE

Free cash flow represents the cash a company generates after accounting for cash outflows to support operations and maintain its capital assets. Unlike EBITDA or net income, free cash flow is a measure of profitability that excludes noncash expenses on the income statement and includes spending on equipment and assets as well as changes in working capital from the balance sheet.

Gift Tax Appraisals

One last note on getting an appraisal for your business—you absolutely must get a formal appraisal with an appraisal report if you plan on transferring a portion of your business (by gift or sale) to a family member or a *trust* for their benefit before the transaction closes. You may also want to get an informal appraisal to help you understand your business's value ahead of a transaction. This may not be necessary if you hire an investment banker or a business broker to help you sell the business, simply because they will go through their own valuation analysis and provide you with an estimated range of expected values. However, if you don't plan on using an investment banker or a business broker, getting an appraisal is not a bad idea if the appraiser gives you a range of values with backup to help you articulate the financial value of your business to your prospective buyer.

THE STORY OF GEORGE AND HANNAH
ADJUST EARNINGS TO BOOST VALUE

Harkening back to our example in Chapter 1, let's change the facts so that George's business, 3DP, has $100 million in revenues but only shows $4 million in net income (after taxes, interest, depreciation, and amortization). This reflects a 4% net profit margin for the business. This margin may be too low for many prospective buyers and might result in a significant discount to the business's value.

George's CPA informs him that he had interest expenses on long-term debt of $90,000 and depreciation and amortization expenses of $45,000 for the year. The entity had no tax liability because it was taxed as an S corporation. So 3DP's EBITDA is $4,135,000 ($4,000,000 + $90,000 + $45,000).

Once George digs into his books and records, he finds that many expenses of the business should be added back. For example, he found that he claimed

- $100,000 per year for personal vehicles for himself and Hannah;
- $25,000 per year for country club memberships;
- $75,000 for personal travel;
- $50,000 in charitable donations;
- $10,000 in other personal expenses;
- $60,000 in life insurance premiums for policies on him and other key employees;
- $1,000,000 in bonuses paid to him and other key employees;
- $150,000 in salaries and bonuses of relatives (other than Hannah) who were hired in the business but weren't working full-time and probably will not continue after the sale of the business (uncovering these expenses also may reveal that George may have claimed improper tax deductions that may require additional representations and warranties to protect the buyer from any IRS challenge in the future);
- $500,000 in litigation fees and expenses for an unusual lawsuit that was filed against the business and settled;

- $300,000 in unsuccessful research and development or marketing efforts that resulted in onetime charges; and
- $35,000 in onetime severance payments to employees under some form of settlement agreement to resolve disputes.

ADJUSTMENTS TO EBITDA

DESCRIPTION	AMOUNT
Net income	$4,000,000
Add back:	
Interest	90,000
Depreciation and amortization	45,000
EBITDA	*$4,135,000*
Add back nonrecurring and personal items:	
Personal vehicles	100,000
Country club dues and expenses	25,000
Personal travel	75,000
Charitable contributions	50,000
Other personal expenses	10,000
Life insurance premiums	60,000
Excess bonuses	1,000,000
Relatives' salaries	150,000
Litigation and settlement	500,000
Research and experimentation	300,000
Severance	35,000
Adjusted EBITDA	*$6,440,000*

These adjustments increased George's bottom line by $2.305 million ($6.44 million − $4.135 million EBITDA). If the buyer applies a multiple of 7x EBITDA to determine the purchase price, George just added $16.135 million ($2.305 million × 7) to his potential purchase price! In other words, each dollar added back to the bottom line is worth the multiple of earnings being applied in the deal.

MULTIPLES, INDUSTRY QUIRKS, AND WARREN BUFFETT

Most clients ask what the proper multiple of EBITDA is for valuing their business. Investment bankers and appraisers remind me (and I remind you) that applying multiples in a vacuum is not the right approach for valuing a business. It may be a shorthand method to determine the valuation of a particular business in a particular industry at a particular point in time. However, multiples rise and fall as market conditions fluctuate, as facts change regarding your business and industry, and as the market for *mergers and acquisitions* (M&As) in your industry evolves. Again, the best measure of a business value starts with a discounted cash flow analysis.

If you want to read some expert white papers and articles on valuing software as a service (SaaS) companies, e-commerce companies, and online and internet business valuation generally, check out Thomas Smale's articles on the website feinternational.com. For example, one paper on SaaS valuation debates whether to use a multiple of seller discretionary earnings (SDE), EBITDA, or revenues. SDE multiples are typically reserved for younger companies with valuations of less than $5 million.[37] EBITDA is generally the standard used to value businesses worth more than $5 million. For SaaS companies, if the business must rely heavily on the owner, revenues are growing at less than 50%

annually year over year, or revenues are less than $2 million per year, then the SDE valuation model should apply. If none of the foregoing metrics apply, the business should either use a multiple of EBITDA or revenues.

Your choice of metric and the determination of the multiple depend on many variables. A higher multiple may be indicated by the age of your business (usually 3+ years is a good starting point), low dependency on you to keep the business going, consistent revenue growth (greater than 10–15% annually), and low customer churn/turnover (not more than 5–7 %).

One side note on cash flow analysis: many of you are developing new technologies, either utilizing patents, copyrights, or some other form of know-how or intellectual property that may constitute a trade secret and that is not easily replicated. The question of the value of such a business clearly depends on the ability of the technology to generate revenues in the future.

As Warren Buffett, "the Oracle of Omaha," once said at the turn of the millennium, "Cash is king and if a business can't generate cash, it may not have any value." I read that quote along with the following quip from Mr. Buffett in an *Associated Press* article when I was serving as CFO and general counsel of NewsReal, Inc., a George Soros–backed internet company that was struggling to generate cash flow:

"If I taught a class, on my final exam I would take an Internet company and ask, 'How much is this company worth?' Anyone who would answer, I would flunk."

Of course, this quote was made in the early days of the internet, and companies without cash flow or profits were being valued using metrics based upon "eyeballs" and "page views" for their websites. Right after the article was published, the tech bubble burst and thousands of companies went out of business.

Technology inventors and investors will argue vociferously that cash flow is not the sole driver of business valuation and that technology should be valued for its potential. But it's the market and the prospective buyers that will ultimately determine what the value of your business is.

> **IDEAS IN ACTION**
>
> Frank recently sold his company to a large government contractor. Frank and his cohorts had developed extremely new technologies to deliver services and gather data that had not been created before. However, the new technologies had not been tested to the point where they were generating meaningful revenues. The company invested millions of dollars in developing the technologies. The buyer did not give much credence to the value of the technologies in the cash purchase price offered. Nevertheless, the buyer did agree to increase the purchase price if the technology generated specific levels of revenues over a finite period.

This is known as an *earnout*, which is used in many cases to protect a buyer if the seller's business doesn't perform as projected. In certain cases, an earnout can be an effective way of capturing future value that is not reflected in current financial results but (you believe) will be realized by implementing the technologies you have developed. The next chapter will delve into earnouts and other strategies to capture the best price and value.

Bottom line: sell your business for what a willing buyer will pay you and what you are willing to accept, and capture any excess value in the form of an earnout.

LESSONS LEARNED

- Talk with other business owners and industry experts to get a better understanding of what you might receive in the sale of your business and what the process is like.
- Consider getting an informal valuation for your business before putting it on the market. You don't need a formal report unless you need the valuation to support pretransaction *estate planning* or gifting strategies; those valuations will be invariably lower than a valuation to determine your strategic value to an interested buyer.
- Identify and fill the value gaps in your business. Consider hiring experts to help you identify the gaps, and consider filling them before you put the company up for sale.
- Understand that going concern value and goodwill may represent the most significant part of the value of your business. Consider selling personal goodwill in a service business to minimize income taxes where appropriate and necessary.
- Appraisers and corporate development officers use discounted cash flow analysis to value your business. They must use a discount rate that measures your cost of capital to predict the present value of your cash flows. The discount rate is a combination of your cost

of borrowing and cost of equity and may involve great subjectivity depending on your business. The higher the discount rate, the lower the value of your business.
- Buyers and investment bankers typically use multiples of EBITDA to value your business. Don't forget to adjust your EBITDA for personal expenses and nonrecurring items that artificially depress (or increase) earnings.
- Remember that cash flow is key in determining the value of any business, but there may be intangibles (e.g., technology) that influence the multiple and value upward.
- Ultimately, the value of your business is what a willing buyer will pay you and what you are willing to accept.

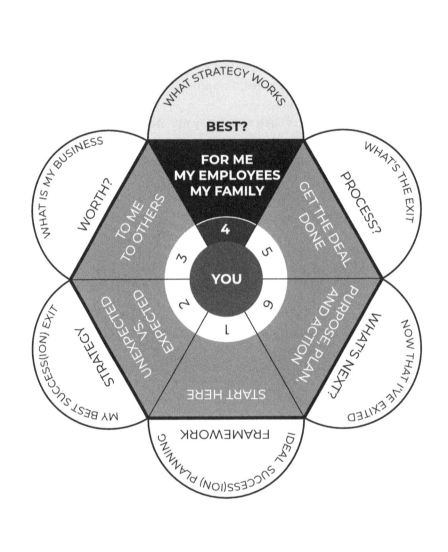

CHAPTER 4

WHAT SUCCESS(ION) EXIT STRATEGY WORKS BEST FOR ME?

"Always start at the end before you begin. Professional investors always have an exit strategy before they invest. Knowing your exit strategy is an important investment fundamental."
—ROBERT KIYOSAKI

WHAT'S THE MARKET FOR MY COMPANY (IS MY BUSINESS SALABLE)?

When I joined the company as employee 13, early childhood education was just starting to get national attention. It had just made the cover of Time magazine. That brain development in the first 5 years was so important. So, during my 15-year tenure at the company, we saw really explosive growth as school systems started to build out public pre-K programs, and Head Start and Early Head Start got more dollars. We started to get an understanding of the importance of those early years, and that they really are the foundation for children's future success in school and life. The company just saw explosive growth, such that when I left the CEO seat and transitioned to the board, we were at about 300 employees.

—Kai-Leé Berke, entrepreneur,
Founding Partner, Hana Education Partners

Scan the QR code to watch the entire interview

youtube.com/ @ZellLaw/videos

After reading Chapter 3, hopefully you have taken some initial steps to determine what your business may be worth to others. Under an ironclad *nondisclosure agreement* (NDA), you may have already contacted investment bankers and business brokers who specialize in your industry to find out what comparable companies are selling for. More likely, they may have contacted you.

One client was getting weekly (sometimes daily) calls from *private equity* (PE) firms looking to buy his company for several years before he decided to sell his business. Others tell me about unsolicited emails they receive weekly or even daily from investment bankers, brokers, PE firms, and potential strategic partners who are looking to purchase or sell their business.

If your email inbox is not overloaded with these solicitations and you are not being aggressively pursued, don't fret. There may be a match for you. Check with your *certified public accountant* (CPA), lawyers, board of advisors, and *board of directors* to see whether they can identify prospective purchasers or introduce you to folks in their networks with whom you can invest your time, leading to potential buyers.

But be careful. You do not want to appear overanxious or desperate by soliciting others to buy your business unless time is of the essence. More importantly, you need to be cautious of competitors or employees finding out about your intentions. This could lead to unintended consequences.

IDEAS IN ACTION

Gina was so anxious to sell her business that she signed a standard NDA with a prospective buyer who was also a competitor, without having an attorney review it. The agreement lacked certain provisions that would prohibit the prospective buyer from soliciting Gina's customers, prospective customers, and employees for a specified period (i.e., 1 year would have worked). Then Gina promptly provided the prospective buyer with a detailed listing of her customers and employees. Once the competitor had this valuable information, they called off negotiations and proceeded to go after Gina's customers and employees. While the confidentiality provisions of the NDA may have provided some protection and Gina arguably could have sued the competitor for violating the NDA, the protections weren't enough to prevent the competitor from poaching her customers and employees and severely damaging her business. Gina learned a painful lesson and suffered deep losses due to her overanxious efforts to sell during a challenging time.

Similarly, you should be cautious about disclosing to your employees your intentions to sell the business. They may fear the change that inevitably comes after an acquisition occurs and seek alternative employment. Yet you will always need to involve a few key employees in preparing for a potential sale. They will assist you in handling the details of preparing financial information, copies of contracts, and lists of employees, vendors, suppliers, and contractors, along with managing the *due diligence* process (discussed in Chapter 5), which can be overwhelming to many entrepreneurs. You may want to have those key employees sign a special NDA that specifically addresses the potential transaction and their duties in connection with the transaction, in exchange for which you might promise them a special bonus if they help you close the transaction. This incentive will keep the key employees engaged during a tumultuous time.

Back to the main question: is your company salable? To understand the process and determine whether there is a market for your company, you've solicited the opinions of professionals and experts in your industry and may have even contacted folks who sold their businesses. If the lights ahead are green, you are ready to dig deeper.

NAVIGATING TOUGH TIMES

Overanxious entrepreneurs may attract "bottom fishers" or "vulture" capitalists who are looking to buy their businesses for next to nothing. Try to avoid these characters if you can, but the exigencies of your situation may force you to make the difficult choice of selling to the lowest bidder. When the economy turns downward, many businesses may not have a choice in the matter.

WHAT SUCCESS(ION) EXIT STRATEGY WORKS BEST FOR ME?

I witnessed this first during the savings and loan crisis in the late 1980s and early 1990s, which resulted in the failure of nearly a third of the 3,234 savings and loan associations in the United States. The failures were precipitated by extreme increases in interest rates, *stagflation*, and increased risk-taking by lenders who were essentially operating in an unregulated market resembling the Wild West.[38] Taxpayers bore the brunt of the crisis, shouldering over $132 billion of the total $163 billion in losses generated by the failed lending environment. Thousands of real estate projects were abandoned, hundreds of thousands of folks lost their jobs, and the economy struggled.

It happened again in the early 2000s when the dot-com and technology bubble burst, technology stock prices plummeted, and again thousands of businesses failed, and hundreds of thousands more lost their jobs. The bubble was predictable, given that companies were being valued at overinflated earnings multiples (or infinite multiples where no earnings existed) without real economics, business plans, or cash flow.[39] Economic failures recurred in 2007–2009 during the *Great Recession* in the wake of the subprime lending debacle, brought on by overexuberance in the real estate sector, fueled once again by lack of oversight and regulation of the lending practices of banks, insurance companies, and investment banks. This led to a worldwide credit crunch and a precipitous drop in bank lending.[40]

And who can forget the massive economic disruption caused by the COVID-19 pandemic? Thousands of viable businesses were forced to close, workers were forced to either work remotely or abandon their jobs, students were sent home to learn over online platforms that teachers were unprepared to manage, and millions died.

If your business is adversely affected during an economic downturn, you may still be able to sell it, but the price you receive will depend on the state of the company and the economy at the time of the sale. In 2022, we are experiencing hyperinflation and entering a period of potential stagflation. Many companies will fail; fewer will succeed.

Certain industries and specialties continue to thrive and garner high multiples. For example, companies engaged in cybersecurity threat detection and protection should thrive even during an economic downturn. Healthcare, food, consumer staples, and basic transportation are examples of industries that can perform well in recessions.[41] You can either try to weather the economic storm and wait until the economy shows signs of recovery to sell your business or sell it now to relieve yourself of the burden of debt and operating in an extremely difficult environment.

THE STORY OF GEORGE AND HANNAH
ADAPT DURING A RECESSION

Let's put our friend George into an economic recession and see how he can morph 3DP to keep it thriving. If George continues to make 3D printers, who will buy them? The demand for his product may decline precipitously during a downturn unless he can use the technology to provide an essential service. Hannah knows there is a global shortage of housing. In such an environment where inflation drives the cost of building materials and labor sky-high, 3D printers have started to use the technology to build houses. The

> *Economist* reported that "not only does 3D-printing allow greater versatility and faster construction, it also promises lower cost and in a more environmentally friendly approach than is possible at present."[42] Houses can be built at a fraction of the cost and time it takes to construct conventional brick-and-mortar dwellings. George and Hannah could adapt the business during changing times to capitalize on the boom in 3D-printed houses and keep revenues and *profits* growing.

Today is no different. We are experiencing hyperinflation and facing another recession. I look at these changes as opportunities to focus on Business Success(ion) planning and other areas that require our skillsets as innovative lawyers who think out of the box.

In your business, you have undoubtedly faced disruption in the wake of economic downturns and will encounter unexpected events in the future. The critical question is this: how can you weather these storms, survive, and succeed where others have failed? **If you have the time (i.e., the runway), then you need to anticipate the downturns and have a plan B or contingency plan to overcome the unexpected events lurking ahead.** What is your plan B? I have one. George now has one. Do you?

Planning for the unexpected deals not only with death and *disability*; it also anticipates economic downturns. Assuming you can sell your business, let's focus on what's in it for you if you do sell.

LESSONS LEARNED

- Solicit opinions of professionals, investment bankers, experts in your industry, and others who have sold their businesses to get an indication of whether you can sell your business.
- Navigating tough times, including economic downturns and pandemics, requires patience, adaptability, and resilience.
- Beware of "bottom fishers" who may sense your desperation to sell your business in tough times.
- Plan for unanticipated economic downturns and other tough times by having sufficient cash reserves and contingency plans to weather the most difficult situations.

WHAT'S IN IT FOR ME?

We were [in business for] 5 years, and we were acquired by Accenture. [Following the] acquisition, I became the head of Accenture's global cyber defense practice, which for me was a lot of fun. I was, you know, a small to mid-size company guy, and for Accenture to say take the largest element of our security practice and go run with it, build it in your image. For me, it was great that Accenture would take that kind of risk on an entrepreneur. But for me, it was fun to see how my skills applied to a big company environment.

—Matt Devost, entrepreneur and cybersecurity expert

WHAT SUCCESS(ION) EXIT STRATEGY WORKS BEST FOR ME?

Scan the QR code to watch the entire interview

youtube.com/ @ZellLaw/videos

WATCH OUT FOR TAXES IN CASH-ONLY DEALS

If you're lucky enough to sell your business for all cash, you need to reserve a portion of the proceeds to pay the *income* tax due on the sale. The tax is based upon the gain you must recognize when you sell the business, the structure of your business, and the structure of the transaction. What's left over is yours to keep, unless the buyer makes a claim against you for undisclosed liabilities or damages incurred because of breaches of promises you made in the sales agreement (see Chapter 5 for details on the representations and warranties that buyers expect you to make in the sale of your business).

The amount of gain you must recognize equals the cash or other property you receive plus any liabilities assumed by your buyer, minus your tax basis in the business interest or assets you sold. If you sell stock or *limited liability company* (LLC) interests to the buyer, your gain on the sale may be treated as long-term *capital gain*, which is currently taxed at a maximum federal rate of 20% if you held your business interest for more than 12 months. If you held the business interest for 12 months or less, you would be taxed at a progressive federal rate of as much as 37%.[43]

In addition to federal income tax, you may be subject to the net investment income tax (NIIT) of 3.8% on the sale of your business interest. The NIIT is imposed on the lesser of

- your NIIT (which generally includes interest, dividends, rents, and royalties, minus related expenses) or
- the excess of modified *adjusted gross income* over the following threshold amounts:
    - $250,000 for married filing jointly or qualifying widow(er),
    - $125,000 for married filing separately, and
    - $200,000 in all other cases.[44]

The NIIT is imposed on income-derived passive activities or trading in financial instruments or commodities, and net gains from the disposition of property (to the extent considered in computing taxable income), other than property held in a trade or business to which NIIT doesn't apply. If you materially participate in your business, the NIIT will not apply to you.[45]

IDEAS IN ACTION

Rita is the managing member of her firm, which is an LLC electing to be taxed as an *S corporation*. She spends substantially all her working time on the business. If she sells her stock (and the transaction is not treated as an *asset sale* for tax purposes), the gain on the sale will not be subject to the NIIT because she materially participates in the business.

Depending upon the structure of the transaction, you may also be required to recognize *ordinary income* on the sale (which is taxed at higher rates than capital gains). If you sell assets that have been depreciated, such as computers or vehicles, and a portion of the purchase price is allocated to those assets, then any gain on their sale will be "recaptured" and immediately taxed as ordinary income. Also, if you sell *accounts receivable* that have not been previously taxed (i.e., because you are a cash-basis taxpayer), the difference between your receivables and accounts payable and accrued expenses will be taxed as ordinary.

Virtually all my clients ask why they should pay any ordinary income tax if they just sell their stock or LLC *membership interest* in the transaction. One client recently said, "I've held on to the stock since I started the company over 20 years ago. I should get long-term capital gains treatment when I sell the stock, right?" My standard answer: "It depends."

Most buyers want the ability to write off (i.e., deduct the cost of) the assets in the business they are purchasing. If they don't acquire assets and simply purchase your stock, the buyers can treat the stock sale as an asset sale for tax purposes by making a special election under the IRC.[46] PE buyers also prefer to structure the transaction so they can write off the assets and *goodwill* using an approach that has been approved by the IRS.[47]

If you operate your business as a *C corporation*, you might be able to convince the buyer to purchase your stock and allow you to qualify for long-term capital gains treatment.[48] If your corporation does not render professional services and is otherwise treated as a qualified small business, you may even be able to exclude all or a portion of the gain on the sale of your stock completely, depending on when you bought the stock, how you acquired it, and how much you paid for it. Among other requirements, you must hold on to the stock for at least 5 years to qualify for this special treatment.[49]

If the buyer insists on purchasing your corporation's assets or treating the stock purchase as an asset purchase (i.e., to write off goodwill and the cost of other assets), then the corporation will pay tax on the sale of the assets. Capital gains of a C corporation are taxed at the same rate as ordinary income at the corporate level (currently, 21% federal, plus state income tax). When the proceeds are distributed, they may be taxed to the shareholders either as dividends (currently taxed at up to a 20% federal rate) or as capital gains (same rate but reduced by the basis or cost of the stock). This double taxation serves as a significant deterrent in using the C corporation structure if a business sale is contemplated.

IDEAS IN ACTION

Rita owns a Delaware corporation that is taxed as a C corporation. She received an offer to purchase her corporation for $10 million net of expenses of sale. The buyer has required Rita to treat the transaction as a sale of the corporation's assets. The corporation's income tax basis in the assets is $2.5 million, and Rita's income tax basis (investment) in her stock is $500,000. When the corporation closes the sale, it will pay federal income tax of $1.575 million ($10 million − $2.5 million tax basis × 21% corporate income tax rate). If the remaining proceeds are distributed in a complete *liquidation* of the corporation, Rita will pay additional federal income tax of $1.585 million ($10 million gross proceeds − $1.575 million corporate income tax − $500,000 tax basis in her stock × 20%), leaving her with net proceeds of $6.84 million before state corporate and individual income tax.

WHAT SUCCESS(ION) EXIT STRATEGY WORKS BEST FOR ME?

If you operate the business as an S corporation or a partnership, you should only have one level of tax,[50] but, depending on your facts, some of the gain you incur on the sale of your business may be treated as ordinary income and not as capital gains, resulting in a higher tax rate on the ordinary income portion of the sales proceeds.[51] In the case of an S corporation, it would be better for you to treat the sale as a pure stock sale, which would generate long-term capital gains on the transaction and be taxed at a lower rate.

You need to determine your state income tax on the sale as well. The state income tax rules and rates vary from state to state and are based upon where you live and where the corporation was organized and operates. Most states tax capital gains at the same rate as they tax ordinary income. The income tax consequences vary significantly among the states. In New York, the highest rate of income tax is 8.82%, and if you live in New York City, the rate is as high as 3.876%, for a total top marginal rate of 12.696%. California's income tax rates are even higher. By contrast, 9 states—Alaska, Florida, Nevada, New Hampshire, South Dakota, Tennessee, Texas, Washington, and Wyoming—do not impose income taxes on capital gains (New Hampshire taxes interest and dividends).

The tax hit is not as severe if you can deduct state income taxes to reduce your federal income tax liability. However, the Tax Cuts and Jobs Act of 2017 (TCJA) temporarily disallows the ability to deduct state income and other state and local taxes above $10,000 per year. This rule sunsets at the end of 2025.

THE STORY OF GEORGE AND HANNAH
GEORGE SELLS 3DP FOR ALL CASH

What should George do if he is offered $30 million in cash for his stock in 3DP and the corporation is treated as an S corporation? If the corporation has no built-in gain (which could trigger corporate-level tax) and the income tax basis of his stock equals $1 million, he will have $29 million in capital gains subject to federal tax at a rate of 20%, or total federal income tax of $5.8 million, if he simply sells the stock.[52] If George lives in San Diego, California, he will have additional state income tax of 13.3%, or an additional $3.857 million. So the total tax George will incur in a straight stock sale would be $9.657 million. Because George materially participates in the business, he would not incur additional NIIT.

If George's buyer insists on treating the purchase as an asset purchase (i.e., to write off the goodwill in George's business), then a portion of the gain on the sale could be treated as ordinary income. Assuming that 3DP's accounts receivable exceed its accounts payable and accrued expenses by $2 million, that amount would be subject to a 37% tax rate (instead of 20%), resulting in $340,000 (37% − 20% × $2 million) of additional tax on the transaction. George's attorney will try to negotiate an increase in the purchase price to compensate George for the additional income tax incurred on the treatment sought by the buyer, but this may be a tough battle to win.[53]

If 3DP is operated as a C corporation and the buyer wants to treat the sale as an asset sale (by making a Section 338 election), and George wants to take the cash out of the corporation after the sale, he may be subject to double taxation on the sale of the assets of the corporation (or if the stock sale is treated as an asset sale and a Section 338 election is made).

Using the facts above and assuming the tax basis of the assets inside the corporation is 0, 3DP would pay tax at a rate of 29.84% on the asset gain if the entity is in California.[54] So 3DP would incur taxes of $8.952 million in corporate-level tax. If George distributes the remaining cash to himself in a liquidation of the corporation, his net proceeds would be reduced by an additional 33.3% (13.3% + 20%), leaving him with $13.372 million after taxes.[55] While there may be ways to mitigate this extremely harsh result, this example clearly illustrates the painful impact of double taxation using a C corporation.

CHANGING STATE RESIDENCY TO SAVE TAXES

Many of my clients have attempted to restructure their affairs to save state income taxes by moving from a high-tax jurisdiction (e.g., California, New York, Massachusetts, Maryland, DC,) to low- or no-tax jurisdictions (e.g., Florida, Texas, Wyoming, Nevada). A word of caution is appropriate here: the high-tax jurisdictions don't like that strategy, are on the alert for taxpayers using it, and may audit you if the dollars are significant. The question of *residency* or *domicile* varies from state to state. What may be required to establish residency or domicile in Florida may not be sufficient to abandon domicile for state income tax purposes in New York or California.

> ### THE STORY OF GEORGE AND HANNAH
> # AVOIDING STATE INCOME TAX
>
> Let's say George starts out as a California resident and wants to avoid the confiscatory taxes imposed by that state. So he devises a plan with his accountant to move to Florida before the sale of his company takes place. Among other things, George abandons his California driver's license and gets a Florida license. He registers to vote in Florida, changes his car registration to Florida from California, opens bank accounts in Florida, and signs a one-year lease for a condo on the beach. He changes his schedule so that most of his time in the calendar year before the sale (at least 183 days) and in the year of sale is spent in Florida, not California. However, George also retains ownership of his San Diego home, which contains his valuable art collection, personal effects, and expensive antiques and furniture.

Has George changed his place of residence from California to Florida? Florida may recognize him as a resident, but California may also argue that he has not abandoned his California domicile and therefore remains subject to California income tax on the sale of his shares in 3DP, simply because he continues to maintain his "primary" residence in California.

"Domicile" is determined primarily by intent, and intent is established based upon the individual's facts and circumstances. Here is an excerpt from Peter Faber's Bloomberg State Tax Portfolio 1240, describing the idea of changing or abandoning domicile:

A change in residence must be genuine, based on facts and circumstances, to be recognized for state tax purposes. A person who lives in New York and who has a winter home in Florida will not be able to become a Florida resident for income tax purposes merely by signing a declaration of Florida domicile and buying a condominium there. A change in domicile for tax purposes generally requires a change in the principal focus of a person's business, financial, social, and family activities in every meaningful respect. A person attempting to show a change in domicile for tax purposes should establish as many contacts with the new state as possible, including joining clubs, establishing religious affiliations, having relationships with physicians, voting, and taking part in local civic and philanthropic activities.[56]

Bottom line: it's not easy to change your domicile to reduce your state income tax. You not only have to establish contacts in the new state, but you also must abandon your contacts in the old state to a significant degree to ensure the desired result. Consult your accountant and tax attorney before taking the drastic step of abandoning your domicile to save state income taxes on the sale of your shares or ownership interest in your business!

CASH AND A PROMISSORY NOTE

Often, the buyer wants to limit the up-front cash payment to you as the seller by paying part of the purchase price in cash and the balance in the form of a *promissory note* payable to you or your company. This technique allows the buyer to reduce its risk in the transaction. The note might include provisions that decrease the principal amount and interest payable on the note if you breach any of your representations, warranties, or covenants made in the purchase agreement. It may also include performance metrics that must be met by your business post-closing to receive the desired purchase price.

Under the installment method of tax accounting, you generally do not have to recognize income on the note until the buyer makes payments to you.

- A portion of the payments will be treated as interest income based upon the interest rate in the note, a portion of the purchase price (whether or not payments are made on the note) immediately will trigger ordinary income to the extent of depreciation recapture or other exceptions to the installment method, and the remainder of the note payments are generally deferred and treated as capital gains income and return of capital.

- If you do not charge interest on the note given by the buyer, the IRS may force both of you to impute interest at the applicable federal rate published monthly by the Treasury Department, depending on the amount of the note and its duration.[57]

- In addition, if the sales price exceeds $150,000, the IRS may charge interest on the deferred tax liability included in the promissory note where the installment obligation exceeds $5 million.[58]

IDEAS IN ACTION

Winona is selling her business for $30 million cash and a $5 million promissory note. The business is treated as an S corporation for federal and state income tax purposes. She is selling her stock to the buyer, and the buyer has agreed not to treat the transaction as an asset sale. The interest and principal on the note will be payable on the second anniversary of the closing. Winona will pay income tax on the $30 million proceeds received in the year of sale and will pay income tax on the note when the note payments are received. The interest on the note will be taxed as ordinary income (taxed at up to a 37% federal rate) but will not be subject to NIIT tax if Winona materially participates in the business. The note principal will be taxed at capital gains rates. Winona's income tax basis in her shares will be allocated between the original sales proceeds and the principal on the note to reduce the capital gains on the sale. Because the note does not exceed $5 million, no interest will be imputed on the deferred tax liability.

EARNOUTS AND CONTINGENT NOTES

Occasionally, buyers will use a *contingent promissory note*, or the purchase agreement will include an *earnout*, on which additional purchase price is payable if certain performance metrics are achieved. A buyer can limit their risk in terms of the up-front cash flow investment that they pay for your business by structuring the purchase as part cash and part note, with the note being the additional contingent sale price. The note portion or contingent sale portion is typically referred to as an "earnout."

The earnout may reflect different aspects of the value of your business.

- In some cases, the earnout reflects the difference between the buyer's estimate of the overall potential enterprise value of the business and the amount of cash the buyer is willing to pay you at closing.

- In other cases, the earnout may relate to contingencies that are not predictable at closing because past financial information may not be indicative of future performance, and your projections may be viewed skeptically.

- In other words, the earnout could relate to the value of technologies or patents you have developed, but you have not yet realized their value by generating revenue or cash flow.

- The difference between what the buyer is ultimately willing to pay you and what the buyer is willing to pay at closing in cash is the earnout.

In most cases, an earnout requires you to achieve certain levels of performance—either in revenues, profits, or a combination of the two—following the closing. If the targets are achieved or exceeded, the earnout gets paid. One of the most heavily negotiated areas is whether, and the extent to which, the earnout has been achieved.

THE STORY OF GEORGE AND HANNAH
GEORGE TAKES AN EARNOUT

Let's say George negotiates an earnout as part of his purchase agreement entitling him to an additional $2 million after the first year following the closing if 3DP sales exceed at least 10% of the trailing 12 months' revenue at closing. Let's assume further that in year 2, the buyer will pay George $4 million if the cumulative sales for years 1 and 2 exceed 20% of the trailing 24 months' revenue at closing, less any earnout payment made in year 1. This means that George can miss the target in year 1, but hit the cumulative target in year 2 and earn the full earnout payment.

What happens if George achieves 9.9% growth as opposed to 10% in year 1? Shouldn't George receive something because 3DP came so close to the target? If not, George is being penalized for not hitting the 10% target but is still successful since 3DP increased revenues by 9.9% per year. Without providing for some form of payout if the targets are not hit, George arguably gets nothing unless the agreement contains language that allows for a partial payment of the earnout if a minimum growth percentage is achieved.

One solution would be for George to negotiate a partial payment if 3DP exceeds 8% annual growth where 10% is the goal. In that case, George could structure the earnout to receive something between 0 and $2 million if the revenue growth rate falls within that range. If revenue growth is 8% or less, George would get nothing.

What if George exceeds the projected target? Can he get more than the agreed-upon earnout payment? Although paying more than the targeted earnout amount is less common, the buyer may be willing to share additional upside with George, which might be inspired by hot market conditions favoring sellers generally or where George has an extremely attractive business in the buyer's eyes. It certainly is a goal that every seller should try to achieve and one the buyer may try to ignore or reject because, according to the buyer, the earnout is the maximum amount a buyer may be willing to pay for George's business.

PROTECTING YOUR ABILITY TO EARN THE EARNOUT

In addition to safeguarding your ability to get something if you come close to the performance target, you also need to protect your ability to receive the earnout in general. You should try to retain some level of control over your business for the earnout period. For example, if the buyer terminates you (or one of your key employees who helped you generate revenue) without cause, then it should arguably be required to pay the entire earnout payment. Or, if the buyer changes your business model or forces you and your employees to work on matters that might detract from your ability to hit the target, the earnout should arguably be accelerated. On the other hand, the buyer will not want to relinquish control of a business that it is acquiring, and such demands may go unheeded.

If the earnout is based on profitability or *earnings before interest, taxes, depreciation, and amortization* (EBITDA), then you will be concerned over whether you have continued control of revenues and expenses.

IDEAS IN ACTION

A buyer was acquiring Quincy's company and wanted to pay a significant portion of the purchase price in the form of an earnout that was based on hitting certain revenue and *profit* targets following the closing. The success of the business and the ability to achieve the earnout was largely dependent on the continued stewardship of Quincy, the CEO of the company, as well as his management team. The purchase agreement included a provision that said if Quincy or certain key employees were terminated without cause (narrowly defined to include only egregious acts) or if they quit with good reason (broadly defined to include changes in compensation or benefits, location for performing services, title, duties, and reporting responsibilities), then the entire earnout would be accelerated. In addition, the agreement contained protections against the buyer loading the company with overhead and expenses that would prevent the company from meeting the profit targets.

This type of protection is difficult to negotiate with buyers, particularly PE firms that may desire to bring in outside management to run the business after the acquisition. However, it was important to Quincy and the other shareholders because it meant an additional $5 million in sales proceeds.

LETTING GO

Are you ready to relinquish control of your business to someone else? What will you do in retirement? Most founders don't want to let go of control because the business is their life. This factor is one of the greatest impediments to Business Success(ion) planning.

Many founders find it extremely hard to break away from the business. They may slow down, take long vacations, and then swoop back in with a vengeance when their energy is restored, only to find that the business has not performed as well as they had hoped. Something has gone awry, so they need to inject their charisma back into the business and "save" it. This is a universal truth of entrepreneurs.

Your entrepreneur's mentality and psychology make it very difficult to transition away from the business you love and to which you have devoted your lifetime with blood, sweat, and tears. However, if you can build and implement a well-devised Business Success(ion) plan and create processes to transfer control of the business, whether to the next generation of your family, to the next generation of managers, or to a third-party buyer, then you must let go of the strings.

You, as the founder-entrepreneur, must reconcile yourself to the fact that your involvement in the business has come to an end or will come to an end unexpectedly and leave the family with much less than if you follow the plan and processes you have spent money, time, and energy developing. It's a process just to get you to accept this basic fact, but it is essential to your successful business exit.

LESSONS LEARNED

- You need to understand what your after-tax proceeds will be if you sell your business vs. what you would earn, after taxes, if you held on to the business. This requires you to understand the structure of the sale and negotiate the most favorable outcome if you are trying to save the buyer taxes in the deal.

- Be careful in changing your state residency to save state and local taxes. Your resident state's auditors will examine a variety of factors, including whether you have retained a permanent residence and presence in your original home state, to determine whether you really intended to establish domicile/residency in another state.
- Earnouts may be an important part of your sale transaction. You need to try to control your ability to earn the earnout and to receive a portion of the targeted payment if you come close to the target.
- Be ready to relinquish control of your business once you sell it. It's hard leaving your passion, but with proper planning, you can do so methodically and in style.

WHAT'S IN IT FOR MY EMPLOYEES?

I started as a CFO, and I had a mentor. We all love mentors and, quite honestly, they taught me the operational aspects of a business. And I quickly migrated from the financial side of the house, much more to becoming an operational executive. They sat me down, taught me about product management, product development, and operations. I think it was pretty intuitive to me.

—John Becker, entrepreneur and CEO

Scan the QR code to watch the entire interview

youtube.com/
@ZellLaw/videos

Every successful entrepreneur has been supported by dedicated employees who have given their time, effort, heart, and soul to help build the business. If the buyer minimizes the vision, values, and culture you've cultivated with your employees, the employees may be discarded like unwanted refuse.

In Chapter 2, I told the story of the managed services provider who sold his business to a PE fund right before COVID-19 hit. As revenues and profits flattened, the PE fund lost confidence in management and subsequently jettisoned virtually the entire executive team. In another transaction, a giant government contractor engineered a massive layoff of my client's entire workforce simply to gain access to key contracts with a 3-letter government agency.

In both cases, the buyers made mistakes, in my view. In these and other cases, the buyers eviscerated the cultures of the selling companies to ensure the primacy of their shareholders and investors. More importantly, they cut off interaction between certain key customers and the companies by eliminating some of the sellers' key contacts and their supporting network.

If you are focused on continuing your culture of collegiality and perpetuating your vision and values, you will be more inclined to sell your business to a buyer who is aligned with you. You, as the successful entrepreneur, will be keenly focused on how the transaction will impact your team.

SHOULD THEY STAY OR SHOULD THEY GO?

You'll need to determine whether your employees will be allowed to continue with the acquiring company after the sale. You should ask this question of any prospective buyer up front. There may be employees who should not stay and should be let go prior to or after the sale.

Be careful—if those employees hold *equity* or stock options in your company, there may be a problem in releasing them immediately prior to the transaction, particularly if they hold unvested equity, which could be lost or bought out at a reduced value because of their termination from employment.

- Many lawsuits are initiated by employees who claim they were wrongfully terminated solely in anticipation of the sale of the business, especially if the sale takes place shortly after their termination from employment and they lose their equity stake because of the termination.

- Many equity plans account for this possibility by giving the terminated employee the right to participate in a portion of the sale proceeds if they are terminated without cause within a short period of time before the sale is closed (e.g., 3 to 6 months).

If all the employees are promised employment with the acquiring company, you will need to get that in writing and try to protect the employees from being terminated "at will" shortly after the closing of the transaction. This might be in the form of a covenant contained in the definitive purchase agreement.

You can protect your key employees by demanding that the buyer enter into employment agreements that provide severance if the employees are terminated "without cause" or they resign with "good reason."

These terms are often heavily negotiated and may not be acceptable to the buyer if it has not and will not extend such protections to employees of other companies it has acquired.

In addition, the definition of "key employee" may be limited to the founders and one or two other employees critical to the success of the ongoing venture. The key employees who receive employment agreements should retain their own counsel, which can further delay and complicate the closing of the sale. Everyone else most likely will be subject to standard nondisclosure and nonsolicitation agreements.

TRANSACTION (OR "CHANGE IN CONTROL") BONUSES

IDEAS IN ACTION

The managers of one business took over for a deceased founder and did not have an equity stake in the business. They were hired at a critical time to ensure the survival and success of the business. Without the managers, the business would not have survived and thrived at the rate and level it did. Understandably, the managers felt they were owed more than just their salaries or a small bonus. They negotiated hard and had their attorney (who was the father of one of them) require that significant bonuses be paid to each of them at closing to encourage them to agree to remain with the company and continue operating the business post-closing.

The family of the deceased founder needed the managers to remain involved for the deal to close but felt they were being held hostage by the managers' last-minute demands. Essentially, the managers knew that they had negotiating leverage, which they would have relinquished

WHAT SUCCESS(ION) EXIT STRATEGY WORKS BEST FOR ME?

following the transaction if they had just proceeded and signed on as mere "at will" employees of the ongoing company.

Rather than waiting until the last minute, you could utilize "change in control" bonuses to incentivize key employees to continue with the business following the sale. More importantly, these bonuses are helpful in recognizing the important contributions of your key employees, particularly if they do not own shares of your business. The buyer will not object to these bonuses if they are paid out of the sales transaction proceeds or from other cash in the company available to make the payments. In other words, a buyer will rarely subsidize the payment of change-in-control bonuses.

The timing of these arrangements is important. If you wait until just before closing to agree to these bonuses, it may appear that you must give them something to keep them with the company. If you enter into the agreement before the key employees know that the company is being sold (i.e., to show your appreciation for their loyalty and hard work), they may take a different view and appreciate the gesture. In any case, the bonus agreement should clearly state that no bonus is payable unless you close the transaction.

There are many examples of change-in-control bonuses in the public domain. You can access them through the SEC's EDGAR filings or via Google searches.[59] I have used change-in-control bonus agreements in at least half of the more than 100 transactions in which I have assisted over the last 30+ years, and they assist in transitioning the business smoothly to the buyers.

RETENTION BONUSES

In many deals, retention bonuses are offered to key employees who are critical to the future success of the business. These bonuses become even more important if you are subject to an earnout based on the performance of the company after the acquisition. If a key employee leaves during the earnout period, they will typically forfeit all or part of the retention bonus. However, if they leave during the earnout period and haven't been promised a retention bonus, there's nothing for them to lose in leaving the company (unless they have equity in the new company, which is discussed below).

Retention bonuses are sometimes paid by the buyer and sometimes by the seller, and often the parties may agree to split the cost, depending upon the situation. The retention-bonus payments might be staged over 12, 24, or 36 months. If the employee leaves voluntarily, dies, or becomes disabled during that time period, they will receive only the portion of the retention bonus earned before their termination and would give up the rest. If they are terminated without cause or leave with good reason, the entire retention bonus might be accelerated. If they are terminated with cause, they usually must forfeit the entire bonus.

IDEAS IN ACTION

You offer an employee a retention bonus of $300,000, promising to pay one-third at the end of 12 months, an additional third at the end of 24 months, and the remaining third at the end of 36 months of continuous employment. If the employee leaves the company voluntarily after the 13th month, she would be entitled to receive one-third of the bonus but lose the remainder. The employee will want to include provisions in the retention-bonus agreement requiring payment of the full bonus if the employer terminates the employee without cause or the employee leaves with good reason. These terms are usually defined in the retention-bonus agreement and often heavily negotiated.

Ideally, you want the buyer to pay the retention bonus; the buyer will want you to pay the bonus out of the total proceeds paid to you and the other owners in the transaction.

SALARIES, PERFORMANCE BONUSES, AND BENEFITS

Your continuing employees will be concerned about several things.

- First, they will want to know how secure their position with the new company is. You can try to guarantee their employment for a short period in the purchase agreement or with an employment agreement, which is reserved only for select key employees. Even then, the employment agreements usually provide that the employees are at will (i.e., they can be terminated at any time for any reason), but they can offer severance benefits in the form of continued base salary, benefits, and bonuses if the employees are terminated without cause or they leave with good reason.

- Other continuing employees will be protected only by the employment policies of the new employer.

- The buyer should credit the continuing employees with prior service at your company in terms of the benefits it offers to them, particularly where severance payments and paid time off or vacation are based upon longevity of employment.

Your employees will also want to receive at least the same salary they're receiving currently, and if they are underpaid, they may demand a raise. If you decide to increase their pay before closing, you will need to disclose any changes in your employees' compensation to the buyer ahead of the transaction. Increases in compensation immediately before closing result in an unexpected drop in EBITDA, decreasing the overall value of your company to the buyer. The buyer may demand a reduction in the purchase price if the changes are material.

IDEAS IN ACTION

Kendra decided to increase the base compensation of several employees shortly before she sold her business and after most of the details in the transaction had been negotiated. When Kendra disclosed this information to the buyer at the last minute, the buyer was livid. The buyer demanded a decrease in the purchase price and other concessions from Kendra, and Kendra capitulated to save the deal. Basically, Kendra undermined the trust she had built with the buyer over months of negotiations and created an environment of mistrust and uncertainty going forward. Fortunately, the parties reconciled their differences and closed the deal, but Kendra's actions caused damage to their relationship.

Your employees will also want to maintain or improve their current benefits following the closing of the deal. During the due diligence phase (see Chapter 5), you should verify the benefits the new employer will offer the employees in evaluating the overall deal from your employees' perspectives. If their healthcare coverage is in any way diminished because of the acquisition or if their ability to participate in or receive employer matching for retirement plans, such as 401(k) plans, is adversely affected because of the acquisition, the employees will be unhappy, and an unhappy group of employees will lead to major problems after the closing.

> **IDEAS IN ACTION**
> Sheila's company offered employees paid sabbaticals after being employed for a certain number of years but was unable to convince the buyer to continue this benefit after closing. The continuing employees were very disappointed when the new employer eliminated this valuable benefit, so Sheila negotiated additional consideration for the employees to offset this lost benefit.

Some employers offer generous 401(k) matching, subsidized education and training, increased vacation or paid time off with longevity of employment, flexible work schedules, remote working, or other perks that incentivize and inspire employees to remain loyal to the company.

If you offer these benefits to your employees, you need to ensure the new employer will continue to offer them or replace them with comparable benefits or value. If you don't offer these benefits and experience high turnover, you may want to evaluate your compensation and benefits strategy to ensure your workforce remains intact and motivated following a sale.

Because you care about keeping your employees happy after you sell your business, you must understand what they will be paid in terms of base salary, benefits, and bonuses. This will require in-depth discussions with the buyer's HR staff while you negotiate other details of the transaction. You should request copies of the buyer's benefits and bonus plans in advance and compare them with your existing plans. If the buyer's plans are deficient, you should insist upon incorporating your benefits and/or bonus structure into the ongoing business.

We've explored the impact of exit strategies on you and your employees. In the next section, let's focus on your family.

LESSONS LEARNED

- Try to identify buyers who will perpetuate your business's vision and values, which include excellent treatment of your employees.
- Your purchase agreement should include provisions about continuing your employees as part of the acquiring company's workforce and providing them with equal or better benefits than they currently enjoy.
- You may want to provide change-in-control bonuses to individuals who have been particularly helpful to you in building the business, preparing the business for sale, and consummating the transaction. These bonuses are paid only if the deal closes and could be based on a dollar amount or a percentage of the net proceeds received in the transaction.
- If you need to incentivize employees to stay with the continuing company, you may want to structure retention bonuses payable over time. These bonuses may be part of the transaction proceeds, paid by the

buyer, or split between you and should be paid out as the employees remain employed after closing.
- In your investigation of the buyer, make sure you understand what your employees will be paid, the benefits they will receive, and any other obligations they will have (i.e., *noncompetes*) after closing to ensure they will remain with the company.

WHAT'S IN IT FOR MY FAMILY?

We've been very fortunate to have been involved in some very high-profile matters, where we spent a significant amount of time in very complex things which would include investigations involving Enron, Bernie Madoff, and Lehman Brothers. In terms of the insurance world, I think if you were to look at probably the 10 largest insolvencies in US history, we've been involved doing forensic work in probably half of them. For a relatively small organization, we developed a reputation for being able to figure out particularly complex things and describe them in a way that was understandable.

—Larry Johnson, entrepreneur, Founder and former CEO of Veris Consulting, a forensic accounting firm

Scan the QR code to watch the entire interview

youtube.com/ @ZellLaw/videos

BASIC ESTATE PLANNING FOR YOUR BUSINESS

Everyone, including the most driven entrepreneur, needs *estate planning* and an attorney to prepare their basic estate planning documents. "Estate planning" involves more than just preparing a will; it is a process of understanding

- what assets and properties you own,
- what they are worth,
- how they are titled, and
- how you want to manage those assets and properties to care for you and your family if you are incapacitated (i.e., disabled) or pass away.

Basic estate planning documents include wills, *trusts*, advanced medical directives, living wills, and financial powers of attorney. There are plenty of resources available to learn about basic estate planning and plenty of attorneys to help you. I urge you to consult with an estate planning attorney to draft your estate planning documents and update them based upon what you read in this section.

Caution: some estate planners may neglect to properly link ownership and control of your business to your estate planning documents. I touched on this topic in Chapter 2. Here is a detailed road map for you to follow in constructing your basic estate planning documents with your business in mind.

If you own your business in your own name, it will have to go through the process known as *probate* upon your death.

- In most jurisdictions, your *executor* will have to file an inventory with the court in the jurisdiction where you reside and reveal the estimated value of your business following your death.

- Your executor may have to pay probate tax in some states, such as Virginia, which is based upon the fair market value of the business.

- In addition, your executor will be required to provide formal accountings to the court at least annually, which typically are reviewed by the court for a fee.

- Your executor will have to pay attorneys, accountants, and the court to complete this process, which may last several years.

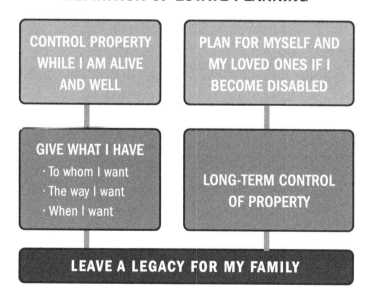

DEEPER DIVE

Some states are very rigid in how accountings must be prepared and submitted if probate is required. The accounting reveals all assets owned in the probate estate and provides excruciating detail regarding all inflows and outflows from the estate. The executor must provide significant backup documentation to the court to support the accounting. This may include bank statements, canceled checks, brokerage statements, receipts, *appraisals*, and the like, and the specific rules vary from state to state. Usually, the executor of the estate must pay an attorney and/or accountant to prepare the accounting and then must pay the court for the time incurred in reviewing the accounting. If any information is unclear or missing, the court will send the executor a list of additional information required to approve the accounting. The executor will have to provide the information to the court on a timely basis until the court is satisfied that it has what it needs to approve the accounting. All these additional reporting requirements will generate additional fees for the estate's accountants and lawyers and for the court.

To avoid probate and minimize delays and costs to your family, you should transfer your business interest and all your other assets (except retirement plan accounts) into a *revocable trust* for your own benefit. You can be the sole *trustee* and sole *beneficiary* of your trust—during your lifetime you will have complete access and control over the assets in the trust, and you will not have to ask anyone for permission to do anything with the assets and properties in the trust. If you transfer your business interest into the trust, it will avoid the probate process upon your death.

In addition, if you become incapacitated and your business is in your trust, you will avoid "living probate," also known as conservatorship or guardianship, where a court must appoint someone to handle your business affairs. Also, if you sign a financial power of attorney, your agent can transfer your business interest to your trust if it is already set up and you did not have a chance to do so.

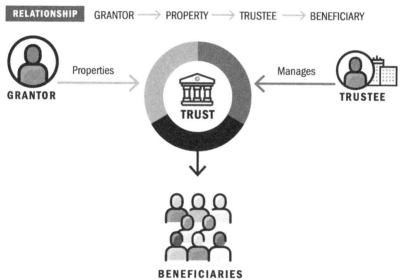

Now, take your basic estate plan one step further. In addition to adding your business ownership interest to your revocable trust, you should sync the provisions of your trust with your *management succession plan* (MSP), which I advised you to draft in Chapter 2. This will ensure that the trustee whom you appoint to succeed you in the event of your incapacity or death not only immediately has control over the business but is also bound by the terms of your MSP.

As an extra precaution, you may want to appoint a business trustee in your revocable trust who has sole authority over your business interest. The business trustee might only have a say in how your business interest is managed; another person or family member can be appointed to manage your remaining assets and make decisions about distributing the assets to your family or other heirs.

You can also have co-trustees serving together. By appointing co-trustees, you create accountability in two persons to watch over your assets and business and do the right thing by your beneficiaries. Usually, the co-trustees must agree upon any actions to be taken, which, unless one of them is not paying attention, protects the beneficiaries from bad behavior by 1 trustee.

DEEPER DIVE

Many states now permit you to separate the duties of the trustees into administrative, investment, and distribution duties. The administrative trustee, who may be a corporate trustee, would be responsible for handling accountings, filing and paying income taxes, and managing other administrative duties that may be difficult for an individual trustee to control. The investment trustee would manage trust investments, and the distribution trustee could make decisions about when and to whom the trust income and principal is to be distributed according to the terms of the trust agreement.

ADVANCED ESTATE PLANNING BEFORE AND AFTER THE TRANSACTION

If the value of your assets and properties, including the value of your business, is expected to exceed $6–7 million, then you should consider some of the advanced planning ideas outlined in this section.[60] Your liquid net worth may not be there yet, but your business may be worth more than you think. If you are like most entrepreneurs, most of your wealth is concentrated in your business, but that can change suddenly when you sell the business.

Upon a sale or another exit, you will realize the value of the business based upon what you receive in the deal, less transaction costs (e.g., investment banking fees, attorneys' fees, and transaction bonuses) and income taxes.

- At your death, the IRS applies rigorous rules to value your business, and the *estate tax* is determined based upon the business's fair market value, even though your estate may not have enough cash to pay the tax.

- Your executor must obtain an *appraisal* from a qualified appraiser to substantiate the value of your business on an estate tax return, which is filed on Form 706.

- There are tools and techniques available to minimize and defer the taxes that must be paid, normally within 9 months after the date of death.

The goal is to determine what portion of your business you can afford to transfer now, well before a transaction materializes, to a trust for the benefit of your loved ones (or, in some cases, yourself) to minimize estate taxes that would be payable upon your death if you simply kept the business interest and didn't spend the net proceeds from the transaction. The valuation of the interest being transferred is more likely to be respected if conducted by a qualified appraiser and the transfer is made well in advance of the exit transaction.

Timing Is Critical

Right before transactions are scheduled to close, founders frequently ask whether there is a way to move assets, including stock or ownership interests of the target company, out of the founder's estate to minimize *gift and estate taxes*. It's usually too late to do anything if it's on the eve of closing. The real question is how far in advance should you be planning these *advanced estate planning* transactions?

To shelter wealth from *estate and gift taxes* and preserve it for your family, there is no hard-and-fast rule regarding when it is "safe" to transfer assets. Your goal is to minimize the likelihood of an IRS audit and the IRS's success if there is a challenge, so you will want to transfer your business interest far enough in advance (using techniques outlined below) to escape the IRS's radar.

Advisors apply a sliding scale of reasonableness. For example, if you plan the transfer of a business interest at least two years ahead of the sale transaction, your likelihood of being audited will diminish—and the likelihood of success in an IRS audit will increase—substantially. Conversely, if the transfer occurs within 1 or 2 months of closing, the risk of audit and the chance of losing to the IRS increase dramatically.

Some of the factors that influence the IRS in deciding how hard to pursue a taxpayer include the following:

- The size of the transaction (larger ones get more attention)

- Whether you have entered into an engagement letter with your investment banker or business broker

- Even if you've entered into an engagement letter with your investment banker or broker, whether they have begun significant work to prepare you for the proposed transaction, including performing an informal valuation of the business (which may be discoverable by the IRS unless you are extremely cautious)

- Even if the investment banker or broker has begun the process of preparing you for sale and soliciting bids for your company, whether any firm offers have been received

- Whether you have started to receive strong *indications of interest* (IOIs) with values or value ranges for your business

- Whether you have received *letters of intent* (LOIs) with specific values and terms of purchase for your business

Even assuming all the factors above exist, ranges of values in IOIs or even specific terms in LOIs where there is no binding or definitive agreement to sell are not fatal and still give you an opportunity to do advanced estate planning. All of this is subject to your tolerance for risk and the specific facts of your situation. Simply put, the closer you get to the transaction closing, the harder it will be to convince the IRS to accept an appraiser's low valuation compared to what the actual transaction yields.

Wealth transfer planning can be completed even after the parties have signed an LOI, provided the LOI is nonbinding on the specific purchase price, terms, and conditions. However, once a definitive agreement for the acquisition has been signed, it's probably too late to engage in any advanced wealth transfer planning.

IDEAS IN ACTION

A group of founders engaged in pretransaction wealth transfer planning. An investment banker had already been hired for the transaction, and the founders had started their discussions with prospective buyers. In fact, they had received two nonbinding offers in the form of LOIs with purchase prices specified and were getting ready to sign one of them. They executed *dynasty trusts* customized for each of them and their families. They gifted shares of stock of the target company into these trusts three months before the transaction closed but before an LOI was signed. Interestingly, a qualified appraiser valued the founders' shares at less than 50% of the actual sales price in the transaction, including discounts aggregating 37% for lack of marketability and lack of control. The IRS never challenged the transactions, and the founders arguably saved millions of dollars in transfer taxes. That's cutting it close.

You are the one who must evaluate the risk of audit and the ramifications of a successful IRS challenge. Your advisors should help you quantify that risk before you proceed with your planning.

Take Advantage of the Valuation Gaps

The appraiser's valuation should be low enough at the time of the advanced estate planning transaction to justify the cost and effort of transferring an ownership interest prior to the sale of your company (i.e., the valuation gap generates a greater shift in wealth and greater tax savings at a federal gift and estate tax rate of 40% times the valuation gap). The valuation gap may include the following:

- Discounts of 20–40%, representing the lack of control and lack of marketability in the ownership interest being transferred in the gift and estate planning transaction

- Reductions in the overall enterprise value because the company is privately held or due to the failure of the appraiser to recognize strategic value or unique assets or opportunities for which a buyer may be willing to pay a hefty premium

IDEAS IN ACTION

Betty transferred an interest in her closely held business to an *irrevocable trust* for the benefit of her husband and children. The transfer was made about a year before she started courting potential buyers. The business had a unique way of processing orders for clients, and the technology, although not patented, was proprietary to the business. When she was ready to sell the business, Betty's investment banker touted the extra value represented by the special technology in the business that was not reflected in the appraisal used for gift tax purposes. This premium yielded an additional multiple of 5x EBITDA in the transaction, which created a huge wealth transfer win for the client. Betty effectively transferred the entire 5x valuation gap out of her estate multiplied by the percentage interest that she transferred to the trust, resulting in transfer tax savings of 40% of the amount transferred, plus any future appreciation on that amount. The wealth transferred to the trust, which had an ultimate value of more than $10 million (generating 40% × $10 million, or $4 million, in transfer tax savings), will be excluded from her estate, her spouse's estate, and her descendants' estates forever.

Because she transferred the business interest into a dynasty trust for the benefit of her spouse, children, and future generations, Betty and her family will reap compounded benefits of avoiding gift tax, estate tax, and *generation-skipping transfer tax* across multiple generations.

The benefits of valuation discounts cannot be overstated, but they have also been in the crosshairs of Congress and the Treasury Department for decades. The IRS has successfully challenged the magnitude and validity of using valuation discounts in many cases involving intrafamily transfers. In 2016, the Treasury Department published proposed regulations that would have effectively denied taxpayers the ability to continue using valuation discounts in intrafamily transfer situations. The regulations were placed on hold and ultimately withdrawn during the Trump administration, and transactions utilizing valuation discounts proliferate today.

The Treasury Department could resurrect these regulations or another set of rules that significantly curtail the ability to use valuation discounting in advanced estate planning situations. It is also possible that Congress may enact legislative changes that accomplish the same result. So keep in touch with your tax advisor to ensure you can still use valuation discounting in your estate planning transaction.

DEEPER DIVE

The discount for lack of marketability (DLOM) and the discount for lack of control (DLOC) are applied to private companies when valuing them. The DLOM relates to the company not being publicly traded on a securities exchange. Publicly traded companies are perceived to have a "market" since the shares can be bought or sold in a centralized marketplace. Owners of privately held companies lack the ability to sell their shares in a public market, and a discount is usually applied to this lack of marketability. The DLOC considers the benefits of control not available to a company's minority shareholders, which may include the ability to do the following:

- Change or appoint officers
- Control the board of directors or managers
- Determine management compensation
- Sell, *recapitalize*, or liquidate the company
- Pay shareholder dividends or distributions
- Lease, liquidate, or acquire business assets
- Negotiate *acquisitions and mergers*
- Control the company's business activities
- Award or challenge contracts
- Sell the company's stock to the public
- Amend the bylaws, operating agreement, or articles of incorporation

The calculation of these discounts is a complicated matter best left to valuation experts, but they are incredibly important in advanced estate planning.

How Much to Transfer?

The three most common questions I get from my entrepreneur clients when considering advanced estate planning transactions are as follows:

1. How much of the business can/should I transfer?
2. How much can I afford to transfer?
3. What does everybody else do?

The first two questions are capable of being answered. The last question, while capable of being answered, is kind of funny because **what everybody else does doesn't necessarily indicate what you should do under circumstances that are unique to your individual situation.**

Regarding the first question, you can transfer as much of your ownership interest in the company as you want. What people forget, though, is when you transfer these interests into an irrevocable trust or a vehicle that is for the benefit of somebody other than yourself, you will run the risk of not being able to access the transferred assets or the proceeds from their sale. However, there are techniques that will allow you to get indirect access to the assets (e.g., loans) and, in some cases, direct access depending on the structure.

You can set up a *spousal lifetime access trust* (SLAT) that allows your spouse to access the assets you deposit into the trust. It can also give your kids and descendants access to the trust assets as well, during or after your spouse's lifetime. A possible downside of this technique is that if you get divorced or your spouse dies, you may lose access to the assets because the kids would be the only beneficiaries. You can give a divorced spouse the right to continue to participate in the trust, but he or she may not want to share the trust assets with you.

> **IDEAS IN ACTION**
>
> Andrea and Joan are married and have two young children. Andrea is ready to sell her business for a significant sum. After consulting with their financial advisor (and well before taking any action to sell the company), Andrea and Joan determined that Andrea can safely transfer 10% of her shares in the company into a trust for Joan's benefit. The trust can also be used for the children's needs, but not to meet either Andrea's or Joan's legal support obligations. They consulted with their estate planning attorney, who assisted in drafting the trust so that Joan can serve as trustee of the trust with the ability to use trust funds for her health, education, maintenance, and support. Any additional distributions would need to be approved by an unrelated, independent trustee. If they get divorced, the trust was drafted so that Joan could remain as a beneficiary and trustee of the trust (although this is not required). This is a form of a SLAT.

In addition, there are ways to structure the trust that allow you to access the trust assets. For example, the trust agreement may permit you to borrow from the trust. Also, in certain circumstances, the trustee or a trust protector may reimburse you for income taxes you have to pay on trust income if the trust is treated as a *grantor trust*. The obvious upside of the SLAT technique is that your spouse can have access, and therefore you can have indirect access, to the trust assets during your lifetimes. If your spouse predeceases you, you will lose direct (but not necessarily indirect) access to the trust assets (i.e., you may still be able to borrow from the trust or get reimbursed for taxes you pay for the trust).

> **DEEPER DIVE**
>
> A "trust protector" provides oversight of certain decisions made by a trustee and allows for a degree of flexibility in otherwise inflexible trust situations. Although the trust protector can be very helpful, there is no standard definition of what a trust protector does. You and your attorney need to be aware of the differing rules applicable to trust protectors—or the lack of rules, depending on where you live.

The trust could state that the assets will be available for your children's well-being or based on some other more rigid standard contained in the trust's terms and conditions. Since this is not an estate planning book, I'm not going to dig into details on the nuances of building these trusts. In brief, you can draft the trusts to give your kids immediate access, deferred access, or very limited access to the trust assets. Most of my entrepreneur clients don't want their kids growing up to be "trust fund babies," so they are rather thoughtful in how they structure their trust agreements so their kids don't have immediate, unfettered access to the trust assets, but their critical needs are met.

Depending on how much is in the trust and your goals and objectives, you may grant your kids and other descendants very limited access to trust assets by leaving distribution decisions to the discretion of an independent trustee. By putting an independent trustee (i.e., someone who is not related or subordinate to you or your trust beneficiaries) in charge of the trust, you achieve two benefits:

1. You can protect the trust assets from the claims of the beneficiaries and their creditors and predators.

2. If the assets are required to be held in the trust—either subject to discretionary distribution standards by the trustee or the ascertainable standard of health, education, maintenance, and support—you can exclude the assets from the kids' and their descendants' estates, saving millions of dollars in estate and generation-skipping transfer tax.

OTHER TOOLS AND TECHNIQUES
Grantor Retained Annuity Trusts

A *grantor retained annuity trust* (GRAT) is an estate planning technique permitted under IRS regulations. This technique allows you, the grantor, to make a gift to a trust over which you may serve as the trustee and receive an annuity payment from the trust for a specified period. Any appreciation on the trust property at the end of the trust term passes to your heirs, estate and gift tax free.

Additionally, if the fair market value of the assets transferred to the trust equals the present value of the annuity payable to you over the term of the trust, you can zero out the gift, meaning that you owe no gift tax on the transfer to the trust. This is known as a zeroed-out GRAT and was allowed by the US Tax Court in a case where the Walmart founder's sister-in-law attempted to make a zeroed-out GRAT gift and the IRS tried to disallow it. The Tax Court overruled the IRS, and since that case, the IRS has allowed taxpayers to use properly structured, zeroed-out GRATs.

You can use rolling GRATs to continuously move the annuity payments and the appreciation on those annuity payments out of your estate. In other words, you set up a new GRAT into which you deposit the annuity payments received from the first GRAT, and any appreciation on those deposits further escapes gift and estate taxes.

The GRAT technique (along with most of the advanced planning techniques described in this section) has survived various legislative attacks over the last several decades. Most recently, in September 2021, the House Ways and Means Committee passed legislation that would have prohibited GRATs from being viable planning techniques unless they were at least 10 years in length and certain other requirements were met. Zeroed-out GRATs would have been disallowed (i.e., some portion of the gift would be subject to gift tax).

In November 2021, the House of Representatives passed tax legislation without including the Ways and Means GRAT proposals, and the Senate failed to pass any tax legislation. Tax legislation passed in 2022 under the budget reconciliation rules excluded any estate, gift, or GST tax changes. To date, Congress has not passed legislation curtailing or limiting GRATs or any of the other advanced planning techniques, and, thankfully for you and my other entrepreneur clients, these estate planning techniques continue for now.

GRANTOR RETAINED ANNUITY TRUST

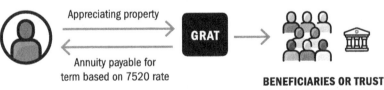

Intentionally Defective Grantor Trusts

An *intentionally defective grantor trust* (IDGT) is a popular alternative to a GRAT. You can gift or sell a business interest to an IDGT. If you don't want to transfer the entire value of your business interest (i.e., you want to retain something for the future in terms of the value that you're transferring today), you could sell the interest to the IDGT in exchange for a promissory note. The trust is "intentionally defective" because it is ignored for income tax purposes as a grantor trust, which means that all the income of the trust is taxed to you as the grantor or creator of the trust. It is effective for minimizing or avoiding transfer taxes, however.

You may ask, "Why would I want to pay income tax on an asset that I've just transferred to my kids?" Good question! If you've retained sufficient wealth aside from the interest you transferred to the IDGT, then you should be able to afford to pay the income tax earned by the trust. The IRS has ruled that your payment of the taxes for the trust is not considered a gift to the trust beneficiaries. So you are using your other assets to indirectly shift wealth into the trust by paying the trust's taxes. As I mentioned earlier, the trustee or trust protector can reimburse you for the taxes that you pay, but you cannot require the trust to do so.

If you sell a business interest to the trust instead of gifting it, and assuming the trust is a grantor trust, then you're treated as selling the business interest to yourself for income tax purposes. That is, the sale is ignored for income tax purposes but respected for gift and estate tax purposes.

If you take back a promissory note from the trust in exchange for the business interest that you've sold to the trust, you don't have to pay income tax when you receive payments under the note. Using this structure, here are some possible scenarios:

- The trust could pay the promissory note over a short (3 years or less), medium (3–9.9 years), or long period (10–20 years).

- If the note is respected as being a bona fide debt, then you can defer the payments on the note until the maturity date.

- The note must be payable at a definite time in the future and bear interest at a rate equal to or greater than the applicable federal rate (AFR) published monthly by the IRS.

- Taxpayers have taken advantage of low interest rates over the last couple of decades, shifting any appreciation above the note interest rate to the trust and its beneficiaries. In 2021, the long-term AFR was as low as 1.6%, and in 2022, it has been as low as 2.6% but is rising rapidly to over 3.8% in early 2023. As interest rates rise, this technique becomes less advantageous, yet I've been using it for decades, even when the long-term AFR was as high as 5%.

Bottom line: if your return on investment on the business interest exceeds the note interest rate, this technique can shift the excess appreciation out of your estate.

If you're getting ready to sell your business but haven't taken significant steps toward completing the sale, and the transaction value is expected to exceed the appraised value of the interest being transferred to the trust, then you should consider selling a portion of your business interest to an IDGT in exchange for a promissory note. The IRS will expect you to fund the trust with enough cash or other assets to give the trust substance and the ability to make payments on the note. Many practitioners recommend the following:

- You fund the trust with assets worth at least 10% of the note obligation as a minimum benchmark of how much to put in the trust.

- This contribution would be treated as a gift and would utilize some of your lifetime gift tax exemption ($12.06 million per person in 2022, rising to $12.92 million in 2023).

- The note would bear interest at the AFR and be fixed and payable over a definite period.

- Then, if you sell the stock in your company for substantially more than the appraised value, you will be able to exclude any appreciation more than the note principal and unpaid interest from your estate.

- This transaction essentially allows you to freeze the value of the asset that was sold to the trust at a discounted, lower value and still get something back from the trust in the form of the note payment if you need it.

INTENTIONALLY DEFECTIVE GRANTOR TRUST

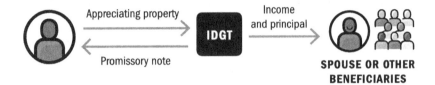

Self-Canceling Installment Notes

A *self-canceling installment note* (SCIN) is a promissory note that contains a provision under which the buyer's obligation to pay automatically ceases in the event that the seller dies before the note's maturity date. SCINs are typically used in family business transfer situations. An installment note is useful if your business is appreciating in value and you would like to sell it, but you'd like to spread the income tax on the gain over a term of years. SCINs are especially useful when one family member, typically a parent or grandparent, wishes to transfer property to another family member, typically a child or grandchild, with minimal gift and estate tax consequences.

Absent the self-canceling feature, the fair market value of the unpaid portion of an installment note on the date of death is included in the estate of the seller. However, if the note contains a properly designed self-cancellation provision, the buyer is under no obligation to make any further payments after the seller's premature death, which leaves no unpaid balance to be included in the seller's estate. The self-canceling feature allows the seller's estate to avoid estate tax on the unpaid balance of the note at the date of death.

DEEPER DIVE

A SCIN will avoid adverse gift and estate tax treatment only if the self-cancellation provision is properly designed. The courts have held as follows:
- The cancellation provision must be bargained for as part of the consideration for the sale.
- The purchase price must reflect this bargain with either a principal risk premium (the principal is increased above the market sales price) or an interest rate premium (above market interest rate).
- The seller may not retain any control over the property being sold after the sale.

DEEPER DIVE

If your self-cancellation provision is not properly designed, you may be deemed to have made a part-sale, part-gift transaction. If any portion of the canceled payments is considered a gift, the entire value of the property sold, less the consideration actually paid, may be included in your gross estate. This problem can be avoided simply by structuring the note as much like a market note as possible, except you must include a principal or interest rate premium.

The sales contract and the note should include the self-cancellation clause. To avoid retained controls (i.e., that would cause the note to be included in your estate), the sales contract and/or note cannot place any restrictions on the use of the property by the buyer, including any restrictions on subsequent sales. (In general, a subsequent sale of the property by the buyer within 2 years of the original sale will trigger automatic recognition of any remaining deferred gain.) Furthermore, you should avoid using the property sold as collateral for the note, so you would have no right to reacquire the property sold under any circumstances.

For income tax purposes, self-canceling installment notes are subject to the installment sale rules. Although these rules are complex, the general rule is that the interest rate on an installment sale note must at least equal the appropriate applicable federal rate with semiannual compounding. Failure to follow these rules may result in reapportionment of interest and principal of scheduled payments and imputation of interest income to you as the seller, even in periods in which you may not have received payments.

Installment Sale to Non-Grantor Trust

As an alternative to a sale of an appreciated business asset to an IDGT or a SCIN or a transfer to a GRAT for an annuity payment, you could sell an appreciated business interest to children or heirs directly or to a non-grantor trust for the benefit of children/heirs in a taxable installment sale. The sale could be made in exchange for a promissory note bearing interest only, with principal being due on the maturity date. The maturity date should generally be no more than 20 years into the future, and the interest rate would be based upon the IRS's long-term applicable federal rate. The note may or may not be secured but would need to be enforceable under local law.

If the buyer is related to you (including your children or a non-grantor trust for their benefit), the buyer must hold on to the purchased asset for at least 2 years for you to get installment sale treatment. Moreover, to avoid an interest charge on the taxes deferred in the installment sale, your installment sale would need to be less than $5 million ($10 million for taxpayers who are married filing jointly) in any one taxable year. Any interest received from the buyer will be taxable at ordinary income tax rates, but the principal will be taxed as long-term capital gains and return of capital only when principal payments are received.

One reason to sell to a non-grantor trust is to lock in capital gains at a fixed value but still defer recognition of the gain until payments are made under the note. This technique can shift appreciation to the trust beneficiaries.

> **IDEAS IN ACTION**
>
> Let's assume you own a business interest for which you paid $250,000 10 years ago and which is now worth $2 million. Let's further assume (1) you sell the business interest to a non-grantor trust for the benefit of your children on July 1, 2022, in exchange for a 20-year, interest-only note, (2) the trust sells the property for $2.5 million cash on July 10, 2024, and (3) current favorable long-term capital gains rates remain in effect in the year of sale by the trust.
>
> The trust would have $500,000 in long-term capital gain ($2.5 million sales proceeds, less the $2 million basis acquired in the installment sale), which would result in $100,000 federal income tax to the trust (i.e., assuming a 20% tax rate). Since the asset was held by the trust for more than 2 years, you can defer the gain on the original sale until the principal payment of $2 million is made in year 20 (paying tax only on the interest income received), and the trust can invest the net after-tax proceeds of $2.4 million from the sale and use the proceeds for the benefit of the children.

This technique works particularly well if the assets appreciate at a rate more than the interest rate being paid on the note. Any future appreciation is removed from your estate at your death, although the present value of the note is included in your estate (unlike the SCIN described above) if you die before it is repaid. As interest rates rise, the technique becomes less attractive.

Private Annuity

In a *private annuity*, two parties enter into an agreement where one party (the transferor-annuitant) transfers ownership of a business (or another appreciated asset) to another party (the transferee-buyer) in exchange for an annuity from the transferee-buyer. The transferee-buyer makes periodic payments to the transferor for a specified period (usually the lifetime of the transferor or the transferor and transferor's spouse).

The private annuity is useful if you want to spread gain from a highly appreciated business interest over your life expectancy, although the income tax planning benefits of this technique were severely circumscribed in 2006 under proposed IRS regulations. The private annuity remains a useful federal estate tax saving tool because, like a SCIN, payments end when you die, and the entire value of the asset sold is immediately removed from your gross estate. In other words, the transferred property is excluded from your estate because it belongs to the buyer from the moment the private annuity document is signed, and no further obligation is owed to you or your estate. Another advantage is that the private annuity allows you to make non-income-producing property productive if the transferee can afford to pay the annuity.

DEEPER DIVE

Ideally, you should consider using a private annuity in these cases:

- You are in a high estate tax bracket or have no marital deduction to shelter the asset from estate tax upon your death.
- The business interest you are selling can produce at least some income and/or is appreciating rapidly, so the annuity can be paid in cash or in kind.
- The buyer is capable of—at least in part—paying the promised amounts.
- The parties trust each other (the private annuity must be unsecured), which means that this technique is normally used only in family business transfers.
- You have other assets and sources of income.
- You have less than a normal life expectancy but are not terminally ill. This makes the arrangement more of a "bargain" for the buyer (i.e., the annuities you receive are less than the value of the asset being transferred).

Charitable Planning

You should include charitable planning in your arsenal of estate planning weapons only if you really are charitably inclined. I know that many people are looking at the tax benefits exclusively and not really focused on the fact that whatever you provide in the form of a trust or a gift to a charity must be permanently dedicated to charitable purposes. Failure to realize this very important fact will cause problems later with the IRS. I'll briefly describe two popular charitable-trust planning techniques where you and your heirs can enjoy the property even after it has been formally dedicated to charity.

Charitable Remainder Trust. Of the various charitable planning techniques that people use either before or after an exit, one of the most popular techniques—particularly as interest rates rise—is known as the *charitable remainder trust* (CRT). In a CRT, you're giving a portion of your business interest to a trust that ultimately, at the end of the term or your life expectancy, will be paid out to the charity.

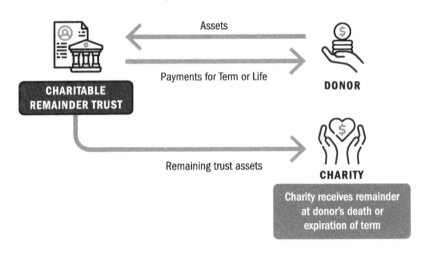

Income Tax Consequences. A CRT is generally funded with appreciated property (e.g., stock in your business).

- You should not use S corporation stock because a CRT is not an eligible shareholder of an S corporation.

- You should avoid a partnership or an LLC interest treated as a partnership if the interest will generate unrelated business taxable income and destroy the tax exemption of the trust.

- If appreciated stock is used to fund the trust, you will be entitled to claim an income tax deduction for the gift of the stock to the CRT in an amount equal to the fair market value of the charity's remainder interest.

- The charitable income tax deduction is limited to 20% of your adjusted gross income for the year of the contribution for gifts made to a CRT, the beneficiary of which is a private foundation (i.e., charitable family foundation), or 30% for gifts involving public charities.

- Any amount not deductible due to the limitation can be carried forward and used in the next 5 tax years. One important requirement is that the value of the charitable remainder interest must be more than 10% of the total value of the trust.

Importantly, as long as the interest being transferred is not subject to debt, you can avoid income tax on the transfer of the appreciated business interest to the trust and on the sale by the trust of the interest.

Moreover, the CRT will not be taxed on any income it generates (provided that the trust invests only in investment assets, such as stocks, bonds, and other income-producing or capital-appreciating assets).

Note: you should avoid reinvesting the proceeds from the sale of the property initially contributed to the trust in tax-exempt securities. If you do so, the IRS may try to tax the sale directly to you, ignoring the existence of the trust. Also, you must not invest the proceeds in other businesses that generate unrelated business taxable income to the trust—this will destroy the CRT's tax-exempt status.

The CRT will generally be required to pay you a percentage of the value of the trust assets annually (i.e., at least 5% per year). The type of trust (unitrust or annuity trust) will determine how much income must be distributed annually. The amount distributed will generally be taxable to you to the extent that it is paid out of the trust's current and prior years' ordinary and capital gains income. Any amounts paid to you out of principal (other than capital gains that are considered part of principal) will not generally be taxable to you.

Estate and Gift Tax Consequences. The transfer of your business interest to the trust will not be subject to gift tax. In addition, neither your income interest nor the charitable remainder interest will be subject to estate tax at your death, provided the remainder interest is distributed to a qualifying charity (i.e., the property is included in your estate, but a charitable deduction is permitted that offsets the value of the included property). The remainder must be distributed to one of the following types of charitable organizations:

- The CRT's agreement could require the trustee to distribute the trust property to your charitable family foundation (see below) if it is in existence and a qualifying charity at the time of your death.

- If a family foundation does not exist or qualify, the trustee will be required to distribute the trust property to qualifying Section 501(c)(3) charities.

- Many entrepreneurs use their own donor-advised funds to receive the remainder distributions and have their heirs suggest charities to receive the proceeds. Importantly, you can serve as the trustee of your CRT.

CRUTs and CRATs. One form of CRT is the charitable remainder unitrust (CRUT). When you establish a CRUT, you transfer an appreciated business interest (usually C corporation stock) to an irrevocable trust but retain (either for yourself or for 1 or more family members) a variable annuity (payments that can vary in amount based upon the value of the trust assets determined annually but are a fixed percentage) from the trust.

At the end of a specified term, or upon the death of the beneficiary or beneficiaries (both you and your spouse can be the beneficiaries), the remainder interest in the property passes to the charity you have specified.

Another form of CRT is the charitable remainder annuity trust (CRAT). In a CRAT, a fixed percentage of the value of assets originally contributed must be paid at least annually to a noncharitable beneficiary. In addition, once you establish a CRAT and make the initial contribution, you cannot make further contributions.

The principal difference between a CRUT and a CRAT is that a CRUT pays a varying annuity based upon a fixed percentage, whereas a CRAT is fixed at the inception based upon the value of the property originally contributed to the trust. In other words, the amount paid by a CRUT is likely to change each year. The amount paid by the CRAT remains fixed.

CRUT assets must be revalued each year, and the fixed percentage amount must be paid at least once a year for the term of the trust, which must be a fixed period of 20 years or less, or must be until the death of the noncharitable beneficiaries (i.e., individuals), all of whom must be living at the beginning of the trust.

Two popular variations of the basic CRUT (which pays a fixed percentage of the value of the trust assets, regardless of income) are the net income CRUT, or NI-CRUT, and the net-income-with-makeup CRUT, or NIM-CRUT, both of which pay the lesser of the fixed percentage of the CRUT's value or the income received by the trust. In a NIM-CRUT, if the income is less than the fixed percentage of value, the deficiency can be paid in a future year, as soon as the trust has income that exceeds the fixed percentage.

An additional variation is a "flip" charitable remainder unitrust (FLIP-CRUT), which is a CRT that changes from a NIM-CRUT to a regular CRUT upon the occurrence of a specific event, such as the sale of a specific asset that was contributed to the trust and was not expected to produce much income or following a term of years. NI-CRUTs, NIM-CRUTs, and FLIP-CRUTs are valued in the same way as a regular CRUT for the purpose of determining income, estate, and gift tax charitable deductions.

DEEPER DIVE

You may prefer a CRUT over a CRAT because it's possible that annual payouts to you from a CRUT may increase if the assets in the trust grow in value. If you're relying on payments from a CRUT for income, you may find it easier to keep pace with inflation. When inflation rises, purchasing power using CRAT distributions can shrink. Also, a CRUT allows you to make additional contributions in future years. If you decide you'd like to leave a larger share of your wealth to charity, then you could do so using an existing CRUT; a CRAT would not give you that option. Last, CRUTs offer more flexibility than CRATs in structuring, evidenced by the NIM-CRUT, FLIP-CRUT, and other variations.

The IRS has also approved in several private letter rulings the use of private derivative contracts to transfer appreciated asset values to a CRT without transferring the underlying business interest. In those rulings, CRTs for a university could not invest directly in the university's endowment fund because it would produce unrelated business taxable income (UBTI), which would cause the trust to lose its tax-exempt status for that year. Instead, the CRT paid the university the cost of an option to receive future payments from the university, in exchange for the university's agreement to pay the CRT any upside based on the performance of the endowment fund. This technique can arguably be used to shift future wealth without transferring the business interest to the CRT.

DEEPER DIVE

"Derivatives" simply refers to financial instruments that give the holder a right to payment from the other party to the instrument if a certain event occurs during the term of the contract. Derivatives can be tied to anything: the price or performance of an asset, the weather, or even a family member's survival for a specified period. In that way, private derivatives can transfer wealth based on the financial performance of an asset.

Finally, many practitioners use the income tax savings generated from the contribution to the CRT to purchase life insurance to be held in a separate irrevocable trust. The insurance and life insurance trust are designed to replace the wealth "lost" by leaving the remainder interest to charity. Your age, health, and circumstances will dictate how much insurance you can buy.

Family Holding Companies

Basically, a family holding company is an LLC or a limited partnership that's established to hold assets for the benefit of family members. The general partner in a family limited partnership (FLP) or a manager in an LLC runs the show; they make all investment decisions. They deploy capital into new investments, and they make decisions about how and when to make distributions, except where an independent third party needs to be involved to avoid inclusion of the holding company assets in your estate.

One goal of this structure is to ensure that assets can be shifted out of your estate and into the hands of future generations or trusts for their benefit. Instead of transferring an asset directly into the hands of the next generation, you can combine family-owned assets into the family holding company and use it as a centralized way of managing the family's wealth. Then you can transfer shares or a percentage interest in the family holding company that owns the assets to the next generation or trusts for their benefit.

The interest in the family holding company usually attracts significant valuation discounts because the entity is closely held, which leads to a lack of marketability discount for the interest being transferred. In addition, if the interest is nonvoting or does not otherwise participate in the management of the entity, the interest can attract an additional lack of control discount, which allows the founder to achieve discounts of up to 40% or more of the value of the interest being transferred.

As noted earlier, the valuation rules for closely held entities have come under attack by Congress, by the Treasury Department, and in the IRC. Although various laws have been enacted to make it more difficult to achieve valuation discounts and shift wealth to the next generation using a family holding company, these techniques still thrive.

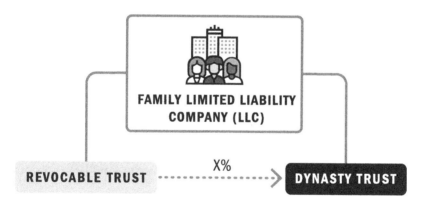

FAMILY LLC WITH DYNASTY TRUST

IDEAS IN ACTION

Let's say you own real estate that has a fair market value of $6 million today and you also own an interest in a closely held company that is worth approximately $10 million. You could contribute these assets to the family holding company, where initially you own 100% of the interests in the LLC or the FLP. Subsequently, you may transfer a 30%

interest to a dynasty trust for the benefit of your kids and grandkids. Intuitively, that would mean that you're transferring 30% of $16 million, or $4.8 million, to the trust. However, you're transferring much less than $4.8 million because a qualified appraiser will review the holding company's operating agreement or partnership agreement and determine that the interest that was transferred is not marketable, is not involved in management, and has no ability to control the investment decisions of the entity.

Because of recent court cases, the independent trustee of the dynasty trust (who is unrelated and not subordinate to you) may need to have a say in whether the entity liquidates and when distributions are made to the owners. But other than that, you can shift $4.8 million in value for $3.12 million if a 35% valuation discount is used and upheld,[61] which would result in initial transfer tax savings of $672,000.[62] All future appreciation would be excluded from your estate as well.

Another significant benefit of owning the assets in a properly structured family holding company is that in many states, your creditors will not be able to force the holding company to liquidate its assets or make distributions to you if they have obtained a court judgment against you or other members of the holding company.

This asset protection benefit comes in the form of a charging order remedy, which prevents the creditor from taking your interest in the LLC or partnership. The creditor can only impose a lien on your ownership interest, so that any profit distributions that would have been made to you are instead made to the creditor. The charging order can prevent you from taking backdoor distributions from the holding company

WHAT SUCCESS(ION) EXIT STRATEGY WORKS BEST FOR ME?

in the form of loans or fees, but you may still be able to take salaries (subject to possible garnishment of wages by the creditor).[63] You will want to set up the LLC in a state where charging order remedies are the most limited, such as Wyoming, Nevada, and Delaware.

In sum, family holding companies will afford you potential transfer tax savings and asset protection and allow you to centralize ownership and management of assets and properties for the family's benefit.

Dynasty Trusts

A "dynasty trust" generally refers to an irrevocable trust that can last in perpetuity. Under old English law rules, the *rule against perpetuities* prohibited trusts from lasting forever and survives today in the United States in various forms. Eight states have eliminated the rule against perpetuities entirely, and many others have adopted flexible interpretations of the rule that allow the rule to be waived or significantly extend the time applicable to the rule.[64] Ten states have adopted longer fixed periods for the rule against perpetuities, sometimes only for certain types of property.[65] In any case, the dynasty trust is designed to avoid the arcane rule against perpetuities and last for many generations.

We often establish trusts in those states where the trusts can last indefinitely. Why would you want to have a trust last forever? Simply, if the trust is properly structured, the assets can be held in trust and used for the benefit of multiple generations without incurring estate tax, gift tax, or generation-skipping transfer tax. The transfer taxes, normally imposed at your death and on successive generations, compound at a 40% rate plus state death tax rates, the effect of which can be enormous.

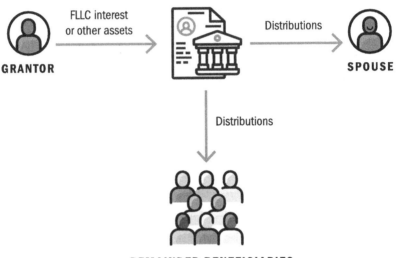

Dynasty trusts are often incorporated into the estate planning of clients who have or are building significant wealth. For example, upon the death of the survivor of you and your spouse, the assets could be left in a dynasty trust for the benefit of future generations. They are also great receptacles for distributions from GRATs that terminate after a period of years. In addition, IDGTs and SLATs are also frequently structured as dynasty trusts. So the term is not mutually exclusive from other trusts described in this section; it's just a useful way of identifying a trust that can qualify for exemption from estate and generation-skipping taxes and last for multiple generations.

Recapitalizations

A *recapitalization* refers to the *reorganization* of a company's equity structure. For example, if your company has only one class of stock outstanding, and that class of stock is common stock, you can reorganize the company to have voting common stock and nonvoting common stock. Or, in a C corporation or partnership, you could freeze the shares of common stock at a certain level and add preferred stock to the mix. You would hold on to the preferred stock. There are many ways of coming up with structures that will allow for you to pass on your ownership in the company to future generations using recapitalization techniques.

THE STORY OF GEORGE AND HANNAH

WHAT'S IN IT FOR GEORGE, HIS FAMILY, AND HIS EMPLOYEES?

Let's help George plan his exit from 3DP and provide him with additional guidance regarding his family, employees, and Business Success(ion). To refresh your memory, George has stage 4 prostate cancer, so assume he is unable to purchase life insurance to help in his planning but is not expected to die within the next 12 months. Given that his life expectancy may be substantially shorter than the IRS life expectancy tables predict, George is a good candidate for a private annuity transaction. He could gift and/or sell a portion of his 3DP shares to his daughter Hannah, who works with George in the business, and a separate portion to a trust for the benefit of Ian and Jessica, who are not involved in the business.

You may recall that 3DP is an LLC taxed as an S corporation, which is only allowed to have one class of membership interest but may have voting and nonvoting common units. Currently, George owns all 10,000 of 3DP's outstanding membership interests. George's estate planner advises George to recapitalize the LLC into 1,000 units of voting interests and 9,000 units of nonvoting interests. George is willing to transfer most of the membership interests to or for the benefit of his children as follows:

- George is willing to gift or sell one-third of the nonvoting units (3,000 units) to each of the children or to trusts for their benefit. The amount of the gifts will depend upon how much lifetime gift tax exemption George has at the time of the gift and the value of the nonvoting units. If the IRS were to challenge the value of the gifts after the transactions are completed, George's attorney has advised George to include an adjustment clause in the gift document that treats the excess over his lifetime exemption as a contingent sale supported by a promissory note bearing interest at the applicable federal rate in effect on the date of the gift.
- George will retain all the voting interests but will give the voting interests to Hannah upon his death, if he still retains them at that time.

George hires a qualified appraiser to value the business in advance of the gift and private annuity transactions. After being provided with historical financial information, projections, and other information relating to the business, the appraiser determines that the business is worth $30 million as an enterprise, and a 1% nonvoting interest is worth $200,000, after factoring in combined valuation discounts

33⅓% for lack of marketability and lack of control ($30 million × 1% × (1 − 33.33%) = $200,000). Therefore, each nonvoting unit of 3DP is worth $2,000 ($200,000 / 10,000 units).

George has not used any of his lifetime gift tax exemption, which in 2022 is $12.06 million and $12.92 million in 2023. So George can give away that amount in total to his children without incurring any gift tax. If George wants to transfer enough nonvoting units to fully utilize his gift tax exemption, then he would gift a total of 6,000 nonvoting units, or 2,000 units to each of his children or trusts for their benefit.[66] His estate planner recommended transferring the shares to separate non-grantor trusts for each child. The trusts would elect to be treated either as qualified Subchapter S trusts or electing small business trusts so they can be permitted as shareholders of 3DP, an S corporation. To provide maximum asset protection and minimize transfer taxes to his children, George structures the trusts as dynasty trusts, allowing distributions to the children and their heirs for health, education, maintenance, and support, requiring the children and their descendants to otherwise keep the assets in trust, and permitting the children to serve as co-trustees with an independent trustee of their choice. The trusts permit George to be reimbursed for income taxes he must pay on the trust income.

In July 2022, George sold his remaining 3,000 nonvoting units to each of the trusts (1,000 shares per trust) in exchange for a private annuity payable by each trust, acknowledging his potentially shortened life expectancy. He enters into separate agreements with each trust. Based upon current IRS rates and standard life expectancy tables, each trust must pay George an annuity of $163,545.67, of which $102,564.10 is treated as long-term capital gain and $60,981.57 is treated as ordinary income.[67] George would receive over $490,000 per year under this structure, compared with the $350,000 he currently receives in salary, but only $183,000 ($60,982 × 3) of the annuity payments would be taxed at higher ordinary income rates.[68] The annuity payments will stop at George's death, and no amounts relating to the property transferred to the trusts will be included in his gross estate for estate tax purposes. If George dies before his IRS-projected life expectancy of 20 years, the trusts and children benefit substantially.

In August 2023, George is contacted by an investment banker he has known for years, who tells George that he can receive substantially more than the appraiser's estimate of $30 million for his business. After talking it over with Hannah and the other key employees, George engages the banker and begins the process of readying his business for sale.

In July 2024, George receives several IOIs from strategic buyers and PE firms, indicating that 3DP is worth between $90 million and $120 million! After several meetings with potential buyers and receiving a few offers in the form of LOIs, George and his management team select a PE firm that has offered a purchase price of $100 million to purchase 100% of the membership interests in 3DP LLC, 80% payable in cash at closing and 20% in *rollover equity*. The 20% rollover equity will be received in a tax-free transaction, where the owners of 3DP will contribute their membership interests in 3DP into a new operating company that is disregarded for income tax purposes (in an F reorganization).

George wants to ensure his key employees (including Hannah) benefit from their hard work in making the company as valuable and successful as it has become, so he constructs 2 bonus packages to recognize their contributions. The first package is a change-in-control bonus of 2% of the net proceeds from the transaction for each of the 3 key employees if they remain employed through the closing of the sale. These bonuses would be taxed at ordinary income rates. The second package is a retention bonus equal to an additional 2% of the net proceeds for each key employee if they remain with the company for at least 24 months after closing. The retention bonus agreements would require that the entire bonus be paid to the key employees if they are terminated without cause or if they leave with good reason. George agrees to pay these bonuses out of the net cash proceeds received at closing.

The net proceeds from the transaction might flow as follows:

TOTAL PROCEEDS TO GEORGE'S FAMILY

Gross proceeds payable in cash ($100MM × 80%)	$80,000,000
Less: Investment banking and other transaction expenses	(5,000,000)
Net proceeds from the transaction	$75,000,000
Less: Change in control bonuses (2% or $1.5MM per employee)	(4,500,000)
Less: Retention bonuses (2% or $1.5MM per employee)	(4,500,000)
Remaining net proceeds	*$66,000,000*
Allocated to George (10%)	$6,600,000
Allocated to Hannah's trust (30%)	19,800,000
Allocated to Ian's trust (30%)	19,800,000
Allocated to Jessica's trust (30%)	19,800,000
Total to George's family (excluding bonuses above)	*$66,000,000*

Assuming zero income tax basis in the membership interests and a 20% flat federal rate (with no state income tax because George has relocated permanently to Florida and the trusts are located in no-tax states), George's net after-tax proceeds would be $5.28 million ($6.6 million × (1 − 20%)), and each trust would receive $15.84 million ($19.8 million × (1 − 20%)), less the annuity payments made to George. In essence, George will have transferred $47.52 million ($15.84 million × 3) out of his estate permanently, saving his heirs $19 million in estate tax on his death. Any annuity payments received before death would be included in his estate if he doesn't spend them.

In addition, George's family fully participates in the 20% rollover equity as follows:

ROLLOVER EQUITY TO FAMILY

Allocated to George	2%
Allocated to Hannah's trust	6%
Allocated to Ian's trust	6%
Allocated to Jessica's trust	6%
Total Rollover Equity	**20%**

If all the ownership interests in the continuing company are later sold for $400 million (4x return for the PE buyer's investors), George would receive an additional $8 million ($400 million × 2% × (1 − 20%), or $6.4 million after tax), and each trust would receive an additional $24 million ($19.2 million after tax), shifting an additional $57.6 million in wealth and saving an additional $23.04 million in estate tax!

Any appreciation on the amount originally transferred, plus any appreciation on the amount transferred on the subsequent sale of the rollover equity, would be permanently excluded from any future estate and generation-skipping transfer taxes.

George will need to work with his estate planner and financial advisor to complete his remaining estate planning, including dividing up his remaining assets (which can be done in any manner for his children and grandchildren). He may be well advised to distribute his retirement assets directly to charity if he is charitably inclined; this will avoid busting a retirement plan to pay estate taxes, which can generate horrific results. He may want to contribute his other assets to a family holding company and sell a portion of the LLC to his kids or their trusts at a *discounted rate* in exchange for a SCIN to avoid inclusion of the note or a portion of the assets represented by the LLC interest sold in his estate when he passes.

Next, let's take a deep dive into the daunting process that you (and George) will experience in preparing the business for sale.

LESSONS LEARNED

- You should structure and time your estate planning well in advance of the sale of or exit from your business.
- You should consider different approaches to minimizing gift and estate taxes on your death yet try to retain control over the assets as much as possible. These techniques may include GRATs, IDGTs, SLATs, and other forms of dynasty trusts.
- If you are charitably inclined, consider giving a portion of your wealth to charity in a manner that allows you or your heirs to receive benefits from a charitable trust either during your lifetime or after you are gone.
- Use advanced estate planning techniques that apply to your specific facts rather than a cookie-cutter approach designed to solve someone else's issues.

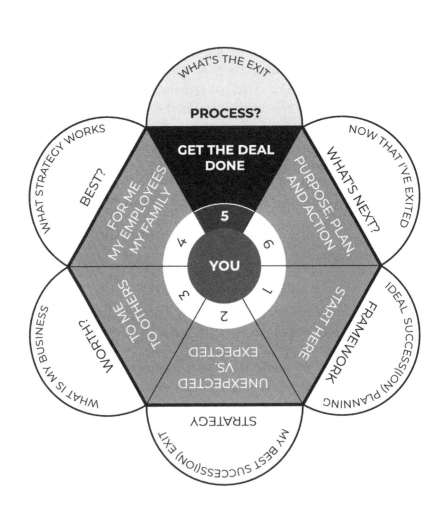

CHAPTER 5

WHAT'S THE EXIT PROCESS?

"The difference between something good and something great is attention to detail."
—CHARLES R. SWINDOLL

SALE/MERGER & ACQUISITION PROCESS

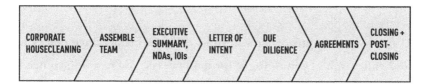

THE BIG LIFT: CORPORATE HOUSECLEANING AND PREPARING FOR DILIGENCE

CORPORATE MINUTES AND CONSENTS

If you're thinking of transitioning your business to a third party, you need to have your corporate legal documents in order. By that, I mean you need to observe the formalities set forth in your organizational documents, including your articles of incorporation or articles of organization, bylaws, operating agreement, or shareholders' agreement, and you must document transactions completed to date.

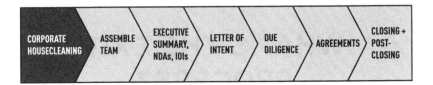

For corporations, consider these questions:

- How many directors are you supposed to have according to your articles of incorporation and your bylaws?
- Has the correct number been appointed?
- How often are you required to have shareholders' meetings or directors' meetings?
- Have you held the meetings and documented actions taken in minutes or consents?

If the bylaws require that you hold these meetings once per year, and you haven't been doing it for many years, you're going to need to create records that approve actions taken and transactions not previously approved. Failure to do this creates an opportunity for creditors to attack your corporation for failing to observe the formalities of the corporate form.

Most small business owners open their corporate minute book and stock ledger for the first time since starting up the corporation in response to diligence requests from prospective buyers. They may find that they never held the required board or shareholder meetings, never formally appointed a *board of directors*, and never issued stock certificates as required by their bylaws.

You will make it easier on yourself, your attorney, and the buyer when you get ready to sell your business if you clean up your corporate house before you even introduce investment bankers or business brokers. Have an attorney conduct a corporate legal audit to make sure that all the t's are crossed and i's are dotted. If you haven't conducted annual meetings, you can prepare catch-up minutes or consents that approve and ratify transactions that were completed many years ago.

If you haven't done so already, make sure that you've appointed a board of directors. After you appoint the board, either hold a meeting that ratifies the prior transactions or prepare a written consent for all the directors to sign accomplishing the same result.

Here's a top 10 list of transactions or items that a corporation's board of directors typically should approve:

1. Electing officers and approving their employment agreements, compensation, bonuses, and other benefits
2. Transactions between the corporation and any member of the board, identifying any conflicts of interest and the fairness of the transaction to the corporation
3. Indemnification and compensation agreements for board members and officers
4. Company's annual budget

5. Employee benefit plans, including qualified retirement plans (e.g., 401(k) and *profit* sharing plans) and welfare benefit plans (e.g., *disability* and life insurance, healthcare, educational reimbursement, and other benefits)
6. Leases and material purchases of equipment and real estate by the corporation
7. Lending or borrowing transactions between the corporation, employees, and third-party lenders
8. Purchases and sales of businesses
9. Investment policies for investing excess cash
10. Issuing stock, stock options, or other securities to employees, board members, and vendors or consultants

For a *limited liability company* (LLC), first determine whether the LLC is required to be managed by managers or by its members. A manager acts like a director on a board of directors and is responsible for running the operations and daily activities of the company. The members are like stockholders in a corporation; they own *membership interests* in the LLC, sometimes referred to as LLC units. The information regarding who runs the LLC can be found in the LLC's articles of organization or operating agreement. If the LLC is managed by managers, what powers do the managers possess?

The operating agreement often contains a laundry list of powers that the managers or members have and indicates when the managers or members must vote on certain matters. Like a corporation, the LLC should document the approval of the transactions that are required to be approved by the managers and members over the years, and if those transactions have not been approved previously, have the managers and members sign a unanimous consent (or lower percentage if authorized by the operating agreement) or hold a meeting approving of these transactions.

ORGANIZATION AND AUTHORIZATION TO DO BUSINESS

Your corporate cleanup should also address whether your company is authorized or registered to do business in the jurisdictions in which it operates.

IDEAS IN ACTION

Let's say you're incorporated in Delaware but operating with employees and property located in Virginia and Florida. You most likely have already registered the entity to pay taxes in each jurisdiction. But that does not mean you're qualified to do business or registered as a foreign corporation or foreign LLC in those jurisdictions. In that case, you may need to formally register to do business in both states, particularly if you have employees and property there.

In some states, failure to properly register as a foreign entity will subject the entity to penalties and potential liability. (By "foreign," I'm not referring to countries outside the United States; rather, I'm referring to states other than the state in which the entity was originally organized.) Failing to register will also prevent shareholders or members from arguing that they are protected by the corporate or LLC shield of limited liability. This could be devastating if a claim arises against the entity in one of these foreign jurisdictions. In that case, creditors may be able to pierce through the corporate shield and pursue the owners directly to collect a judgment against the entity.

Buyers always require good standing certificates from the jurisdictions in which the entity is organized and registered to do business. You won't be able to get such a good standing certificate if the entity has not been properly registered to do business in the jurisdictions where it operates, so you may want to investigate this now. Being in "good standing" means that you have properly registered the entity, filed any required annual or biannual reports with the appropriate state authority, and paid the fees and taxes you owe in that jurisdiction.

KEEPING ACCURATE AND COMPLETE FINANCIAL STATEMENTS

Another important consideration for you as a potential seller is whether your business maintains its financial statements in accordance with *generally accepted accounting principles* (GAAP). You may operate your business using QuickBooks or another accounting software program that allows you to provide information to your accountant to prepare tax returns. Many sellers are on the cash-basis method of accounting, which means they only recognize revenue as cash is received and only claim deductions as cash is paid.

Under GAAP, financial statements must be maintained on the accrual basis of accounting. This means that revenues are recognized in accordance with financial accounting standards as the revenue is earned and often before cash is received. On the accrual basis, your business records *accounts receivable* for services or products that have been billed but not yet collected. Similarly, expenses must be accrued as they are incurred, as opposed to when they are paid.

You may want your accountant to prepare GAAP-based financial statements in advance of a transaction. This will give the buyer

comfort that your business's financial statements, which are usually prepared in accordance with GAAP, can be incorporated into their financial accounting system.

Your financial statements may need to reflect otherwise unrecorded assets and hidden liabilities. Unrecorded assets may include prepaid expenses in the form of security deposits and prepaid insurance premiums. Unrecorded liabilities often include deferred revenues reflecting cash that has been collected for services not yet performed. If they are not properly recorded on the balance sheet, unrecorded assets and liabilities may have to be disclosed in footnotes to the financial statements. If they do not have to be disclosed on financial statements (i.e., because they are too contingent or remote), unrecorded or contingent assets and liabilities must be disclosed in schedules attached to the acquisition agreement. Failure to properly account for these items raises concerns in a prospective buyer, who will want protection from such liabilities by demanding that you indemnify them from any claims or losses arising after closing.

When I'm reviewing a potential investment or an acquisition candidate, I always scour the footnotes to understand whether there are any unique circumstances or risks relating to the business that may not be disclosed in the body of the *income* statement, balance sheet, or statement of cash flows. Footnotes explain the accounting treatment for the business's income, assets, liabilities, and *equity* ownership. They serve as a road map for the reader to better understand the business. Again, unless you've retained an accountant to compile, review, or (even better) audit your financial statements in accordance with GAAP, your financials may be incomplete and potentially misleading if they don't contain detailed footnotes providing these critical explanations.[69]

Clearly, audited financials provide prospective buyers with much greater comfort than compiled or even reviewed financial statements. The quality of the audit also depends on the firm conducting it. Some firms specialize in a particular area. For example, I've represented accounting firms that specialize in the insurance industry and are experts in auditing insurance companies. These firms are not necessarily part of the Big Four accounting firms—PricewaterhouseCoopers, Deloitte, Ernst & Young, and KPMG—yet are quite competent.

I will discuss this below, but many clients hire an accounting firm in advance to perform Quality of Earnings assessments of their business and financial reporting. The Quality of Earnings assessment is designed to reveal accounting anomalies, errors, and nonrecurring events that may skew results either positively or negatively. The assessment often results in adjustments to *earnings before interest, taxes, depreciation, and amortization* (EBITDA), which can affect the value of the business. **You may want to hire a firm experienced in performing Quality of Earnings assessments before marketing your company for sale to help you fill in financial reporting gaps in your business and better understand its value.**

WHO OWNS THE BUSINESS?

The ownership of the equity in your business is probably one of the most important representations you make to the buyer at the time you sell your business. Who owns the shares or membership interests, and how are they titled? Have you promised someone who is not currently a shareholder or member stock, membership interests, or some piece of the sale proceeds?

Prospective buyers always ask whether there are any other owners or prospective owners (through the exercise of stock options) of the business, and the seller often says no. Then, at the last minute, the seller reveals that he or she entered into a side agreement with an investor who put money or other property into the business years ago. Unfortunately, the seller finds that this back-of-the-envelope "hypothetical" investment may constitute a binding written contract between the parties where there may need to be some compensation paid to the individual who was previously promised ownership but never received it. Even an email promising to give an employee or investor an equity interest in your company that says no more than that could constitute a binding agreement.

At a minimum, you should disclose these arrangements to your attorney and try to correct them before beginning due diligence with a prospective buyer. You will have to provide a representation and warranty in the purchase agreement regarding the ownership of your business, and if one of these outlier owners surfaces after you close the deal, you will be personally liable for any subsequent damage to the buyer or the company from your failure to resolve this issue in advance.

Entrepreneurs will debate over whether these quasi-promises of equity really constitute a right to claim an ownership interest in their company. They may, and therefore they need to be resolved in advance. Believe me, you don't want to wait until the last minute to find out that you've got a hidden owner who is now making a claim to 5 or 30% of your company. If you don't honor your promise or settle on a reasonable resolution with the other party, you could end up in litigation with them. It's just not worth it to have these ownership issues lingering.

IDEAS IN ACTION

Jack successfully negotiated the sale of his business to a buyer with significant experience and resources. Two weeks before closing, Jack disclosed to his attorney that he had agreed to share ownership of his business with a former "partner" in a signed, handwritten one-pager that could have been easily construed as a contract. Jack told his attorney not to worry about it because the partner had already received significant benefits from the company and would not pose any problems in closing the deal. Jack's attorney wisely advised Jack to get closure with his former partner by entering into a settlement agreement with the former partner, only after disclosing the material terms of the deal with the buyer. Fortunately, Jack's good relationship with the former partner allowed him to pay the former partner a small fraction of what he would have owed had the former partner demanded what he would have been entitled to under the handwritten letter, and the former partner released Jack and the company from any future claims he may have had to ownership in the company.

CONTRACT TRANSFERS, VIOLATIONS, AND BREACHES

In a legal audit, your attorney should request and inspect all the agreements of the business. Your reaction: "You wanna see what? There's no way I can get my hands on all these agreements that I've signed over the many years that I've been in business."

WHAT'S THE EXIT PROCESS?

The attorney's response should be unequivocal: all your active agreements that currently apply to the operation of your business should be cataloged and reviewed. This includes customer agreements, supplier agreements, vendor contracts and agreements, and employment agreements. A prospective buyer will also want to see every *nondisclosure agreement* (NDA) that you've signed, particularly those with employees and consultants who have access to your know-how and trade secrets.

You should have your attorney carefully review these agreements for provisions that would preclude you or your company from competing with any business in the future. Prospective buyers will be looking for *noncompete* provisions to ensure that you and your business are not restricted in any way from conducting the business after closing.

Other important provisions in the agreements include limitation on liabilities and indemnification from loss, warranties you may give on your products or services, and term and termination provisions. The buyer will want to know when and how a customer can cancel a contract, and when a project or service is deemed to be substantially completed so that revenue can be recognized properly on your financial statements.

Your attorney should also review the transfer or assignment clauses in your agreements. For example, do any of your customers have a provision in their agreements that requires them to consent to the transfer not only of the agreement to a buyer but also of your ownership interest in the company to a buyer? This change-in-control provision in a customer contract can impede the transaction if the customer is important, raising additional concerns regarding whether they will resist granting their consent. Often, landlords must consent to a change in control in real estate leases; many equipment leases and software licensing agreements require such consents as well. In a recent transaction, a seller's contract required them to obtain the consent of a major software vendor so that project management software critical to the smooth operation of the seller's construction projects could continue to be used seamlessly following the sale of the business.

COMPLIANCE WITH LAWS

Your attorney should check that you comply with all laws applicable to your business.

IDEAS IN ACTION

Willa unsuccessfully tried to sell her for-profit school to a third party. When due diligence began on this project, the school only complied partially with federal regulations relating to its operation and finances. Noncompliance was due in part to Willa's deficient financial statements. This deficiency delayed and ultimately killed the transaction. At a minimum, Willa should have retained a regulatory specialist to ensure her company was in compliance with federal law and, more importantly, whether the third party knew of the strict financial standards imposed by the government on such organizations.

When you're trying to figure out whether there are any legal issues or risks relating to your business, you need to review compliance with workers' safety laws, Department of Labor and IRS rules under the *Employee Retirement Income Security Act of 1974* (ERISA), federal and state securities laws relating to the issuance of securities to your owners, and other regulations that may apply to your industry or practice.

For example, federal and state securities laws regulate *registered investment advisors* (RIAs) and brokers, and state and local licensing and certifications may apply to construction companies, engineers, architects, lawyers, *certified public accountants* (CPAs), physicians, dentists, and other professionals.

Your company may be subject to environmental laws, federal interstate commerce licenses, franchise disclosure rules, and other requirements unique to your business.

If your lawyer is a general practitioner or a specialist in an area that does not cover all the areas applicable to your business, you will want to retain a firm that has the expertise to conduct the legal audit and ensure you comply with applicable laws before you start looking for buyers. I've served as quarterback in many transactions where the client hires outside counsel from different firms to provide the appropriate assistance, but it often comes at a substantially increased cost if you are on a very tight deadline.

TAXES

And then there are taxes. The very mention of the word inspires fear in the heart of the bravest woman or man. **You will want a tax lawyer working with your CPA to review your tax reporting, tax payment history, and overall tax compliance.** By taxes, I'm referring to all taxes that could apply to your business, including federal and state income tax, sales and use tax, payroll taxes, tangible property tax, gross receipts tax, excise taxes, and other federal, state, and local levies.

Income Tax

You need to verify that all required tax returns have been filed in all relevant jurisdictions and that all taxes and estimated taxes have been paid on a timely basis. If you were operating as a regular *C corporation*, you must have filed Form 1120, the corporation income tax return, annually. If you had profits, you were required to pay estimated taxes and additional taxes owed on the appropriate due dates to ensure no penalties or interest is due.

S corporations file Form 1120-S annually.

- Although they are not typically taxed, *S corporations* may owe income tax in certain cases, such as where built-in gain is taxed following conversion of a C corporation into an S corporation.

- When certain transactions occur within 5 years of the conversion, passive income (e.g., real estate rental, interest, dividends, and *capital gains* on investments) is taxed when it exceeds 25% of the entity's gross receipts.

- S corporations are taxed in certain states because they do not recognize the S corporation election.

- The buyer will also want to see the original IRS letter recognizing your S corporation status.

If you operate a partnership or an LLC treated as a partnership for income tax purposes, you must file Form 1065 every year.

WHAT'S THE EXIT PROCESS?

- This partnership return of income serves as a conduit through which all the income, losses, credits, and deductions pass to the partners or LLC members.

- The buyer will try to determine whether the partnership or LLC has income tax payment obligations at the state and local level, and has filed its returns in a timely manner. In some states, partnerships are not recognized for income tax purposes and may owe tax. For example, the District of Columbia imposes an unincorporated business franchise tax on partnerships and LLCs.

- In other states such as Virginia, the partnership or LLC must withhold tax on income allocable to nonresident partners.

You may have issued stock options, membership interests, or other equity-type property rights to your employees or other consultants or vendors in exchange for services.

- You should have reported this as compensation income on the recipient's Form W-2 or Form 1099 and withheld payroll taxes on the value received by employees. This often comes as a surprise to sellers in the due diligence process.

- Even worse, under IRC Section 409A, the IRS will impose a 20% excise tax, interest, and penalties on top of income tax if an option to purchase stock or LLC interests was provided or *phantom stock* or *phantom equity* interests were granted with an exercise or strike price below fair market value on the grant date.

DEEPER DIVE

You can avoid the harsh penalties of Section 409A if you issue options with a strike price below fair market value and they are only exercisable on a change in control, as defined under Treasury regulations. If the option strike price is less than the fair market value of the underlying stock on the date the option is granted, it will trigger immediate income tax recognition, plus penalties and interest under Section 409A. In many cases, 409A violations are not discovered until the due diligence process begins. At that point, the buyer will require the seller to make a corrective filing with the IRS, where the seller may still incur significant penalties depending on the lapse of time between the grant of the option and the filing date.

I encourage you to obtain some form of valuation when you issue equity that justifies the value that you're claiming on the individual's Form W-2 as well as on your tax returns.

State and Local Taxes

A good accountant will require you to report and pay state and local income tax in any jurisdiction where you maintain employees, property, or both. These income tax returns may also trigger an obligation for you and your other owners to report and pay income taxes as a nonresident in states where your business operates. If you operate as an LLC treated as a partnership or an S corporation, you may be required to file and pay tax in multiple states.

Payroll Taxes

Many of my clients treat individuals who are performing work for them as independent contractors instead of as employees. This raises an age-old question of whether the consultant or contractor should truly be treated as an independent contractor or as an employee for payroll tax purposes as well as for employee benefit purposes. I represented a major Fortune 500 company when I was in public accounting in an IRS audit of their treatment of independent contractors. We ended up settling the case, but millions of dollars of back taxes were involved for thousands of misclassified workers.

In many cases, failure to properly treat an individual as an employee could result in detrimental consequences to your company as well as to your other employees.

- If the IRS treats an independent contractor as your employee, and if you have not properly covered them under your employee benefit plans that are governed by Department of Labor and IRS rules, you may have tainted the plan and caused the plan to be out of compliance with federal law.

- In that case, the qualification of those plans could be jeopardized, which would be devastating to your remaining workers. Contributions to a plan that is disqualified for failing to cover eligible employees could be treated as taxable income to the plan participants. Moreover, the company may not be able to deduct the contributions, the plan *trust* will become taxable on its earnings, and other disastrous consequences may result.

According to the IRS, there are 20 factors that go into determining whether an individual should be properly treated as an independent contractor vs. employee. No one factor is dispositive of the treatment of the individual. However, if you control the activities of the individual who performs services for you, and you provide a place for them to work and resources for them to use in performing those services, you will probably be required to treat them as an employee. This is particularly true if you're supervising the output or work product they create.

When businesses get in trouble, they sometimes stop paying their required payroll tax withholdings to use the funds for other purposes, which is a classic blunder. If an individual responsible for reporting and withholding payroll taxes to the IRS or to state and local governments fails to do so, that individual can be held personally liable for the taxes. You should always ensure that business payroll taxes are paid to the federal government and the state and local governments first before diverting funds to other uses.

Sales, Use, and Other Taxes

State and local jurisdictions have become very aggressive in taxing activities that were not previously deemed to be subject to tax. For example, if you're operating an online sales or e-commerce site, the state in which you're selling the products may try to impose sales tax or use tax.

A state may also impose sales and use tax on certain services or amusements or events that you conduct that attract these types of taxes. Like payroll taxes, if you have not properly withheld and remitted sales and use tax, you could be personally liable to the states for taxes, interest, and penalties. You should consult an accounting firm with state and local tax expertise to ensure you follow these ever-changing laws.

Maryland recently enacted a digital advertising tax on businesses with at least $100 million in global revenue and $1 million in gross receipts from digital advertising services in Maryland. Literally hours after the legislation passed, the US Chamber of Commerce and several trade associations filed a federal lawsuit in the US District Court for the District of Maryland challenging the constitutionality of the tax. In April 2021, Comcast and Verizon Media Inc. filed a separate lawsuit in Maryland Circuit Court challenging the Maryland Digital Advertising Tax under the Internet Tax Freedom Act (ITFA) and the US Constitution's due process clause, commerce clause, and First Amendment. The Maryland Circuit Court ruled from the bench in favor of Comcast and Verizon.

Similar legislation is pending in other states, and similar challenges undoubtedly will be made to overthrow these new laws.

IDEAS IN ACTION

John ran a successful retail online florist and gift business in Virginia that was selling to customers in most of the 50 states and the District of Columbia. His company used fulfillment houses located in various states throughout the United States. While John collected sales tax in Virginia on sales made to Virginia residents, he did not collect sales tax on sales made outside the state. He did not realize that fulfilling the orders in other locations created a nexus for sales tax purposes in the state where the fulfillment house is located. The presence of inventory in a state creates a nexus for not only sales tax but also for income tax purposes.

In addition, the US Supreme Court case of *South Dakota v. Wayfair, Inc.* allowed all states to require tax collection from online retailers and other remote sellers, even if they do not have a physical presence in their states, if they have an economic nexus with the state. Looking strictly at the South Dakota economic nexus legislation addressed in the case, South Dakota's law minimizes the burden on online and out-of-state sellers and makes it easier for them to collect sales taxes from online sales activities with residents of the state. The legislation provides a safe harbor for small sellers: a remote seller must make in-state sales exceeding $100,000 or 200 or more separate sales transactions in the previous or current calendar year for the nexus provision to apply. The legislation also ensures that the nexus provision does not apply retroactively.

Many other states have enacted economic nexus legislation like South Dakota's to capture sales tax on internet sales.

John recently hired an accounting firm with strong expertise in multistate sales taxation to begin the painful and arduous process of filing delinquent sales tax reports and paying back taxes, interest, and penalties. The accounting firm will utilize its vast resources and ability to have penalties waived for John's noncompliance before he tries to sell or transfer ownership of his company.

LITIGATION AND POTENTIAL CLAIMS

Your legal housekeeping should include a close examination and documentation of whether there has been any litigation or investigations, threatened or otherwise, by any governmental authority or party against your business. This may include governmental agency audits, claims, or complaints made by employees, vendors, and customers. The buyer wants assurance that no claims are currently active or pending. If you are in the process of settling or resolving actual or threatened claims, you will need to indemnify the buyer for any losses that arise from these claims.

INTELLECTUAL PROPERTY

Your intellectual property (IP) includes copyrights, trademarks, trade names, service marks, patents, know-how, trade secrets, and other confidential information. Every potential buyer wants to be sure that you have nondisclosure or confidentiality agreements with every employee of your company. This includes former employees, whether they left on good or bad terms. Your trade secrets and other intellectual property are critical to the value of your business. The buyer does not want to buy the business if any of the intellectual property or other valuable intangible assets are jeopardized because of a failure to properly monitor and maintain confidentiality and protection of these assets. **You should also ensure that you own or have valid licenses to the intellectual property you use in your business.**

Let's say you have hired a contractor to help you develop something that you consider proprietary to your business. Hopefully, your contract with the developer clearly states that you own whatever the developer creates. In addition, if the developer uses any kind of open-source software or licensed intellectual property from third parties in building your product or service, they need to identify these components separately in your product documentation, and you may need to get separate licenses or permission to transfer your product or service platform that incorporates these components. The buyer will often bring in a technical or technology expert to audit your intellectual property, including any internal software that you're using to run your business. You may want to prevent any surprises by hiring such an expert before you begin due diligence with a prospective buyer.

DEEPER DIVE

"Open source" generally refers to something people can modify and share because its design is publicly accessible.[70] The term originated in the context of software development to designate a specific approach to creating computer programs. Today, open-source projects, products, or initiatives embrace and celebrate principles of open exchange, collaborative participation, rapid prototyping, transparency, meritocracy, and community-oriented development. "Open-source software" is software with source code that anyone can inspect, modify, and enhance. "Source code" is the part of software that most computer users don't ever see; it's the code computer programmers can manipulate to change how a piece of software—a "program" or "application"—works. Programmers who have access to a computer program's source code can improve that program by adding features to it or fixing parts that don't always work correctly.

The buyer will require you to represent in the definitive purchase agreement that not only do you own or have valid licenses to all the intellectual property that you use in your business, but that you are also not infringing any third party's IP rights. With copyrights, patents, and trademarks, either you own the registration to these items or you have hired an intellectual property lawyer to ensure that you can claim ownership over what you're selling.

In the case of software, you can't claim ownership of software developed with open-source code; you can only own the original pieces you built on top of the open-source code, which may be hard to identify and segregate.

REAL ESTATE

If your business owns real estate and you are selling it with the business, you will have to establish your ownership through a title search and proof of title insurance when the business acquired the property. If you lease real estate, you will want to ensure that you're in compliance with all provisions of your leases.

If you're leasing property from yourself (i.e., you own the property in a separate LLC that's leasing it to your business), make sure you have a valid, signed lease agreement between the two entities, even if you own 100% of both entities. If you don't have a lease in effect, execute one before offering your business for sale. Your leases should allow you to sell the business without any constraints. In most cases, leases with third-party landlords contain change-in-control provisions that will require a landlord to consent to the transfer of the business, even if the lease itself is not being assigned. This may come into play where you're just selling your stock or ownership interests in the business and not the assets.

IDEAS IN ACTION

Corinne ran a general contracting business that leased one of its locations from her LLC. Before selling her business, her company entered into a long-term lease with the LLC that charged rent based upon comparable rents charged by similar landlords. Corinne had a local commercial real estate agent survey the local market and develop comparable rental rates to back up the rental terms used in the lease. Having the lease in place in advance of the business sale made it much easier for Corinne to negotiate the assumption of the lease by the buyer.

If your business holds or generates any kind of hazardous substance that is regulated under federal law, you're going to have to provide assurance to the buyer that there is no continuing environmental liability because of your activities.

IDEAS IN ACTION

In one deal involving the sale of a shopping center, the owner-landlord, Paul, had allowed a dry-cleaning company (which had left the premises) to occupy one of the stores for many years and it was found to have dumped dry-cleaning effluent on the property. Paul was forced to hire environmental experts to remediate the problem and then had to obtain certifications from the state environmental protection agency that the problems in fact were fixed before a sale of the property could be completed. This effort took almost two years and cost hundreds of thousands of dollars.

Environmental issues arise frequently in sales of real estate. If you're conducting any kind of construction activity or store equipment where gasoline or oil is stored on the property, you may need to conduct phase I environmental studies of the properties, and if any defects are uncovered, you will have to fix them in advance of a sale.

EMPLOYEES

Perhaps the most important asset that you're transferring to a buyer will be your human capital—that is, your employees. The buyer will want to ensure that you're in compliance with federal and state laws relating to your employees. Make sure you are keeping accurate records of employee vacation or paid time off; you are complying with applicable labor laws; employees are maintaining confidentiality of your trade secrets and processes; no workers' compensation or other liability exists; you're paying payroll taxes and unemployment insurance; and, again, all employees are being properly classified as employees and not as independent contractors.

DEEPER DIVE

Did you know that members of an LLC taxed as a partnership are not allowed to be treated as employees of the LLC? This rule dates to a 1969 IRS ruling that is arguably outdated but has not changed in over 50 years. So if you are a member of an LLC taxed as a partnership and you've been treating yourself as an employee and receiving W-2 income and benefits, you are not in compliance with federal tax law and will need to take steps to correct this issue. You can plan around this issue from the very beginning by either creating a C corporation subsidiary that houses the employees or creating a separate LLC that offers equity to your employees and owns a piece of the operating LLC that employs your workforce.

CUSTOMER SATISFACTION AND RELATIONSHIPS

The buyer will want assurances that the customers are satisfied with your company and that the relationships are sound. At the same time, you do not really want a prospective buyer snooping around your clients. After you have the terms and conditions of the definitive agreement fully negotiated, you may let the buyer contact certain key customers who are critical to the ongoing success of your business within a certain number of days before closing. Or you can sign the purchase agreement and make closing conditional upon the buyer being reasonably satisfied that your customers will remain with the company. In either case, you should wait until the last minute to give the buyer this critical access and information.

To reemphasize what was noted earlier, your ironclad NDA will prevent the potential buyer from stealing your secrets, customers/clients, and employees before due diligence begins.

VENDORS

If you rely on certain vendors, subcontractors, or suppliers to help you conduct your business, you should ensure that the relationships with these folks are sound and strong. The buyer will examine the contracts with your vendors and suppliers to make certain there are no hidden items that would prevent the transaction from going forward safely and smoothly. As with your customers, the buyer will want to talk with your vendors and suppliers before the deal is closed. Depending on the situation, you may want to delay these communications until due diligence is completed on all other matters.

If you have a single source of supply for raw materials, manufacturing, or services to conduct your business successfully, your buyer will be concerned about the concentration of risk in that single source. If the source dries up or goes out of business, the value of your business may decline precipitously. So, having diversified sources of supply will mitigate this risk. The risk of losing your source of supply may adversely affect the purchase price or, alternatively, result in a breach of the purchase agreement if you have promised that the source of supply will remain stable after the closing.

> ### IDEAS IN ACTION
> In 1991, I represented one of the first "pen computing" companies, TelePad, based in Reston, Virginia. They were a startup with a spectacular vision that was ahead of its time. To mass-produce their new product, they had few choices in manufacturers and turned to IBM. The costs were prohibitive, and control over the manufacturer was minimal. As a result, the company could not survive the pressures of building and selling its product profitably, in part due to the sole source of manufacturing supply.

Once you've completed your corporate housecleaning, you can complete the assembly of your Rock Star team to help you to a successful exit.

> ### LESSONS LEARNED
> - Get your corporate house in order before approaching prospective buyers.
> - Update and complete your corporate minute book and stock ledger and approve of important prior transactions.
> - Eliminate any outlier-owner problems you may have, based on prior promises made to employees and investors.
> - Check with your attorney to make sure you are properly qualified to do business in every jurisdiction in which you operate.
> - Review your contracts with customers and suppliers to make sure you don't have any noncompete,

change-in-control, or other obligations that would impede or prevent the sale from occurring.

- Have your attorney conduct a legal audit to ensure you are in compliance with all applicable laws and the provisions of your contracts, leases, and other agreements; no litigation or other claims are pending or threatened; you own or have valid licenses to your intellectual property; and you have no environmental or other problems that will haunt you in the due diligence process or that can be corrected before starting due diligence.
- Make sure your financial statements comply with GAAP and contain footnote disclosures prepared by your CPA. Remember, an audit gives your buyer greater assurance that your financial information is true, accurate, and complete, and a Quality of Earnings assessment provides even further assurance to the buyer.
- Check to ensure your income tax, sales tax, payroll tax, and other tax returns have been filed and taxes have been paid on a timely basis. Be prepared to disclose any current or past audits and the results.
- Verify that your employees have completed all necessary paperwork, including Form I-9, W-4, and NDAs that protect your confidential information and trade secrets.
- Check in with your customers and vendors regularly to ensure your strong relationships with them, before the buyers have a chance to contact them.

ASSEMBLE THE TEAM, DEFINE THEIR ROLES, AND BEGIN THE PROCESS

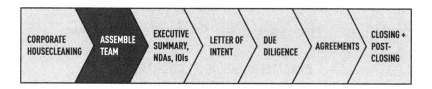

You should assemble a strong team to assist you in negotiating and preparing you and your business for sale.

ATTORNEYS

There are many kinds of attorneys who can assist you in selling your business. The most important one is the lead attorney, who should have experience in *mergers and acquisitions* (M&As). You may also need specialists to assure you that you're conducting your business in a way that doesn't violate federal or state law and you're in compliance with these laws. Having an expert in tax, ERISA, labor laws, real estate and environmental laws, technology and data privacy, government contracting, and other industry expertise is critical to the success of a transaction.

> **IDEAS IN ACTION**
>
> I was the lead attorney to an independent RIA firm on the West Coast that was sold to a *family office*. We hired an industry expert who made sure that our client was protected both in negotiations specific to the industry and in securities law compliance. His experience in selling and buying RIAs and his knowledge of the federal securities laws proved invaluable to our client and me as the lead.

As I discussed in Chapter 4, your *estate planning* lawyer will also play a critical role on your transaction team. They will ensure that you take advantage of any planning opportunities available to you well in advance of the transaction. They are also going to want to make sure your basic estate planning is in place ahead of the transaction.

CERTIFIED PUBLIC ACCOUNTANT

Your CPA may be an integral part of the transaction if they have experience in handling mergers and acquisitions. **An experienced CPA firm will not only help you ensure that your financial statements are in good condition and that your tax situation is sound, but they can also add value by reviewing the financial statement disclosures, tax representations, and working capital calculations and adjustment provisions in the *letter of intent* (LOI) and purchase agreement.** The CPA can also assist in evaluating Quality of Earnings analysis by the buyer's accounting firm.

FINANCIAL PLANNER

You should involve a financial planner early in the sale process. There are two basic kinds of financial planners. The first and more common financial planner helps with individual or personal financial planning and advises on investments and asset allocation within your investment portfolio. A valuable second type is one who understands the transaction process and can work effectively with your estate planning attorney and your tax accountant in helping you plan for the transaction. **The financial planners will help you understand the economic consequences of the transaction and how to deploy the net proceeds received in the transaction after taxes. They will assist in investment, tax, and overall financial planning pre- and post-transaction and should be part of your team.**

INVESTMENT BANKER VS. BUSINESS BROKER

Depending on the size and complexity of the transaction, you may want to enlist an investment banker or a business broker to help you find and market your business to prospective buyers. An investment banker will have broad, deep connections within the universe of potential investors and buyers, and will hopefully provide strong expertise in your industry. They will help you prepare for and conduct a road show where you and your key managers meet with prospective buyers to sell them on the valuable attributes and great opportunities your business presents and why you're a great acquisition candidate. They will also help you in constructing, evaluating, and negotiating *indications of interest* (IOIs) and LOIs from prospective buyers. The best investment bankers are also closely involved in helping you build your data room to share critical information about your business with prospective buyers and their representatives.

Investment bankers typically charge an up-front, nonrefundable fee, which ranges anywhere from $30,000 to $150,000. This fee ensures you are committed to the process and may or may not be applied against the ultimate contingent fee that they receive if the transaction is closed. You should have your corporate attorney closely review the investment banker's contract before you sign it. Remember, many of these contracts are negotiable, not only in terms of the scope of services that will be provided by the investment banker but also in terms of the fees being charged.

Fees often are structured using a sliding scale where the percentage decreases as the size of the deal increases (the so-called Lehman or double-Lehman formula).

DEEPER DIVE

The single-Lehman formula, named after the now-defunct investment banking firm, works like this: the fee is 5% of the first $1 million of transaction value, plus 4% of the next $1 million, plus 3% of the next $1 million, plus 2% of the next $1 million, plus 1% of all amounts thereafter, in all events relating to the total purchase price. A double-Lehman formula simply doubles the percentages: 10% of the first $1 million of transaction value, plus 8% of the second $1 million, plus 6% of the third $1 million, plus 4% of the fourth $1 million, plus 2% of everything thereafter. So if you sell your business for $30 million with the help of an investment banker who uses the Lehman formula, the fee paid to the banker would equal $166,000, which is the sum of $50,000 on the first $1 million (5% × $1 million), plus $40,000 on the next $1 million (4% × $1 million), plus $30,000 on the next $1 million (3% × $1 million), plus $20,000 on the next $1 million (2% × $1 million), plus $26,000 (1% × ($30 million − $4 million)).

If a double-Lehman formula is used (i.e., double the Lehman formula fee), the fee would be $332,000, which is the sum of $100,000 (10% of the first $1 million), plus $80,000 (8% of the next $1 million), plus $60,000 (6% of the next $1 million), plus $40,000 (4% of the next $1 million), plus $52,000 (2% × ($30 million − $4 million)).

A normal range for investment banking fees is from 0.5% to 1% for very large deals (i.e., over $1 billion) up to 8% for smaller deals (less than $5 million). In some deals, the banker may be willing to use a reverse scaled fee that increases as the price increases. This creates a strong incentive for the banker to find the highest possible bidder for you.

WHAT'S THE EXIT PROCESS?

> ### DEEPER DIVE
> A reverse scaled fee looks like this: If the seller receives a $50 million offer that meets the seller's minimum value expectation, the investment banker would get a modest success fee of 2%. However, if a much higher offer of $65 million is received, the investment banker might receive an additional 10% on the difference between your minimum value expectation and the premium offer. Total success fees in this transaction at $65 million would be $2.5 million (or 3.85% of the total deal).[71]

In either case, the investment banker usually charges a minimum fee for undertaking the transaction if the deal closes; in most cases, no fee is due (other than the up-front payment) if a transaction isn't closed. This may eclipse the Lehman formula or double-Lehman formula amount, depending on the size of the deal.

> ### IDEAS IN ACTION
> Georgia recently negotiated a termination of an engagement with an investment banker who was charging an exorbitant fee for doing nothing. The investment banker was willing to relinquish a tail provision in the contract that would have entitled him to a significant share of any fees paid on any subsequent transaction within a lengthy period, even after termination. Georgia was able to pay a very small up-front fee to eliminate the tail payment.

Should you use a business broker or an investment banker in the transaction? In my experience, business brokers may understand your industry and have ready a list of prospective buyers that you may want to consider. However, they may not be as sophisticated

or experienced as investment bankers. Their minimum fees are often less than what investment bankers charge, but as a percentage of the transaction, business brokers still get paid well. Just as you would do with an investment banker, have your attorney review the bona fides of the business broker as well as the contract that you intend to sign with them.

Whether you use an investment banker or a business broker, they usually serve as the lead negotiator on the business terms of the transaction. They will have candid, difficult conversations that you may not otherwise feel comfortable having with prospective buyers. It's their job. That's why they're paid the "big bucks." They should also assist you in the due diligence process, maintaining your information in a secure data room that's accessible to prospective buyers, and in helping you compile the information for the disclosure statements that ultimately become an integral part of the purchase agreement. The data room should provide staged, limited access, which becomes more accessible as the transaction and due diligence proceed toward completion.

Many attorneys serve as business advisors in transactions without generating an investment banking fee. That raises the question of whether you really need an investment banker or a business broker in the transaction. Clearly, if you have identified a prospective buyer based on your own relationships, you may not need an investment banker to charge you for finding prospective buyers or conducting an auction process. That is particularly true if you have a good lawyer and a good CPA assisting you in negotiating the deal.

WHAT'S THE EXIT PROCESS?

Nevertheless, an investment banker will be invaluable to you if you plan on conducting an auction process for your business. Basically, in an auction process, the investment banker

- learns your business inside out;
- helps construct an executive summary of the business with financial, quantitative, and qualitative information;
- identifies and contacts prospective buyers;
- has them sign NDAs;
- circulates the executive summary to procure initial interest;
- orchestrates a road show for you to demonstrate your value proposition to prospective buyers;
- solicits indications of interest; and
- narrows down the top candidates to engage in a competitive bidding process with LOIs and further meetings until a final candidate is selected.

After assisting in negotiating a nonbinding LOI, the investment banker helps you build your data room and responses to due diligence requests and leads the remaining business negotiations in completing the definitive agreements. A good investment banker is clearly worth the investment.

The same goes for business brokers. They come in all shapes and sizes. The bottom line is that the best business brokers will find you the best buyer and assist heavily in the sale process. **Business brokers typically work well in smaller transactions (e.g., less than $15 million), whereas investment bankers are critical in larger, more complex transactions where an auction process with an expansive listing of prospective buyers is involved.**

BUSINESS APPRAISER

If you're going to conduct pretransaction, *advanced estate planning*, you will need a business appraiser to value the business and the interest that you might be transferring to a trust or to your family directly. You may also want to hire a business appraiser if you're not using an investment banker or a business broker to understand how a third party might value your business. These two types of valuations are very different.

The estate planning valuation requires a detailed *appraisal report* that contains schedules of assumptions, calculations, and detailed analysis. It is used to support a *gift tax* return that you must file with the IRS to report the advanced planning transaction.

By contrast, the business appraiser serves as your advocate to give you a range of values that you can use to support a higher purchase price than the buyer may be willing to offer.

If an *employee stock ownership plan* (ESOP) owns all or part of your company, the ESOP *trustee* will require a fairness opinion and separate appraisal supporting the purchase price being offered by a third party to buy your business. This is required under ERISA and Department of Labor rules.

COLLABORATION

Members of the team must be allowed to communicate with each other openly and frequently throughout the process to ensure everyone is aware of business, tax, accounting, and other issues that may affect negotiations. A strong team will support you in reaching the best business exit possible.

The next step in the sale process is to draft an ironclad NDA for use in the deal and engage your team members to solicit IOIs and LOIs to purchase your business.

LESSONS LEARNED

- Your team should include attorneys of various disciplines, CPAs, a financial planner, an investment banker or a business broker, and possibly a business appraiser if you need an indication of value in advance or if you engage in pretransaction gifting.
- Your CPA will need to have experience in preparing clients for acquisitions, a deep understanding of tax laws, and the capability to prepare GAAP-compliant financial statements.
- The choice of whether to use an investment banker or a business broker may depend on the size of the transaction and whether you intend to engage many or few potential buyers.
- A financial planner will help you understand how a transaction will impact your financial future.

NDAS, INDICATIONS OF INTEREST, AND LETTERS OF INTENT

If you've hired an investment banker, let the auction process begin! If not, you should still focus carefully on this next section, which emphasizes the importance of ironclad nondisclosure agreements, seeking indications of interest, and negotiating nonbinding letters of intent.

NONDISCLOSURE AGREEMENTS

Your attorneys or investment bankers should circulate ironclad NDAs with the candidates who are interested in buying your business. The NDAs should contain prohibitions on the buyer poaching your employees or customers for some time period after the NDA is signed and also protect your confidential information from being used or disclosed outside the scope of the agreement.

Once you have signed NDAs, you can start disclosing your identity and an executive summary of your business to potential buyers. A word to the wise: you should understand that, notwithstanding the ironclad NDA you may have with prospective buyers, you may not be able to keep the proposed transaction a secret, particularly if your investment banker canvasses a large group of potential buyers. Information may leak into the marketplace that you're selling, and your competitors may find out. In turn, they may seek to lure your employees and customers away from you.

You should develop a contingency communication plan for your employees and customers to allay their fears if word leaks out. You could also communicate your intentions up front—that is, be transparent that you are exploring a possible transaction with a third party that may not result in a sale of the entire company but only a partial sale and an investment. In either case, the greater the population of potential suitors, the more likely your secret will be exposed.

For this reason, some clients prefer to pursue a limited auction process. The investment banker could narrow the universe of prospective buyers to limit the possibility of unwanted disclosure.

IDEAS IN ACTION

We used a limited auction approach in the proposed sale of a large retail chain whose chief rival was a publicly traded company 10 times its size. The founders were quite concerned about knowledge of the transaction leaking to their key competitor, who did not hesitate to interfere with the business operations of the potential seller when it learned of the potential transaction. In fact, the smaller company initiated and ultimately settled potential litigation that arose because the competitor improperly solicited management employees who were bound by tight noncompete agreements.

INDICATIONS OF INTEREST

Your investment banker may disseminate over 100 NDAs, and you may get almost as many agreements signed. But the number of interested parties who want to bid on your business (IOIs) will vary and probably represent only a fraction of the universe contacted, depending on how attractive your business is in the marketplace, whether you have strategic value for prospective purchasers, and the market in general for the sale of businesses. It will also depend on how well you and your investment banker capture and convey your value proposition in the executive summary.

You may receive 5 to 10 IOIs that tout the benefits and synergies of selling your business to the bidder and provide a range of values they may be willing to pay for your business before conducting preliminary due diligence. The ranges of values can vary wildly from one bidder to the next. In one deal, we saw six IOIs with ranges in values from $60 million to $140 million, and one IOI in that deal with a range from $110 million to $140 million.

You will want to talk to the bidders whose IOIs resonate with you, not only in terms of ranges of values but also in terms of what they can offer you, your employees, and your customers post-transaction. They will woo you with their prior accomplishments and other successful deals they have engineered. You should look for language in the IOI that matches your values and vision for the business.

- Are they going to keep your values, employees, and culture intact?
- Why are they so interested in your company? What do they have to gain? What do you and your employees stand to lose?
- What are their plans for your company after the closing?

You should ask these questions and many more before narrowing your choice to the final candidates who will present you with LOIs.

LETTERS OF INTENT

In over 37 years of representing mostly sellers, I have seen myriad LOIs, from bare-bones versions to extremely detailed and comprehensive LOIs. A more detailed LOI may serve you best, simply because it makes negotiating the definitive purchase agreement and ancillary agreements easier. A detailed LOI looks something like the example found on my website at *www.waynezell.com/resources*, but it typically contains the following components and answers the questions raised below.

Nonbinding Provisions

- **Purchase Price and Terms of Payment.** A well-drafted LOI should include the total purchase price to be paid for your business and how that price will be paid.
    - Will the buyer pay you 100% in cash at closing (which would be your best case)?
    - Will the buyer require a portion of the purchase price to be held in escrow (typically 5% to 10% of the purchase price for private deals) to protect the buyer from breaches of your representations and warranties and covenants? (You want the escrow to be as low as possible.)
        - When will the escrow terminate so you can get additional proceeds if no claims have been made? (You would prefer to have it end after 12 months, but the buyer wants longer.)
    - Will there be a target working capital amount (current assets minus current liabilities) that must be present at closing? (You want this as low as possible, preferably 30 to 60 days of working capital; the buyer will seek much higher levels.)
        - If so, do you get to keep the excess?
        - When will that amount be finally determined (the sooner the better)?
        - Will the buyer demand an additional escrow (reducing your cash proceeds further) to ensure the required working capital is present? (You will want to resist this.)
    - Will a portion of the price be paid in a *promissory note*?
        - What is the interest rate and term (should be market rate interest and paid in 1 to 3 years)?

- Can the note be increased or reduced if results are better or worse than expected after closing?
- Is the note secured or enforceable without your having to sue the buyer in court?
- Will there be an *earnout* or additional payment if certain performance metrics are met?
  - What are the performance metrics, and will you be able to control them after closing?
  - Can you receive more than the earnout if you blow away your targets?
  - Can you receive a portion of the earnout if you come close to the targets?

- **Structure.** Your LOI should clearly state how the buyer intends to structure the purchase of your business. This may directly impact your tax treatment on the transaction.
  - Will the buyer simply buy your stock or membership interests so you can qualify for long-term capital gain treatment on most, if not all, of your proceeds?
  - Or will the buyer purchase assets or treat the stock/membership interest sale as a sale of assets for tax purposes (e.g., in an F *reorganization* or by making Section 338/336(e) elections)?
    - If the buyer treats the transaction as an asset purchase, will it gross-up your proceeds with the additional tax you must pay to structure the deal so it can amortize *goodwill* and other assets deemed to be purchased?

- If you are negotiating with a *private equity* (PE) firm, will you receive *rollover equity*, and will you have to pay income tax when you receive it? (You want to avoid this.)
    - What rights will you have to protect your interest in the rollover equity (i.e., can you ensure that you get no less than the value of the equity on the closing date)?
- If the deal involves an exchange of stock for your ownership interest, is all or a portion of the deal tax-free to you?
    - If so, can you sell the securities you receive in the public market soon after closing (to provide you with liquidity from the transfer of your business)?
    - If you receive nonpublicly traded stock, can you force the buyer to redeem your shares in certain circumstances? If so, at what price?

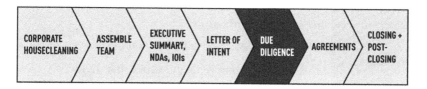

- **Due Diligence.** The LOI should include a section describing the buyer's plan for conducting a due diligence investigation of your business and the time frame to complete its investigation.
    - When will the buyer have access to your customers and employees (hopefully, not until the very end of the process)?
    - When does the buyer expect to complete its investigation, assuming you provide the requested information on a timely basis? (30 to 45 days after signing the LOI is reasonable.)
    - Will the buyer have an accounting firm conduct a Quality of Earnings analysis to scrub your financial statements

and determine areas of risk and weakness? (This will delay closing, but the buyer may insist.)
- Will the buyer have a technology expert evaluate your technology and systems?
- Will the buyer require you to produce copies of every active contract you have with customers, employees, contractors, and vendors? (You want to set a floor value over which you will be required to provide contracts.)

- **Purchase Agreement.** The LOI will reference the purchase agreement, which will contain representations, warranties, covenants, agreements, conditions, indemnities, setoffs, and escrows normally associated with transactions like yours. Ask these questions in the LOI:
  - What approvals will you be required to obtain before closing on your transaction?
    - Will you need to obtain approval of your board of directors/managers and other shareholders/members?
  - Will you be subject to confidentiality, noncompetition, and nonsolicitation covenants?
    - How long will the covenants apply after closing? (Noncompete covenants typically range from 3 to 5 years post-closing.)
    - Will the noncompete restrict you from engaging in any activity related to the business, or will it be limited to the customers you service?
  - Will you be required to pay off your borrowing and debt before closing? (This is typically required.)

- Will you need to obtain tail insurance to cover liabilities that arise after the transaction is closed but relate to events occurring before closing?
- Will you be able to continue benefits and plans currently provided to employees, or will you need to terminate your existing plans? (It will be easier and preferable to continue your plans for at least 1 year after closing.)
- How will the purchase price be allocated to your assets in an asset purchase or in a stock purchase treated as an asset purchase? (You want to allocate as much as possible to goodwill, which is treated as a capital asset entitled to long-term capital gains treatment.)
- What liability protection will the buyer demand if you breach or violate your representations, warranties, or covenants in the agreement?
    - Will you be able to limit your liability to a percentage of the purchase price?
    - Will the agreement contain a deductible, above which you are liable and below which you aren't?
- How and where will disputes under the purchase agreement be resolved?
    - Would you prefer arbitration over litigation?
    - Where would disputes be litigated or arbitrated? (You would prefer to hold any proceeding at your location.)

- **Employment Agreements and Other Ancillary Agreements.**
    - Will you or any of your key employees enter into employment agreements or consulting agreements with the buyer after closing?

- What will everyone's salaries be? Bonuses? Benefits?
- Will there be severance provisions if they are terminated without cause or they leave with good reason?
- Will the employees be required to sign separate noncompete agreements? How would the noncompete affect an employee if they are terminated from employment? With cause? With good reason? Without cause? What is the duration of the noncompete? What are the geographic restrictions and scope of the noncompete?
- Will key employees be entitled to receive change-in-control bonuses, retention bonuses, or equity in the buyer?
- Will you continue leasing any owner-occupied real estate to the buyer post-closing?
  - What is the term of the lease?
  - What are the rental payments over the term?
  - Can the lease be terminated without cause?
- Will there be an escrow agreement?
  - If so, who will the escrow agent be, and who will be responsible for paying the escrow agent's fees?
  - How and when can the escrow be released?

Binding Provisions

- **Exclusivity Period.** If the buyer expects to spend substantial time, effort, and expense in conducting due diligence, it will want to bind you to a provision that prevents you or any of your key employees from entering into or conducting discussions with other prospective buyers for a specified period of time after the LOI is signed. This is known as an exclusivity provision. The buyer will want at least 90 days, but you will want to negotiate a shorter period (e.g., 45 days) simply to avoid the due diligence process from diverting your attention from your business. Because it is binding, this provision allows the prospective buyer to sue you for damages if you violate the agreement and if you solicit competing offers from others after signing the LOI.

- **Confidentiality and Nonsolicitation.** If you were unable to include strong nondisclosure and nonsolicitation language in your NDA with the prospective buyer, you should try to get them added as part of the LOI's binding provisions. The nondisclosure obligation will prevent either you or the buyer from disclosing the existence or contents of the LOI or any other confidential information exchanged to anyone other than your representatives in the transaction. The LOI should also prohibit either party from soliciting, hiring, or otherwise interfering with the employees or customers of the other party.

- **Other Binding Provisions.** The LOI usually contains provisions that
    - require each party to bear its own fees and expenses incurred in negotiating or closing the transaction,
    - indicate how and where disputes over the LOI will be resolved, and
    - instruct each party how to notify the other party in the event that a dispute arises or to terminate the LOI.

- In many PE transactions involving rollover equity, the buyer will demand that you bear a proportionate share of the fees incurred in the transaction after closing (e.g., if you retain rollover equity of 20%, you will bear responsibility for 20% of the fees incurred by the buyer).

- In less than a quarter of private company sales, the LOI (or the purchase agreement) may include a termination or "breakup" fee (which may be based upon a fixed amount, a percentage of the purchase price, and/or reimbursement of expenses incurred in pursuing the transaction) if the buyer backs out of the deal without justification. The seller rarely must pay a termination fee in deals worth less than $100 million, and even if it must pay (for failing to proceed with the transaction without cause), the seller pays only in a small minority of cases.[72]

Once you sign an LOI, you are effectively "engaged" to your prospective buyer for a limited period. Just like any engagement, you should be able to break it off at any time. However, if due diligence goes well, you may end up signing a definitive purchase agreement with your buyer. Let's see what that might look like.

LESSONS LEARNED

- You need a strong NDA to prevent prospective buyers from disclosing or using your confidential information, and from soliciting or engaging your employees, contractors, and clients.
- If you conduct an auction process, your investment banker or business broker will solicit IOIs from various parties that will provide you with an indication of who

- may be interested in buying your business and what range of values they might be willing to pay for it.
- Once you narrow down the list of potential buyers, you will seek LOIs from your top choices.
- The LOIs will contain nonbinding provisions relating to the purchase price, the deal structure, key employee compensation and restrictions (e.g., noncompete provisions), escrows, holdbacks and earnouts, working capital targets, and other deal-specific matters.
- LOIs will also include binding provisions that give the prospective buyer exclusive rights for a limited time to conduct due diligence and move toward a definitive purchase agreement, ensure confidentiality of the LOI terms, and other important provisions relating to fees and dispute resolution, among other things.

KEY AGREEMENTS

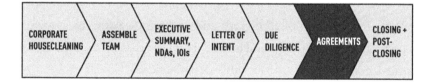

THE PURCHASE AGREEMENT

The purchase agreement is the focal point of the transaction and may be called by different names, including acquisition agreement, merger agreement, stock purchase agreement, asset purchase agreement, or sales agreement. It contains details on every important aspect of the transaction, substantially expanding the scope of the LOI to reflect comprehensive negotiations between your attorney and the buyer's counsel. Most folks don't appreciate the level of detail covered in the purchase agreement and, as a result, become impatient with the process, particularly on such arcane topics as representations and warranties (also referred to as reps and warranties) and indemnification (discussed below).

Usually, the buyer's attorney presents the first draft of the purchase agreement to your lawyer. I have closed small, "friendly" transactions with 5-page agreements and complex agreements involving millions of dollars in payments with more than 100 pages. The level of detail usually increases when the buyer is unfamiliar with you and the purchase price is substantial; the buyer's lawyer is trying to protect the buyer from risks inherent in your business.

The buyer's attorney will say that he is simply attempting to allocate the risk of the transaction to you by including every possible representation and warranty under the sun and asking for you to indemnify the buyer (i.e., promise to cover any liability) for claims and damages arising from breach of those reps and warranties. After all, it's your business and you should stand behind it (at least that's what the buyer's attorney will say).

Your attorney wants to limit the scope of the agreement and your potential liability to the buyer.

The ability of one side to prevail in this negotiation depends on how badly the buyer wants your business, how much you want to sell it to the buyer, and the amount of money and other considerations in changing hands.

PURCHASE PRICE AND PURCHASE PRICE ADJUSTMENTS

The nonbinding provisions of the LOI morph into the binding terms and conditions of the purchase agreement. While the LOI may include the purchase price and how it will be paid, the purchase agreement contains excruciating detail on

- how the purchase price can be adjusted upward or downward,
- the mechanics on how and when it will be paid, and
- definitions of terms that may have been used in the LOI but require exhaustive elaboration and explanation.

It should also include provisions explaining exactly how disputes regarding working capital (i.e., current assets, such as cash, accounts receivable, and inventory, minus current liabilities, such as trade payables, accrued expenses, vacation pay, and other short-term liabilities) and other purchase price adjustments and earnouts will be resolved.

As noted earlier, one of the most heavily negotiated provisions in the purchase agreement relates to the calculation of working capital and adjustments that are made to that number post-closing. As noted above, "working capital" refers to the difference between current assets and current liabilities, as determined under GAAP. If you are not using GAAP-based financial statements, your accountant will add accrual-based items to your balance sheet. On the asset side of the balance sheet, you will include accounts receivable, prepaid expenses (e.g., insurance premiums paid in advance), and inventories, among other things. On the liability and equity side, you will add accrued expenses and accounts payable (e.g., vacation or PTO accruals and payroll accruals), deferred revenue collected in advance of rendering services, and trade accounts payable.

Cash-basis taxpayers are usually surprised by the magnitude of changes caused by the proper calculation of working capital, since they typically do not show them on their balance sheets. If there is a disagreement as to what the parties believe is the appropriate number, the purchase agreement will have dispute resolution provisions enabling an independent accountant to resolve it without going to court.

IDEAS IN ACTION

Robin ran a service business that was on the cash-basis method of accounting. He signed an LOI that required him to have working capital of $500,000 at closing, determined in accordance with GAAP. He really didn't know what GAAP or working capital was, but he signed the LOI anyway. He thought he was going to be able to withdraw over $1 million in cash from the bank at closing, but when the first draft of the purchase agreement arrived from the buyer's attorney, he realized that if he withdrew all his cash, it would leave the company short of working capital. Instead, he would have to leave it in the company at closing. He was very surprised and disappointed that he hadn't paid more attention at the front end in negotiating the LOI. He had been counting on that extra cash for an addition to his home.

If a portion of the purchase price is to be paid in the form of a promissory note given to you by the buyer (i.e., the buyer is holding back a portion of the purchase price and paying you over time), the note should contain protections for you in the form of a *security interest* in the stock, or membership interest being sold with penalties for default by the buyer.

- The buyer will try to reduce the principal amount of the note if certain promises aren't kept or if revenues or profits decline below your current or predicted levels.

- You will want the note to increase the purchase price if you exceed your targets. The same concepts apply in drafting an earnout provision. In either case, you will want to control the business as much as possible post-closing so you can ensure receipt of the note payments; the buyer will be reluctant to allow you to do so.

DEEPER DIVE

A "security interest" acts like a mortgage on real estate. The lender—you, in this case—would get protection in the form of security in the buyer's property or the stock you sell if the buyer defaults on the promissory note. If the buyer fails to pay on time, you could sue the buyer and use the security interest to generate cash to pay off the debt owed to you by the buyer. If you get a confessed judgment provision in the note, you could collect on the note without going through a full legal process involving notices, hearings, and a trial.

The purchase price is usually reduced by transaction costs to be paid at closing, including your investment banker/business broker fees and attorneys' fees. The net proceeds are allocated among the owners and others who will be receiving funds at closing, such as key employees who may receive transaction bonuses (if not paid from your regular cash flow, which may be better from a tax perspective), net of applicable tax and payroll withholdings.

The buyer will work closely with you and your staff to construct detailed wire instructions so the funds can be deposited directly into the appropriate bank accounts at closing. Most closings today occur virtually, with the attorneys and financial people working hard to manage last-minute changes and details required to give the clients assurance that closing can occur.

Closing is usually handled in a ceremonial conference call since all the work has been done in advance. The parties agree to release signature pages and permit funds to flow from the buyer to the seller and other payees. All these mechanics are typically spelled out in the purchase agreement.

REPRESENTATIONS AND WARRANTIES

Perhaps the longest and most complicated (and heavily negotiated) sections of the purchase agreement deal with representations and warranties you must give to the buyer regarding your business. These include "fundamental" reps and warranties, such as these promises:

1. Your company is organized and properly registered in its state of formation as well as all jurisdictions in which it operates.
2. The ownership and capitalization of the company is fully disclosed to the buyer, and there are no other owners or potential owners.
3. You and the company have the authority to enter into the transaction, and by doing so, you are not violating any laws or contracts to which you may be a party.
4. Any brokers or investment bankers are fully disclosed, and you are responsible for paying your investment banker's/broker's fees.

WHAT'S THE EXIT PROCESS?

Usually, your potential liability for breaching fundamental reps and warranties is limited to the purchase price and is unlimited in some cases. The buyer frequently demands that reps and warranties regarding taxes and employee benefits fall into this category as well.

The top 20 "nonfundamental" reps and warranties usually include these assurances:

1. Any consents of third parties required to close the deal have been obtained.
2. There are no conflicts that would arise from closing the deal.
3. Any change-in-control payments due at closing have been disclosed.
4. Your financial statements are true and complete and prepared in accordance with GAAP.
5. Your business has good title to its assets, and the assets are all that is needed to properly conduct the business.
6. Certain important transactions have been fully disclosed.
7. All income, sales, payroll, and other taxes have been paid; all returns have been filed in a timely manner; and there are no pending tax audits or investigations.
8. You own or have valid leases to the equipment and real estate used in your business.
9. You own or have valid licenses to the intellectual property used in your business.
10. All material contracts have been disclosed.
11. All clients and vendors/suppliers are listed and have good relationships with you.
12. All employee benefit plans and welfare benefit plans comply

with federal and state law, all required returns have been filed in a timely manner, and no government audits or investigations are pending or threatened.

13. All employees and their compensation, bonuses, and benefits have been disclosed; they are properly categorized as exempt or nonexempt employees; all required forms and filings have been maintained or filed with the appropriate authorities; and they have all signed NDAs that prevent them from improperly disclosing or using your confidential information, trade secrets, or intellectual property outside the business.
14. No litigation is pending or threatened.
15. Your business complies with all applicable laws, and you have the required permits to operate your business.
16. You maintain adequate liability and other insurance required to protect the business from various risks.
17. Your accounts receivable have been disclosed and are fully collectible.
18. Your inventories are not obsolete and are valued properly.
19. There has been no material adverse change in your business or financial prospects after a specified date.
20. There are no related party transactions between the business and you or your family.

Of course, the buyer may demand additional representations and warranties, depending upon the industry in which you operate.

For example, if you provide services or products to the federal or state government (i.e., you are a government contractor), you will have to provide these special assurances to the buyer:

WHAT'S THE EXIT PROCESS?

- Your business is in compliance with export control and sanctions laws.
- You haven't violated any anti-bribery, anti-corruption, or anti-money-laundering laws.
- You have all facility and individual security clearances required to serve your government customers.
- None of your officers or employees have been debarred or suspended from practicing before the government.
- All bids, certifications, and statements submitted to the government are materially correct.
- No contracts have been terminated for default.
- There are no organizational conflicts of interest.
- You generally comply with the federal acquisition regulations.

For a registered investment advisory firm, you will have to represent and warrant the following:

- You have disclosed any notices received from the SEC.
- You haven't violated any SEC rules.
- All your investment advisor representatives are properly licensed.
- You have appointed a chief compliance officer who handles all compliance issues.
- You have adopted and maintained a code of ethics.
- You have adopted written cybersecurity and identity theft provisions and carefully monitor enforcement of those provisions to protect your clients' personal identifiable information.
- You maintain data privacy controls and procedures.
- You require written supervisory policies and exercise supervisory control in managing your business.

In construction firms, the buyer focuses heavily on product liability and service warranties. The buyer wants to make sure no pending claims by customers exist or that any such claims that are pending are accurately quantified. Buyers also want to be sure you have recognized revenues properly, particularly if you use the percentage-of-completion method in recognizing revenues on an accrual basis from unfinished jobs.

DISCLOSURE SCHEDULES

Your reps and warranties tie directly into the disclosure schedules that support the purchase agreement. Basically, if you identify an exception to a particular representation, you must disclose it in a schedule attached to the purchase agreement. Likewise, the buyer may require you to list every material contract between you and your customers and vendors, every employee and their compensation and benefits, every benefit plan, every insurance policy, every piece of intellectual property, every lease, every asset—everything!

In other words, the disclosure schedules become the buyer's road map of your business, which originated from the information you posted in the data room and provided during due diligence.

Many sellers lose patience in the process of creating and populating the disclosure schedules. Conversely, the buyer's counsel becomes the buyer's bloodhound in ensuring that every item raised in due diligence—including the Quality of Earnings analysis, legal review, and technology review—and described in the representations and warranties is disclosed fully. It is common for the buyer and its attorneys to be requesting additional information and forcing the seller to update the disclosure schedules through and including the closing date.

My advice to you is to hang in there and be patient. Let the lawyers and your key financial staff do their jobs to complete the disclosure schedules in a manner acceptable to the buyer and its counsel and get the deal to closing.

You should also have one or more dedicated employees assigned to assist in the preparation of the disclosure schedules. Although the investment banker and your attorneys will also assist, your employees know your business the best and know of any hidden skeletons or issues that ultimately must be disclosed to limit potential claims of fraud or misrepresentation by the buyer.

INDEMNIFICATION CAPS AND BASKETS

Closely related to the representations and warranties you make in the purchase agreement is the scope of your potential liability to the buyer if your reps and warranties prove to be false or incorrect. This is known as your "indemnification obligations." Unless you have committed fraud, the indemnification provisions included in the purchase agreement usually serve as the buyer's sole recourse against you to recover losses or damages suffered because of your breaches of reps and warranties or covenants. There are 2 basic ways to limit your liability as a seller: "caps" and "baskets."

Sellers Want a Low Cap

A "cap" is the upper dollar limit of your potential liability to the buyer. It represents the total amount of losses and damages a buyer is entitled to recover from you if reps and warranties are untrue. You want the cap to be as low as possible; in contrast, the buyer will seek a high cap or no cap at all.

Caps typically apply only to losses arising from breaches of certain representations and warranties and not from covenants or promises to do something or not do something in the future. Caps also do not generally apply to tax liabilities, ERISA liabilities, and any fraud you may have committed, and they usually do not apply to fundamental representations and warranties. If the cap does not apply, either your liability is uncapped (meaning the buyer can recover the full amount of its losses, even beyond the purchase price) or the purchase agreement contains a second, typically higher cap that applies to these items. In many cases, the higher cap equals the purchase price.

Caps range from as low as 1% to 100% of transaction value. A recent survey showed that over half of all reported deals involving privately held sellers had caps of 10% or less of the total transaction value. The size of the cap often relates to transaction size. For example, nearly 75% of the transactions with a cap of more than 20% of total transaction value involve deals of less than $75 million. Larger transactions (i.e., more than $100 million) have caps that are consistently at or below 10% of transaction value.

May I Please Have a Basket?

A "basket" (also referred to as a "deductible") is a minimum amount of losses and damages that a buyer must incur before you must pay the buyer. In a "tipping basket," the buyer can recover all losses, from the first dollar of losses, once the buyer incurs losses more than the floor.

IDEAS IN ACTION

If your deal has a $75,000 tipping basket and the buyer incurs $74,000 of losses, the buyer would not be entitled to any recovery. But, after incurring an additional $10,000 of losses, the buyer would be entitled to recover all $84,000 of losses. If the basket doesn't "tip," meaning that it acts like a true deductible, the buyer would only be able to recover $9,000 (i.e., the amount more than the deductible). In some cases, you and the buyer might agree to a partial tipping basket, which combines the tipping basket with a true deductible.

For transactions having a value more than $10 million, a true deductible (recovery only more than the floor) is the most common type of basket, appearing in more than 60% of all reported transactions of that size. Baskets typically equal 0.5% or less of total transaction value in 67% of the deals over $10 million, and from 0.5% to 1.0% of transaction value in the remaining deals over $10 million. In deals under $10 million, nearly 70% of the reported transactions have a tipping basket or no basket. If you can get a basket in a smaller deal, the basket is usually higher as a percentage of deal value.

NO LIMITS FOR FRAUD

I've mentioned the word "fraud" several times, so it bears explaining because if a seller defrauds the buyer, the seller will have unlimited liability in most cases. Fraud can be based on a misrepresentation of fact that was either intentional or negligent. For a statement to be an intentional misrepresentation, the person who made it must either have known the statement was false or been reckless as to its truth when he made it. The speaker must have also intended that the person to whom the statement was made would rely on it. The recipient of the disclosure then must have reasonably relied on the disclosure and been harmed because of that reliance.

A technical definition of fraud:

> All multifarious means which human ingenuity can devise, and which are resorted to by one individual to get an advantage over another by false suggestions or suppression of the truth. It includes all surprises, tricks, cunning or dissembling, and any unfair way which another is cheated.[73]

In the sale of your business, fraud may also include an omission of a material fact that, if known by the buyer, may have caused the buyer not to proceed with the transaction. The bottom line for you and every seller is this: when in doubt, disclose! Disclose everything! Accurately! Completely! Be transparent and you will avoid claims of fraud and unlimited liability.

R&W INSURANCE

More and more, buyers and sellers are using Representation and Warranty (R&W) insurance to shift the risk of liability for breaches of reps and warranties to an insurance company and away from the seller. One investment banker I recently worked with indicated that 90% of the deals he managed in 2021 had R&W insurance, and all were private deals.

The sweet spot for R&W insurance is for a deal that is between $20 million all the way up to $2 billion. A seller-side transaction R&W

insurance policy covers the seller's liabilities that arise from the seller's breaches of reps and warranties that he or she has made in the purchase agreement. It does not cover a breach of, say, a noncompete agreement or other covenants, but it can remove some contingencies from negotiations between the buyer and the seller, particularly relating to tax issues. Additionally, it minimizes the buyer's potential liability for successor liability that might arise in an asset deal.

DEEPER DIVE

Buyers will often look to structure the deal as an asset purchase to avoid inheriting liabilities as part of the purchase. The general rule is that a buyer of assets is not responsible for a seller's liabilities simply due to the ownership of the assets. Buyers can, in certain circumstances, be held responsible for the liabilities of the seller if a court determines that the facts and circumstances support one of the following exceptions:

- The buyer expressly or impliedly assumes the liabilities.
- The transaction in substance constitutes a merger or consolidation of buyer and seller under state law (also known as a de facto merger).
- The buyer is a mere continuation of the seller's enterprise.
- The transfer was fraudulent or intended to defraud creditors.
- The buyer continues the same product line of the seller.
- The nature of the particular obligation, arising by virtue of a statute, is such that public policy demands a finding of successor liability.

I've found that the presence of R&W insurance makes the buyer's counsel amenable to negotiate and relax the reps and warranties you must provide as the seller.

R&W insurance helps the buyer compete in an auction process, particularly if the buyer bears the cost. It allows for longer survival periods without being nervous about having to make reps and warranties over a period longer than a year or two. The coverage limit may be higher than the cap on liability you might be willing to give in the transaction, so it helps bridge the gap between you and the buyer when it comes to negotiating caps and baskets on liability. R&W policies typically include coverage for loss from claims that are made. The market will typically dictate what's acceptable depending on whether many claims are being made under these policies.

R&W insurance usually covers defense costs, including attorney fees and expenses. It almost always excludes certain known issues. So, for example, if there's a problem that was identified in the disclosure schedules to a purchase agreement, the R&W insurance is not going to cover that problem. It also doesn't cover purchase price adjustments, such as net working capital adjustments that might be included in the deal. R&W insurance policies rarely (if ever) cover fraud by the seller, employee benefit plan liabilities or underfunded pensions, Foreign Corrupt Practices Act claims, and certain environmental and product liability claims that might arise.

Various factors influence the cost of R&W insurance, including

- the risks involved in the transaction,
- the amount of diligence needed to make sure that the insurer and the buyer are both protected in the deal,

WHAT'S THE EXIT PROCESS?

- results of the Quality of Earnings analysis, and
- the size of the deductible under the policy.

The price for an R&W policy typically ranges from 2.5% to 4% of the liability limit, and liability is often limited to 10% to 15% of the overall transaction value. In large or complicated deals, the underwriter wants a fee to protect them from the deal not going forward, so they may charge a minimum nonrefundable fee ranging from $25,000 to $50,000 plus additional fees depending on the scope and type of coverage demanded under the policy.

Just like most insurance policies, there is a deductible in an R&W insurance policy under which the buyer or seller is responsible for any loss. The deductible (which may be different from the basket deductible described above) is essentially a retention amount. It generally ranges from 1% to 3% of the transaction value and varies based on the risks involved. If the risk in the transaction is low, the deductible might be structured as an escrow, so instead of requiring a deductible of 1%, the buyer might demand that you escrow funds equal to 0.5%, which would be returned to you if no claims are made during the escrow period. Using a combination of an escrow and a deductible is not unusual. The seller usually bears the risk of the deductible.

R&W insurance policies are usually underwritten rapidly. A lot of the people who handle R&W insurance are former M&A lawyers with familiarity of the deals and their complexities, so they're good at making the process move quickly. Having a good insurance broker is also helpful.

It might take a couple of days to get a nonbinding indication that R&W insurance will be available for your transaction. The insurer then gives you a list of due diligence requests, which hopefully will be like what the buyer asked you to produce after signing the LOI. The insurer wants access to all the due diligence you provided the buyer, so usually they'll demand access to the data room where you posted all your information. A week or two later, the insurer will discuss any due diligence issues with the buyer, and possibly you, and then they'll want to make sure that the purchase agreement conforms to the insurance policy and vice versa so that there are no hidden time bombs in the deal.

Regarding claims made under R&W policies, there's no real specific data, but anecdotally we've heard that claims notices are received in about 25% of the cases in the United States and about 12% in Europe and Asia. Usually, of the claims that are made, half are settled or resolved within the deductible amount. However, recent literature suggests that claims being made under R&W policies have been increasing due to the increased volume of transactions using R&W insurance and adverse changes in the economy.

COVENANTS

Every purchase agreement contains promises to do or not do certain things after the transaction is closed. These are known as "covenants." For example, virtually every purchase agreement I've negotiated includes a covenant by the seller not to compete with the buyer for a specified period, usually 3 to 5 years, after closing. The geographic scope and duration of the noncompete is usually a heavily negotiated provision. The larger the transaction proceeds payable to you, the more likely the buyer will demand that you are subject to a comprehensive noncompetition clause. You should try to limit the noncompete to apply only to your existing business and customers.

Other covenants may include the following:

- Tax covenants that require both parties to allocate the purchase price in the transaction in an agreed-upon manner, the seller to file tax returns relating to operations before closing, the buyer to file post-closing returns, and the buyer to refund any taxes to the seller for the period prior to closing
- Nonsolicitation of customers and employees for an agreed-upon period
- Confidentiality of the transaction, the documents, and their terms
- Public announcements of the transaction as mutually agreed upon by the parties
- Tail insurance to be purchased by the seller to cover post-closing claims on matters that arose before closing
- R&W insurance obligations and who bears the cost
- Integration matters, including whether employee benefits, management, and accounting will continue or be provided and transitioned to the buyer
- Rollover equity provisions

On the latter issue of rollover equity, if you receive equity in the continuing company as part of the purchase price, you will typically be required to sign an operating agreement for the continuing entity. You need to be extra careful to review and try to negotiate the terms of the operating agreement, which may include the following considerations:

- Can the buyer force you to sell your equity interest if it terminates your employment without cause or otherwise violates your employment agreement or other terms of the purchase? (Try to avoid this.)

- At what price will the buyer be able to repurchase your interest if you leave employment? (Fair market value should not be discounted because you hold a minority interest in the entity. Also, you should receive no less than what the rollover equity was valued at when you closed the deal.)

- Can you force the buyer to purchase your interest (known as a "put" right) if you are terminated without cause or you leave employment with good reason? (You may not be able to convince the buyer to give you a "put," but you should try for it anyway.)

- Will you be permitted to serve on the buyer's board of directors or managers, and will you have any leverage as a member of the board? (You might be able to serve as a minority member of the board or as an observer without any voting rights unless you continue to control a majority of the equity interests after the transaction.)

- Other than voting power, will your equity interest have the same rights and privileges as the buyer's investors? (It should.)

- Will you be entitled to receive cash distributions to pay any taxes on income that is allocated to you? (You should be able to get this.)

You will also need extra time for your attorney to review the operating agreement, so you should request that the buyer have their counsel deliver the operating agreement at the same time drafts of the purchase agreement are being circulated. These and other issues assume great importance if your rollover equity is a significant portion of the overall purchase price.

ESCROW AGREEMENT

Transactions involving closely held sellers usually have a survival period for the seller's representations and warranties under the purchase agreement. After the close of the deal, the buyer has a period, typically 12 to 24 months, when they can inspect your company to ensure the accuracy of your representations. The escrow fund provides the buyer with direct recourse to recover losses incurred due to your breach of those representations and warranties.

If the buyer requires an escrow to protect it from breaches of reps and warranties, violations of covenants, or protection of the ability to receive targeted working capital under the purchase agreement, it will set aside funds out of the purchase price into an escrow account that is usually managed by an independent third party, such as a bank. In many cases, an escrow will protect you as well, since funds will be isolated in a separate account managed by a neutral party, rather than relying on the buyer to fulfill its obligation to pay you funds it may hold back from the purchase price to secure your performance and promises. The neutral third party will be appointed to hold and disburse the funds according to the escrow agreement, and not based on the buyer's unilateral enforcement of a holdback note or amounts it may otherwise want to hold back under the purchase agreement.

The escrow agreement should tie closely into the purchase agreement. If the details of the escrow are left to the attorneys to negotiate, both sides should identify a clear, unambiguous list of events that trigger the release of escrow funds. Once the conditions are fulfilled, the escrow agent will deliver the escrowed assets to the relevant parties. A trigger event can be as simple as joint signatures from the buyer and seller or may be more complicated, such as third-party law firm or audit firm confirmations. In any case, if a third-party escrow agent is involved, your attorney and the buyer's counsel should select the escrow agent and initiate drafting the escrow agreement early in the process to avoid unnecessary delays.

Another issue is who should bear the cost of the escrow. Usually, the cost of hiring an independent escrow agent is insignificant if the escrow consists only of cash and is not complex; in that case, the parties usually agree to split the escrow agent's fees. In a minority of cases where the buyer demands the escrow, the buyer will agree to pay the fees.

In deals that include stock as part of the purchase price consideration, the stock may be deposited into an escrow account. One way to structure a stock escrow is to create a new stock certificate issued in the name of the escrow agent and then reissue certificates to the shareholders if the escrow is allowed to be disbursed following satisfaction of the escrow conditions (or cancel the escrow agent's certificate if the buyer takes back the stock under the terms of the escrow agreement). The buyer could also issue separate stock certificates in the name of each selling shareholder based on their pro rata ownership of the escrow fund. If you use the second option and the buyer reclaims shares from the escrow fund, then every stock certificate would need to be reissued

WHAT'S THE EXIT PROCESS?

with the newly calculated and reduced ownership amounts for each shareholder. Because of the potential administration burden of the second approach (particularly if there are a lot of shareholders), you may want to choose the first option. When the escrow payments are released, the buyer can cut new certificates for each shareholder based on the remaining value of the escrow fund and each shareholder's pro rata ownership.

One last note on escrow agreements: tax reporting can be complicated if dividends or interest must be paid to the escrow agent or stock options are involved. If stock options are granted in the transaction, your attorney should know whether they were canceled or exercised during the escrow period and, if exercised, whether there are any disqualified dispositions, which may require income tax withholding. In addition, nonemployee option holders and employee option holders are treated differently.

EMPLOYMENT AGREEMENTS

Certain key employees—including you if you're asked to stay with the buyer after closing—should have employment agreements with the buyer. Aside from establishing your duties and responsibilities, who you report to, and your base salary, the employment agreement should specify any benefits or bonuses you may receive, circumstances where you may receive severance payments for early or wrongful termination by the buyer, and whether the terms of your employment are linked in any way to your ownership of rollover equity in the continuing company.

You will want your agreement to provide you with severance payments for a reasonable period if you are terminated without cause

or you leave employment with good reason. This begs the question: what is "cause" and what is "good reason"?

The buyer will want a broad definition of "cause," such as the following excerpt from a buyer-favorable contract:

"Cause" means the occurrence of any of the following events:

(A) Your willful or continued failure (other than such failure resulting from incapacity during any period of disability) to substantially perform your duties with or for the company, which failure continues after your supervisor at the company has given you written notice of the same and which notice includes, without limitation, acts of insubordination or failure to follow a supervisor's directives or instructions.

(B) Failure to adhere to any written company policy if you have been given a reasonable opportunity to comply with such policy or cure your failure to comply.

(C) The appropriation (or attempted appropriation) of a business opportunity of the company, including attempting to secure or securing any personal profit or gain in connection with any transaction entered into on behalf of the company.

(D) Any act by you of fraud, breach of fiduciary duty, misappropriation, dishonesty, moral turpitude, embezzlement, or similar conduct against the company or that would damage the company's reputation.

(E) Any act or omission that results in having a customer or client of the company demand that you be removed from any project on which you are working for such customer or client.

(F) Any commission by you of (or his or her submission of a nolo contendere plea in connection with) a felony.

(G) Use or consumption of illegal drugs or excessive use or excessive consumption of alcohol.

(H) Your material breach of this agreement or any noninterference, nondisclosure, and nonsolicitation agreement with the company (the "Noninterference Agreement"), which breach is not cured (if such breach is capable of being cured in the opinion of the company) by you within ten days of written notice by the company of such breach; provided, however, that the breach of any of the provisions of the Noninterference Agreement shall be deemed automatically to be a material breach incapable of being cured. The company shall make all determinations of "cause" in good faith.

On the other hand, the following definition of "cause" drawn from a seller-favorable contract might look like this:

"Cause" means (i) your conviction of a felony, either in connection with the performance of your obligations to the company or which otherwise materially and adversely affects your ability to perform such obligations; (ii) your commission of an act of fraud or embezzlement against the company, which act causes material damage to the company; or (iii) a material breach by you of any material provision of this agreement which breach is not cured within thirty days after delivery to you by the company of written notice of such breach, provided that if such breach is not capable of being cured within such thirty-day period, you will have a reasonable additional period to cure such breach. Any determination of "cause" hereunder will be made by two-thirds of the board of directors voting on such determination. With respect to any such determination, the board will act fairly and in utmost good faith and will give you and your counsel an opportunity to appear and be heard at a meeting of the board and present evidence on your behalf.

For "good reason," you may want to insert the following language from a seller-favorable contract into your employment agreement:

"Good reason" means (i) a change in the principal location at which you provide services to the company, without your prior written consent; (ii) your failure to be nominated for election to, or to be elected to, the board of directors or any other board or committee requested by you pursuant to your employment agreement; (iii) failure of the board of directors to appoint you as [insert your title] of the company, or removal from the board of directors or any other board or committee requested by you pursuant to your employment agreement as [insert your title] of the company provided that such failure or removal is not in connection with a termination of your employment hereunder by the company; (iv) a material adverse change by the company in your duties, authority, or responsibilities as [insert your title] of the company which causes your position with the company to become of less responsibility or authority than your position as of immediately following the commencement date of your employment agreement, provided that such change is not in connection with a termination of your employment hereunder by the company; (v) a change in the lines of reporting such that you no longer report to [your named supervisor]; (vi) the assignment to you of duties not commensurate or consistent with your position as [insert your title] of the company without your prior written consent; (vii) a reduction in your compensation or other benefits; (viii) a material breach of this agreement by the company that has not been cured within [30] days after written notice thereof by you to the company; (ix) [if the company is publicly traded] the company no longer having a publicly traded class of equity securities and/or no longer being subject to reporting requirements under the Securities Exchange Act of 1934; (x) the company ceasing to be engaged in the business of [your business]; (xi) a change of control [as defined in the employment agreement] of the company; or (xii) failure by the company to obtain the assumption of this agreement by any successor to the company.

Of course, the buyer's counsel will try to pare back the scope of this definition substantially; your bargaining power will dictate how far you can go.

The employment agreement usually also includes separate nonsolicitation, noncompetition, and nondisclosure provisions. If you are not in a jurisdiction that prohibits noncompete agreements in connection with an employment arrangement (e.g., California and DC), the buyer typically adds a 1- to 2-year noncompete of equal or greater scope as may be in the purchase agreement. I would try to resist this or tie the noncompete period to the severance period, if possible.

OTHER AGREEMENTS

In addition to the purchase agreement, escrow agreement, and employment agreements, you and your counsel (with the participation of your investment banker or business broker) may need to negotiate the following additional agreements in connection with the transaction:

- Lease with your related LLC or other entity that owns property that will continue to be leased to the buyer after closing
- Promissory note and security agreements if the buyer defers a portion of the purchase price or wants to hold back a portion of the price to secure your promises and performance
- *Noncompetition agreement* for you and other shareholders that may be carved off separately from the body of the purchase agreement
- Confidentiality and covenant agreements and offer letters for employees continuing with the buyer
- Option cancellation agreements for stock option holders who agree to cancel their options in exchange for a pro rata share of the net proceeds they would have received had they exercised their options, less applicable tax withholdings
- Retention agreements with key employees (discussed in Chapter 4)
- Operating or shareholders' agreements for the ownership of rollover equity (discussed above under "Purchase Agreement")
- Loan agreements and other financing documents from third-party lenders in connection with financing the purchase transaction

As the old saying goes, "The devil is in the details," and the agreements are where the details are addressed. The next section will address those situations where some details are improperly or inaccurately disclosed, or unexpected claims arise, or other matters must be dealt with after the closing.

LESSONS LEARNED

- The purchase agreement is the focal point of the transaction. It includes details on the purchase price, how and when it will be paid and whether any purchase price adjustments must be made, representations and warranties you and the buyer will need to give each other about your respective businesses, covenants (i.e., promises) such as noncompetition, confidentiality, and tax filing covenants, and indemnification and liability limitations.
- You may want to consider having the buyer obtain R&W insurance to limit your liability for breaches of nonfundamental reps and warranties.
- You will need to prepare detailed disclosure schedules to back up the purchase agreement and that map closely to the due diligence process. Be patient with this part of the process!
- In addition to the purchase agreement, you may need to enter escrow agreements, where a portion of the purchase price is held back to protect the buyer from breaches of representations and warranties and to ensure there is adequate working capital left in the business.
- The buyer may also need to enter into employment agreements with you and other key employees. The agreements should provide protections in the form of severance payments and continued benefits if they are terminated by the buyer without "cause" or they leave with "good reason."

- A variety of other separate agreements may also need to be negotiated and signed, including leases, notes and security agreements, noncompetition agreements, confidentiality agreements, option cancellation agreements, and operating or shareholders' agreements if you acquire rollover equity.

POST-CLOSING MATTERS

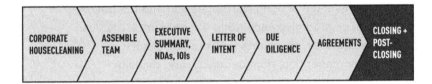

Congratulations! You and your team have done the heavy lifting of cleaning up and organizing your company's affairs and books and records, selected your team, prepared for the exit, selected your buyer, completed due diligence, negotiated and signed all the key agreements, completed the disclosure schedules, and finally received the net proceeds from the sale. You may still have a few yards to go before you get to the finish line. That is, there are still several items you must complete or track after closing your deal.

ANNOUNCING THE TRANSACTION

Your purchase agreement likely contains language regarding when and how the buyer may announce completion of your transaction. Depending on how the provision was written, you will want to review the public announcement to ensure accuracy and that it paints you in the best light possible.

ASSET SALE FOLLOW-UP

If you sold the business's assets and kept your company, you will need to change the name of the company so the buyer can continue using the business's name and branding. Your attorney should have you sign and file articles of amendment to your articles of incorporation or organization to complete this simple step.

The bigger question is, if the buyer purchases your assets, how long should you keep your company alive after the closing? At a minimum, you should keep it going beyond the survival period for nonfundamental representations and warranties, which may be 12 months to two years. In that time, any unknown claims or liabilities are likely to have surfaced. You should also keep it going if you received a promissory note for a portion of the purchase price. Otherwise, tax on the gain from the sale would be accelerated if you distributed the note before it is paid.

Additionally, depending upon the company's tax structure, you need to be very careful about how and when to distribute the proceeds from a sale of assets. For example, if your company was a C corporation, distribution of the net proceeds from the sale may be treated as dividends rather than as capital gains under certain circumstances. Also, if you had to reorganize your S corporation into a holding company (e.g., in an F reorganization) and you are holding rollover equity in your company, you should not distribute the rollover equity to the owners; otherwise, you will trigger immediate taxation on the fair market value of the rollover equity before you get a chance to sell it and generate cash to pay the taxes.

If the buyer required that you terminate your employee benefit plans in the transaction, you will need to coordinate the proper termination of the plans with your benefits provider and plan administrator, perhaps with the assistance of an employee benefits attorney.

BUYER CLAIMS, HOLDBACKS, AND ESCROW TERMINATION

As discussed in detail earlier in this chapter, the buyer may hold back a portion of your purchase price or deposit a portion of the purchase price into an escrow account. **If the buyer fails to assert a claim within the appropriate survival period or asserts a claim but the matter is resolved favorably, the holdback should be paid or the escrow distributed to the company or you and the other owners directly, depending on the tax structure of the deal.**

If the buyer makes a claim against the escrow or offsets the holdback for a claim and you disagree with the buyer's conclusions, you should contact your attorney immediately and get them involved to help you resolve the disputed claim efficiently and economically, but in accordance with the purchase agreement.

IDEAS IN ACTION

In one deal, the parties could not agree on how to allocate the purchase price in the purchase agreement before closing, so the parties agreed to defer resolution of the issue (i.e., "kick the can down the road"). The buyer promptly hired a Big Four accounting firm that aggressively tried to over-allocate a portion of the purchase price to the non-competition covenants in the purchase agreement. This would have caused the sellers to pay significantly more income tax since the noncompete generated *ordinary income* taxable at a 39.6% rate (in that year) vs. capital gains taxable at 20%. We were able to limit the amount allocated to the noncompete to 10% of the amount the accounting firm suggested, saving the client nearly $1 million in taxes.

With escrow agreements, the parties often must issue joint instructions to the escrow agent to distribute the escrow funds. If the buyer drags their feet, there should be a remedy in the purchase agreement that would allow you to force the buyer to issue the instructions or sue for damages caused by the buyer's unjustified delay.

EARNOUT DISPUTES

Hopefully, your purchase agreement contains significant detail on how to measure and calculate the earnout payments and how and when those payments will be made. If the purchase agreement is unclear or ambiguous on these issues, you may dispute the buyer's interpretation of how to calculate the earnout. Again, you may need to involve your attorney to resolve any differences in interpretation so you can be paid what you've earned.

There are several areas where disputes over the earnout may arise.

1. **ADR vs. Litigation.** If the purchase agreement requires the parties to resolve earnout disputes using alternative dispute resolution (ADR) involving an accountant or arbitrator, the matter could still go to court. This could occur where you assert that the dispute does not involve the earnout calculation, but rather that the buyer acted in bad faith, making it difficult or impossible for you to meet the performance standards

outlined in the purchase agreement. For example, if the buyer overloads your business with indirect costs and overhead to artificially depress profits or EBITDA, or delays closing of profitable contracts or performing tasks under existing contracts until after the expiration of the earnout period, you might argue the buyer took those actions in bad faith. Or, if the buyer represented in the purchase agreement that it had the requisite skill, expertise, and ability to operate your business—but it did not—you may argue in court that the buyer fraudulently induced you to enter into the agreement (which is very hard to prove) because it did not have the ability to reach the earnout performance target. This could cause the entire agreement to be set aside. Obviously, these situations arise rarely, particularly where the parties have done their due diligence on each other and have negotiated the terms of the earnout carefully.

2. **Implied Covenant of Good Faith and Fair Dealing.** Every contract includes an implied covenant of good faith and fair dealing, which precludes each party from engaging in conduct that will deprive the other party of the benefits of their agreement. In an earnout dispute, you could argue the buyer violated this covenant by undermining your ability to attain your performance thresholds, such as by substituting its products or employees to perform services your business would have otherwise provided. Similarly, if the buyer transfers your contracts to a different, affiliated company or division or converts your intellectual property in a manner that diverts revenues or profits away from your company and

outside the purview of your earnout, you could argue that the buyer has breached the implied covenant of good faith and fair dealing.

3. **Access to Information.** You may have to go to court if the buyer doesn't provide you with enough information so you can verify the earnout calculations. If the earnout is based only on achieving revenue targets, it may be easier to get the information you need, but there may be disagreements in how the buyer recognizes revenue. Usually, this is left to an independent accountant who must resolve the revenue dispute. The same goes for earnouts that are based on profits or EBITDA, but you must be vigilant in getting every relevant piece of information to determine whether the buyer properly calculated revenues or misallocated and overloaded expenses to your operations.

4. **Business Judgment vs. Contract Interpretation.** As noted earlier, you might argue that the buyer took actions that impaired profitability and therefore failed to use its best efforts to maximize the attainment of the earnout. The buyer may respond that its business judgment in operating your business was totally within its discretion, unless the purchase agreement contains special provisions that prevent the buyer from firing you or another key employee or from changing strategic direction of the company post-closing. The buyer will argue that your counsel should have included these protections in the agreement, and the failure to do so precludes you from making this argument.

You shouldn't leave interpretation of earnout provisions to chance, litigation, or ADR. You need to ensure that the purchase agreement adequately addresses your concerns and your ability to reasonably achieve the earnout.

INTEGRATION

A significant obstacle in achieving a successful result after the closing is integrating your purchased business into the buyer's operations. Some clients can walk away from the buyer with significant cash in their pockets and little concern about the future of the legacy they built. But the most successful entrepreneurs—like you—deal with integration issues well before closing.

You want to know which employees, if not all, will continue with the buyer after closing. You want to secure their compensation and benefits and prevent the buyer from prohibiting the employees from being gainfully employed if they must leave (i.e., through a rigid noncompete agreement). Most importantly, you want to preserve the culture you have spent years cultivating. Failure to consider the employees and their needs can lead to loss of employees and clients during the critical early days of integration when your competitors will go after both your employees and your clients.

Equally important is understanding how your existing accounting and financial reporting systems will combine and transition to the buyer. Will your CFO or controller continue to play an integral role in recording transactions, collecting revenues, and disbursing expenses in the same or similar manner as before the closing, so you have a reasonable chance of meeting your performance criteria under a holdback note or earnout? Or will your data be imported into disparate systems using different accounting conventions? These details should be discussed and resolved during the due diligence process and before an agreement is signed. In other words, you need to determine before you sign on the dotted line how the buyer plans to handle accounting and financial reporting after the deal is done.

In addition to accounting and financial reporting systems, you and the buyer should consider how to combine your technology, systems, and processes with the buyer's. You should understand how orders will be taken and processed; how your marketing group and sales personnel will function in the buyer's ecosystem; how services and products will be created, developed, and delivered; how your employees will be trained, evaluated, and placed within the buyer's organization chart; and myriad other matters.

There are many experts in the field of integration, and depending upon your industry and specialization, you may want to retain someone to help you before the closing to address your concerns and provide suggestions on how to approach integration with your chosen buyer. DealRoom by M&A Science (dealroom.net), many public accounting firms, and other vendors can provide state of the art tools to help you plan and manage the entire integration and M&A process, pre- and post-closing.

Next, we'll explore another comprehensive example of Business Success(ion) planning, involving George, Hannah, and 3DP.

LESSONS LEARNED

- Make sure your purchase agreement has provisions that allow you to work with the buyer in announcing the combination of your two companies in a manner that satisfies both parties.
- You need to avoid adverse income tax consequences in deciding when and how to distribute proceeds received by your company, particularly if you have received a promissory note or rollover equity as part of the sale proceeds.
- Don't forget to follow the process on a timely basis outlined in your purchase agreement to obtain any proceeds held back by the buyer either in an escrow or in the form of a promissory note, and to timely dispute any claims raised by the buyer if you disagree with their assertions.
- Try to avoid disputes in calculating the earnout by including clear and unambiguous language in your purchase agreement regarding how the performance metrics will be measured and controlled after closing.
- Spend time before closing learning how your business will fold into the buyer's, in terms of how employees will be compensated and treated, technologies will be synchronized, and financial reporting and accounting systems will be coordinated and integrated. This will save you and the buyer time and effort and minimize anxiety that invariably surfaces after the deal has closed.

THE STORY OF GEORGE AND HANNAH
GEORGE AND 3DP'S EXIT

3DP'S HOUSECLEANING AND ASSEMBLING THE 3DP TEAM

George had a long-standing relationship with his lawyer, Bob, who was the managing partner of a small firm (40 attorneys) that offered various disciplines, including general tax planning, estate planning, trademark and copyright registration, commercial litigation, and corporate representation. Bob's firm handled all of George's and 3DP's legal needs over the last 20 years, including helping with George's estate planning described in Chapter 4.

George had heard that companies like 3DP were great candidates for a sale in the current market, so he called Bob and asked him what he should do. Bob was a little nervous about losing George (due to George's advanced illness) and 3DP (due to a sale) as clients, so initially he tried to convince George to have Hannah take over the business and run it successfully on her own. However, Bob neglected to bring Hannah into the conversation.

When George reported the results of his conversation with Bob to Hannah, she was flattered that Bob felt she could handle the task of running 3DP, but she was uncertain regarding whether she wanted to assume the risk of running the business George had managed all these years. She was afraid the stress would adversely affect her health. She was also hoping to spend more time with her young family and was concerned that assuming an increased management role would have the opposite effect. Accordingly, Hannah recommended to George (with

Bob's blessing) that they talk confidentially with other experts who were familiar with their industry and what a possible exit might entail.

George confidentially and gratefully paid for an hour of time ($1,200 per hour per lawyer!) to meet with two experienced M&A lawyers at larger firms (recommended by Bob), and (under NDAs drafted by Bob's firm) reached out to a few investment bankers whom the M&A lawyers referred to George. He included Hannah in all these meetings and conversations. They found that the market was ripe to sell 3DP. Even though the appraiser had valued the company as an enterprise for gift tax purposes at $30 million, the M&A lawyers felt they could get a multiple of 3 or 4 times that amount if they sold it to an interested third party, with the help of an experienced investment banker. After interviewing investment bankers about their experience in George's industry and what their process and fees would look like, they chose one investment banker, Randy.

Randy knew the 3D printing market well. He had advised several buyers and sellers of businesses in that industry successfully over the past several years. George invited Randy to send an engagement letter for Randy's firm to represent 3DP and George. Randy immediately sent George the engagement letter, outlining his process and the fees that George would be required to pay. Hannah advised George to send the engagement letter to Bob for review and comments.

Bob had his M&A partner review and revise Randy's engagement letter. They suggested several helpful and constructive changes. George asked Bob to have his partner contact Randy and negotiate the terms of the engagement letter, including reducing the tail provision in the letter if George terminated Randy before a transaction was completed. Randy was concerned that he would introduce his valuable contacts to George without receiving any compensation if George terminated the engagement letter and then hired someone else to help him with the transaction using Randy's contacts. The parties bridged the gap by shortening the duration of the tail from 24 months to 12 months and only applying it to contacts that Randy introduced to George and his attorneys. Further, George asked Randy to carve out 2 contacts with whom George had prior relationships, and Randy compromised by reducing the overall fee and any tail fee if a transaction was closed with either of the 2 contacts.

3DP paid Randy's nonrefundable retainer of $50,000 and signed the engagement letter, and Randy eagerly leaped headfirst into this exciting project.

With George's blessing, Randy first met with Bob and his team to gain an understanding of the work Bob's firm had done in the past for 3DP. After the meeting, it became clear that Bob's firm could handle George's tax and estate planning and its basic corporate needs, but it lacked expertise in selling technology firms like 3DP and did not have lawyers who were technically superior in ERISA and intellectual property matters. George did not want to marginalize Bob or his firm, but Randy made him realize that greater expertise was needed on the legal front to maximize the value of the transaction for George and his family.

George came up with a brilliant idea: why not let Bob, whom George trusted implicitly, be the quarterback of the deal and bring in other legal experts as needed to back him up? Randy was concerned about this approach (i.e., "too many cooks in the kitchen"), but he agreed to try it in part to placate George and in part because it was a creative approach to ensure cooperation between 3DP's regular lawyers and a more sophisticated law firm that brought the needed experience and expertise to manage the deal.

Randy then dug into 3DP's finances, contracts, systems, and processes. He brought his best analysts and partners into meetings with George, Hannah, and their other key employees to ensure 3DP was getting the absolute best representation. After about a month of learning all aspects of the business, Randy's team produced an excellent executive summary of 3DP's business, which provided background information on its technologies, processes, and systems; historical financial results; projections; and a detailed summary description of its business, industry, competition, and management team. This work revealed that Hannah and the other key employees were critical components to the ongoing success of the business and that, although he had been integral in 3DP's growth and success, George's absence would not harm prospects for the business or a potential buyer.

Randy tasked Bob's firm with updating the company's corporate legal records, making sure there was no outstanding litigation, investigations, or threats of litigation; all appropriate consents, minutes, stock certificates, and other organizational documents were in place; and the business was in good standing in every jurisdiction in which it operates. Randy's team also began building a secure data room, instructing certain key employees of 3DP chosen by George (who were under tight, enhanced nondisclosure restrictions) to help populate it with all the information (contracts, bids, proposals, marketing data, customer data, financial statements and records, tax returns, etc.) a prospective buyer would request in due diligence. Randy provided a detailed checklist to assist the key employees in gathering and organizing information for the data room.

The process of building the executive summary, cleaning up the corporate records, assembling reasonable projections of the future, and building and populating the data room took 60 days.

While he was vetting 3DP's business and understanding its opportunities, Randy realized the business had 2 potential exits, depending upon the prospective buyer. One possible exit was the complete sale of the business, which would be easier to negotiate but may not result in the best financial outcome for George and his family.

Another exit strategy was to (1) keep ownership of or obtain a license to the technologies used in building 3D-printed houses, separate this segment of the business from the whole, and let Hannah run that segment; and (2) sell the remainder of the business. This latter strategy required more creativity, but it also avoided a potential buyer marginalizing the value of this new business, since the revenues associated with the 3D housing printer technology and manufacturing only accounted for $4 million revenues with losses of $250,000, due to extensive research and development costs being incurred to further develop and implement this new line of business. The second approach also greatly excited Hannah, who could devote her working hours to further develop 3D housing printer technology and manufacturing, which she created and was very passionate about growing. It also gave her an opportunity to remain involved with the family business and the legacy she helped create.

Randy wanted to be sure the financial statements and accounting systems and records were in good shape, so, with George's permission, he asked to meet with the company's accounting firm that had prepared income tax returns but had never prepared financial statements. The company properly used the accrual method of accounting in preparing tax returns because it was maintaining inventories and selling products. But Randy also needed to have 3DP and the CPA firm prepare financial statements in strict accordance with GAAP for presentation to prospective buyers. At the same meeting, Randy and his team began asking questions about where tax returns were being filed, and whether the company was current in its payroll taxes, sales taxes, and other taxes and filings that were required.

Last, Randy coordinated with 3DP's controller to have his team review internal controls and accounting systems, insurance coverages, banking relationships, and financial policies and procedures. They met with the marketing manager to review the marketing files, branding, trademarks, and domain name registrations, in addition to business intelligence and competitive research files. They met with the sales manager to review the sales process and the pipeline and backlog of projects and customers and with the HR manager to better understand the organizational structure of the company and to ensure employee files and records were up to date and contained the required information, including NDAs and Form I-9s for all employees. They also met with the head of operations to review manufacturing processes and systems processes and with Hannah to review technology documentation, ownership, and licensing issues.

Randy engaged Bob's team to help review the HR files from a legal compliance perspective. Randy also convinced George to hire an ERISA attorney from another firm to review the employee benefits files and reporting, a product liability and insurance expert to review the insurance coverage and ascertain whether the manufacturing operations posed any risks and the extent of warranty liability, and an intellectual property expert to ensure the company owned its technology and had valid licenses to other technologies used in the business. Randy also brought in an integration expert with expertise in the 3D printer industry to learn about the key components of the company's critical operating systems, HR systems and benefit plans, and dependencies on technologies, software, and third-party vendors and suppliers, and to help formulate a plan of integration when the prospective buyer was chosen.

The team assembled their findings and issued a memo to George and Hannah, identifying the *value gaps* in the business. The biggest gap was in the financial statement reporting, for which the accounting firm began to update and prepare GAAP-compliant, accrual-basis-compiled financial statements. Everything else was in good shape.

Randy wanted the company to be ready for the auction process.

THE AUCTION OF 3DP

Randy compiled a list of 50 companies and PE firms he thought might be interested in 3DP. He asked Bob's firm to prepare a detailed NDA, with provisions prohibiting poaching of clients and employees, to circulate to the list of prospective buyers. Forty of the 50 suitors had comments on the NDAs, many of which were different, but not problematic. The attorneys worked through the NDAs and signed up 45 of the 50 to binding NDAs.

With input and guidance from George and Hannah, Randy refined the executive summary and circulated it to the list of 45. Two weeks later, he followed up with them and learned that 10 of the 45 were interested in pursuing further discussions. After extensive rehearsing, Randy then arranged for a road show to visit the top 10, with George,

Hannah, and the 2 key employees in tow. They met with representatives of the top 10 over a period of 3 weeks and wowed them with their preparation, knowledge, and vision.

Four of the top 10 responded with IOIs, with the lowest of the range being $80 million and the highest being $120 million. Two of the final 4 were interested in spinning off the 3D-printed housing division, and one indicated that they would offer a range of $90 million to $110 million, with the housing division spun off to the family. Hannah was excited about this latter IOI.

Randy provided additional financial information to the final 4 suitors and gave each of them the opportunity to speak with the 3DP management team.

In response, Randy requested that the final 4 candidates present draft, nonbinding LOIs if they were still interested. Three of the 4 presented LOIs that were close in price, but one of the 4 (Acme Printing, which was a PE-backed rollup of printing firms) was the firm that was disinterested in the 3D-printed housing division. Acme offered $100 million in value, consisting of $80 million in cash and $20 million in rollover equity. Acme originally wanted an indemnity escrow of $10 million (10% of the enterprise value); Randy negotiated and convinced Acme to obtain R&W insurance coverage and reduce the escrow to an amount equal to the deductible on the R&W policy, which was expected to be $500,000 or 0.5% of the enterprise value. The parties also agreed to include a true deductible of $100,000, and claims for breaches of nonfundamental representations and warranties above the deductible which would be subject to recovery from the indemnity escrow and below which there would be no liability. In addition, the parties agreed to a liability cap of the indemnity escrow amount ($500,000) for breaches of nonfundamental reps and warranties, the purchase price for breaches of fundamental reps and warranties, and no limit for fraud.

Acme pushed hard for an earnout of $15 million of the cash portion of the purchase, but Randy's team successfully negotiated for no earnout in the final LOI. (See *www.waynezell.com/resources* for an example of Acme's LOI.)

After a couple of weeks of negotiating (with Bob and his M&A and tax partners involved throughout), the final version of the LOI contained details on the structure of the deal (sale of membership interests but treated as an *asset sale* for the cash portion and an F reorganization of 3DP to allow for tax-deferred treatment of the rollover equity and a partial gross-up on the additional taxes generated by the structure), along with salaries and benefits of the continuing key employees, with an understanding that, due to his illness and the strength of the remaining team, George would not continue with the business.

The LOI also contained a proposed targeted working capital amount equal to the prior 12-month rolling average. If working capital at closing was higher than the target, George could keep the difference; if lower, George would owe additional money. The parties agreed to a separate working capital escrow of $1 million to cover any deficiency.

Most importantly to Hannah, the LOI permitted the family (i.e., Hannah) to retain control of the 3D-printed housing division and agreed to carve out an exception to the non-compete to allow the family to continue this business and take the related technology unique to the business.

Hannah and George talked it over with Randy and his team and agreed to sign the LOI with Acme. This began an exclusivity period of 60 days to allow Acme to conduct due diligence.

DUE DILIGENCE

Due diligence was intense and arduous, but it was made much easier by the advance preparation led by Randy, his team, and devoted 3DP employees. (It would have been easier had they been anticipating the exit from the beginning and prepared even further in advance.)

The buyer brought in a nationally recognized public accounting firm to conduct a thorough Quality of Earnings analysis of 3DP's financial statements, tax returns, and accounting records and systems. This effort alone took 4 weeks to complete. The buyer's accounting firm came back with a list of proposed corrections to the financial statements, which were reviewed and debated by both sides until final agreement was reached. No change in the purchase price or the escrows was required.

The buyer also hired industry technology experts who spent two weeks with Hannah and with the technology experts brought in by Randy to study and debate the merits and weaknesses of the platform that would remain with the company.

Meanwhile, the team worked hard to populate the data room and give Acme's counsel and its representatives access to everything but the source code, employee names, and customer names.

Acme's lawyers used the data room to begin drafting the definitive purchase agreement and the ancillary agreements and began its barrage of requests to Bob's team for additional information not included in the data room. Bob's team worked furiously with Randy's team and the company's team to provide information throughout the process. They were getting weary of the repeated requests from different people for some of the same information, but they kept their cool, remained patient, and complied with the requests.

Then the R&W insurance company's attorneys began their due diligence, requesting much of the same information that had been provided to the buyer's counsel and the Quality of Earnings accounting firm. Everyone remained patient and complied with the additional information requests.

THE DEFINITIVE AGREEMENTS

Negotiations on the purchase agreement commenced after due diligence was substantially completed. The biggest concern for both sides was the coverage and exclusions under the R&W insurance policy. To the extent there were material exclusions from coverage, the lawyers would have to focus closely on 3DP's reps and warranties. George's counsel negotiated materiality and knowledge qualifiers to the reps and warranties; Acme's counsel rejected or opposed such qualifiers or tried to negate them using materiality and knowledge scrapes.[74] If no material exclusions (including tax matters) appeared in the proposed policy coverage, the negotiations on the reps and warranties and related indemnification provisions were streamlined substantially.

The employment agreements were another story. Acme's counsel rejected Bob's request to narrow the definition of "cause" or broaden the definition of "good reason" in the agreements. They also refused to tie the noncompete in the employment agreements to the severance payments, and they only offered a limited severance period if someone was terminated without cause or left with good reason. The lawyers fought hard and got the parties to increase the severance period to 12 months, but the noncompete period remained at 2 years from termination of employment. Hannah's noncompete had a special carve-out for the 3D-printed housing division, and her employment agreement allowed her to spend up to 15 hours a week on this activity. Her remaining 25 hours were to be devoted to the purchased business.

The other agreements fell into place easily, including a lease agreement between George's LLC and Acme to continue leasing a portion of the property to Acme for a period of 5 years, with a 5-year automatic renewal at market rental rates in effect at that time. A portion of the property was reserved for the 3D-printed housing division. The parties also negotiated 3 retention agreements for Hannah and the other 2 key employees in the amount of $1 million each payable solely out of George's proceeds, with one-third of the bonus being paid after 12 months, one-third payable after 24 months, and the balance payable after 36 months of continuous employment with Acme.

POST-CLOSING

George's health declined after the closing, and he spent his final months spoiling himself, his kids, and his grandchildren with awesome trips around the globe. Hannah resigned from Acme after 3 years of helping to transition the business successfully (and receiving her full retention bonus) and focused her efforts on the 3D-printed housing division and her family. The remaining 2 key employees successfully transitioned into executive positions with Acme. No claims were made against the escrows, and all remaining funds were disbursed to George.

Now, it's time to turn to our final chapter—what's next after your successful exit?

LESSONS LEARNED

- Clean up your corporate books and records in advance of a potential exit.
- Conduct a legal audit to assist in your corporate housecleaning.
- Pretend as if you are going to be audited soon or anticipate a Quality of Earnings assessment and restate your financial statements in accordance with GAAP.
- Build your own data room with your contracts, customer lists, employee lists, pipeline of customers and prospects, operations and processes, technology, insurance policies, financial statements, tax returns, employee benefit plans and reports, and more, and update it periodically to keep the data room fresh.
- Start talking to parties who are willing to assist you in the process of defining your perfect exit, including attorneys, CPAs, investment bankers, business brokers, and individuals who may be willing to serve on your board of directors or board of advisors to assist you in the exit.
- Before the exit process begins, assemble your dream team who will participate in the exit process.
- Execute ironclad NDAs that prevent potential buyers from stealing your secrets, employees, and customers.
- Hire an investment banker if you think an auction process is the way to go for your business. If not, you still need an M&A lawyer, other specialists, and a CPA to assist you in the negotiation of your definitive agreements, preparation of disclosure schedules, and getting you to closing.

CHAPTER 6

NOW THAT I'VE EXITED, WHAT'S NEXT?

"Mighty causes are calling us—the freeing of women, the training of children, the putting down of poverty—all these and more...May we find a way to meet the task."
—W.E.B. DU BOIS

WHAT'S YOUR ULTIMATE PURPOSE?

You obviously understand the meaning of hard work to have gotten where you are in your life. You've devoted countless hours, days, months, and years pursuing your entrepreneurial dreams. Once you take the off-ramp from the entrepreneurial highway, what will be your next exit? Will you drive back onto the fast-paced entrepreneurial highway to pursue yet another exit? Or will you take a different path to pursue your goals? What other passions do you want to pursue? What dreams do you still have that you haven't fulfilled yet? What is your ultimate purpose?

One of my favorite books is *The Ultimate Gift* by Jim Stovall. I've read it many times and will continue to go back to it for inspiration. I hope you get a chance to read it too. Spoiler alert: if you don't want to know how the book ends, you may want to skip down a few paragraphs.

Stovall's fictional story is about the enlightenment of Jason Stevens, the self-absorbed, selfish great-nephew of billionaire oil and cattle magnate Red Stevens. Red has just died and his attorney, Ted Hamilton, is reading Red's will to the family that Red has supported financially throughout their lives. The entire family is a group of ungrateful, entitled individuals dependent on Red's financial support, and Red gives each of them—except Jason—a generous inheritance notwithstanding their ingratitude.

Instead, Red focuses his attention on Jason, believing that Jason can still be redeemed. He conditions Jason's inheritance on completing 12 monthly tasks in the year following Red's death. If Jason fails one task, he loses his inheritance, which is not revealed to him until he completes all 12 tasks. The tasks are designed to teach Jason that the true gifts of life are not financial or economic but are the gifts of hard work, friendship, empathy, family, giving to others, gratitude, dreams, time, and love. Jason reluctantly but successfully completes the tasks and, to his surprise, becomes the *trustee* of a $1 billion charitable *trust*.

Red Stevens leaves Jason the following task in one of his many prerecorded videos:

> Jason, this month, I want you to begin experiencing the gift of dreams. Assume everything is possible. Make a list of all the things

you would like to do and be and have in your life. Then begin to prioritize that list as you discover the ones that generate the most passion in your soul.

Think *The Bucket List*—a popular 2007 movie centered around a list created by Morgan Freeman's terminally ill character, Carter Chambers, that prioritizes the activities Carter wants to complete before he "kicks the bucket." Jack Nicholson, as terminally ill billionaire Edward Cole, encourages Carter to complete the items on the list, adds some of his own items, and finances a globe-trotting final vacation for the 2 of them.

What does your bucket list look like?

I challenge you to continue dreaming beyond your goal of being a successful entrepreneur and create your "bucket list." Then prioritize the things that give you the greatest passion and satisfaction in life and pursue them with the same passion you have for building your business.

Some of the items on your list will continue to emphasize hard work. After all, hard work and focus enabled you to achieve your successful exit. But hard work without a purpose or mission is wasted energy.

> *We actually bought a farm in 1979 in Loudoun County, southwest of Leesburg [Virginia], for my daughters who were 4-H kids, and we wanted the farm so the daughters could raise 4-H animals. It was a small, rocky farm. There was no way we can farm for profit, but I had to have a high-value crop. And people were beginning to talk*

about the possibility of growing European wine grapes in the eastern United States.

—Lewis Parker, entrepreneur and winemaker

Scan the QR code to watch the entire interview

youtube.com/
@ZellLaw/videos

I love doing what I do, and I cannot see myself stopping any time soon. It involves hard work and preparation, not to mention fanatical attention to detail. Yet my work also allows me to be creative and provide solutions to people who need help. Being able to help people realize their dreams of wealth and freedom (whatever that means to them) fuels my passion for practicing law and counseling clients.

I really didn't discover this passion until I was diagnosed with prostate cancer at age 43. After successful surgery to remove the cancer, I had time to reflect on my life, my family, and my ultimate purpose. I realized that life was so much more than working for a living, simply to support a family and pay the bills; it was about consistently giving something back to my clients, my employees, my family, my community, my kids' schools, my students, and everyone I meet. Helping you and others achieve your goals and dreams of wealth and freedom is more important to me than anything else. It gives me a sense of purpose and fills my days with joy and gratitude.

As Jim Stovall put it, "What is more important than the dreams, themselves, is the process of becoming a dreamer." Most entrepreneurs I've met are dreamers. Some spend their entire lives dreaming and creating new ideas, new businesses, and new models for making money or making the world a better place. The key is to keep your dreams alive while you are alive. And make sure that you never stop dreaming or trying to fulfill them.

Once you've exited your business successfully, you may have more money than you've ever had. Do something good with it. Start a donor-advised fund to donate to charities you want to support. Better yet, start your own charity or private foundation dedicated to a cause that you are passionate about.

- One entrepreneur client dedicated a portion of his newfound wealth to supporting a military school he attended that turned his life around completely.
- Another newly minted entrepreneur has begun designing a multifamily housing project in rural Virginia that will support refugees escaping oppressive governments abroad.
- Yet another entrepreneur has founded an orphanage that provides work-study benefits to the orphans while creating products and providing services that can support the orphanage.
- Many have funded incubators for startup businesses in their fields of expertise.
- Others have invested in startups and provided mentorship to the startup founders.
- Some have become teachers, sharing their experiences and life lessons with others.

Perhaps there's a way for you to rekindle old friendships and involve your friends in your future activities, whether they are entrepreneurial, charitable, or just fun.

If you have an insatiable desire for learning and knowledge like I do, you can take online or in-person courses in cooking, history, math, science, art, music, law, finance, accounting, anthropology, political science, astronomy, astrology, religion, or whatever you are interested in learning.

Perhaps you can teach a class and impart your wisdom to younger generations of entrepreneurs. I am an adjunct professor in the Business Department at George Mason University, in Fairfax, Virginia, teaching undergraduate students *estate planning* in their quest to become *Certified Financial Planners*. It is one of the most rewarding things I've done in my career. What can you teach to younger generations?

In addition to giving your money to worthy causes, consider donating your time and effort as well. I was invited to attend a charity gala many years ago for Northern Virginia Family Service (NVFS), an unsung hero in helping thousands of individuals and families in need in our area. I sought out volunteer activities and settled on driving a van once a month for NVFS's SERVE program, where my sons and I collected and delivered groceries and food for NVFS's food distribution center in Prince William County, Virginia. I can't tell you the satisfaction we felt in helping feed over 900 families per month. Volunteer activities abound, and your contributions of time and effort will help those in need.

Giving back makes me think immediately of former NFL and University of Virginia football star Chris Long. In May 2015, Long launched the Chris Long Foundation, which helps raise money for the Waterboys.org Initiative, an effort dedicated to building wells for communities in East Africa. In 2017, Long donated his entire season's salary to charity, with the money going to myriad different causes, including Waterboys.org and educational initiatives. Long stated: "I hope it won't stop here, but that more people will become inspired to commit energy and resources to our educational system. It will be the number of people invested in this cause that will be the difference maker for a quality education for every student in America. Education is the best gateway to a better tomorrow for *everyone* in America." Talk about commitment to good causes—Chris Long and his commitment are awesome!

Here are some more questions to ponder as you define your personal purpose going forward:

- What would you like to accomplish in the next year, over the next 3 years, and over the next decade?
- What part(s) of your life today give(s) you incredible pleasure and enjoyment?
- What do you want to do before you die?
- What would the "best day ever" look like for you?
- Who do you want to associate with socially and in business?
- What and whom are you grateful for?
- Where do you want to live and why?
- What material things do you need/want to make you happy and content?
- What are your most important values?
- What aspects of your life give you the greatest pleasure?
- How do you want to be remembered when you're gone?

Now make a list of your answers to these questions and start prioritizing what is most important to you in these categories. Then let's make a plan!

Volunteers are not paid, not because they are worthless, but because they are priceless.

—Sherry Anderson

Enjoy the gift of your family. Nothing in this world is stronger than the bonds that can be formed by family. I'm not just referring to your blood relatives but also to the families you have built at work, in sports, in religious worship, and in volunteering. Give your time and love to them; it will come back to you 1,000 times.

CREATE YOUR PLAN AND TAKE ACTION!

What we have done for ourselves alone dies with us; what we have done for others and the world remains and is immortal.

—Albert Pike

The previous section allowed you to brainstorm your personal purpose and where your next exit will be. Now, let's organize your thoughts, create a plan, and act.

WHAT IS YOUR VISION?

Just as you must create a clear vision for your business, you need a vision for your life after entrepreneurship. To create the vision, you must first identify your values, which originate from your purpose. Your core values consist of a small set of "vital and timeless guiding principles" for the way you live your life.[75] They may be very different or quite like your business's values.

For example, my top personal values are (1) be grateful, (2) live with integrity, (3) have a positive mental attitude, and (4) be creative. Not too far behind are being growth-minded, empathetic, passionate, energetic and fun, family focused, spiritual, a teacher/mentor, and always doing the right thing. You may have similar values or very different ones.

Your religion may assume a prominent role in your daily living. You may feel great compassion for people or animals that are suffering. You may want to focus on creating or participating in new entrepreneurial adventures or teaching young entrepreneurs what you've learned. You may need to immerse yourself in learning of all kinds or specific topics like language, music, art, or history that you loved when you were younger. You may want to give back to the community using your money, expertise, or both. You may feel compelled to share your experiences by writing a book!

Narrow down your values list from your top 15 to your top 10, top 5, and top 3. Then decide how you can incorporate these values into your daily, monthly, and yearly vision for the rest of your life. Next, marry these values with your purposes that you outlined from the previous section. If your purpose is to create the next awesome startup, then (after your *noncompete* is over or no longer applies) you are going to start planning the next big thing. But if your purpose is filled with focus on family, spirituality, and charity, then you may use your talents and energy differently.

For example, Jon—who worked in public accounting for the same firm for 38 years and is now retired—plans his activities in thirds: one-third of his time is spent on family and personal health and exercise, one-third is devoted to volunteering and using his skills to assist charities; and one-third is allocated to consulting other entrepreneurs and companies on their business and financial matters. The fractions and focus may change over the years, but he will have plenty to keep him busy. This is not your normal view of retirement, where you wake up, work out, play golf, read books, eat a nice meal, have a nightcap, and go to sleep. Where is the purpose in that? Relaxation? OK, but 99% of my clients do not spend too much time relaxing; they love to work and stay active.

Bob "retired" from the military and spends his time giving speeches, consulting, and writing books in his area of expertise. A different retired military officer–client is passionate about his church; he has no surviving family, so he helps the church with audiovisual presentations, recordings, and productions, and the church lifts his spirit every day.

One client, Neal Simon, ran for the US Senate and wrote a book, *A Contract to Unite America*, which you should take time to read. It forever influenced the way I look at politics.

Some of us love what we do so much that we will never really retire. We might slow down some, because we aren't as young as we used to be, but we still approach our professional and business lives with great passion and energy.

Let's build your plan using the following checklist.

NOW THAT I'VE EXITED, WHAT'S NEXT?

My core values are:
1.
2.
3.
4.
5.

My purpose for living is to:

My goals for the next year are:
1.
2.
3.

And for the next 3, 5, and 10 years are:
1.
2.
3.

My plan for achieving each of these goals broken down by quarters is:

Goal 1, Year 1, Q1:

Goal 1, Year 1, Q2:

Goal 1, Year 1, Q3:

Goal 1, Year 1, Q4:

And so on for your other goals, until you have built a strategic action plan to accomplish your personal goals, which very well may include new business goals. Make sure these goals and strategies for achieving them are specific, measurable, achievable, relevant, and time-based (SMART).

Examples of SMART goals might include the following:

1. Physical Health: Lose 20 pounds or reduce body mass index to below 20 in 6 months; drink no more than 1 to 5 glasses of wine per week; eat only healthy foods and decrease sugar and carbohydrates; conduct intermittent fasting; do a body cleanse; work out at the gym 3 to 5 times per week to increase muscle mass and functional fitness; swim 1+ miles per day at an intentional pace of 30 minutes, 6 days a week; visit the doctor and dentist at least once per year; finish a triathlon; bench-press 200 pounds 15 times; run/walk 10 miles a day/week; ride your bike to the park and back home every day; and so on.

2. Financial Health: Continue working or volunteering part-time 10 to 20 hours per week doing something you are passionate about; meet with your financial advisor/planner quarterly; update your *estate plan* every 1 to 5 years; update your financial plan annually; purchase a vacation home in 2 years for cash or with a modest mortgage; add an addition onto your home for a relative; purchase long-term care insurance and additional life insurance if necessary; visit your family and friends who are dispersed around the country/world; travel to every state/continent; buy a fancy car for $100,000; donate $x annually to your favorite charities; and so on.

3. Learning/Teaching: Become an expert chef or sommelier in a year; teach at the local high school or university in your area of expertise; learn to play guitar, piano, or another instrument proficiently enough to perform live or join a band; teach religious school; get an advanced degree in mathematics or philosophy; learn to speak Chinese, Russian, Arabic, Hebrew, French, or Spanish fluently; and so on.

All these goals are SMART; some may take more than a year to accomplish, but they are all specific, measurable, attainable, and relevant to you. The goals need to be time-based, that is, achievable within a specified period.

Next, build a strategic plan to accomplish your personal goals. This is not different from the business planning you have been doing with your business for years. You still need to hold yourself accountable to the goals you have set. I will not belabor the planning phase here; you are probably more proficient than me in designing a perfect post-exit plan.

THE STORY OF GEORGE AND HANNAH
GEORGE'S POST-EXIT PLAN

George knows that he is suffering from a terminal illness and his time on this earth may be limited. He is planning his best life possible over his remaining months or years. His core values are family, faith, and healing the world. His purposes include making sure the transition of the business is smooth for his employees, devoting his time and efforts to his faith, and spending the bulk of his time enjoying his family.

His first goal is to provide for a smooth transition of his business to the purchaser and to enable his employees to continue enjoying the benefits of working for 3DP in the culture they have built together. So he will continue working for 8 to 10 hours a week at most for the first year after the sale to ensure a smooth transition.

One day a week, George plans to volunteer at his local church. He wants to serve on the budget committee, plans to donate a significant sum of money to the church during his lifetime and after he's gone, and will update his estate plan accordingly. He knows that the camaraderie of the church and its parishioners will fulfill his spiritual needs and provide the friendship and support to help him through tough days ahead.

Most importantly, George plans to spend the rest of his time with his family, visiting with them at their homes, playing with his grandkids, and traveling with them to special places that they've never been before as a family. He has always wanted to travel to his parents' homeland in Switzerland and hopes to take the family with him. He wants to enjoy the family as much as possible and wishes for them to remember him as the happy, energetic person that he has always been. He has approached this last goal with a sense of urgency, so he's planning a big trip and will consult with his financial advisor to ensure that everyone's travel costs and lodging will be paid for out of the proceeds from the sale of his business.

LESSONS LEARNED

- Retirement is simply the beginning of a new, exciting chapter in your life, so approach it that way.
- Having a sense of purpose for your personal life, apart from your business, will give you a compelling reason to live.
- Outline the purposes, values, vision, and goals for the next year, 3 years, 10 years, and beyond, and create a strategic plan that allows you to achieve the goals you set.
- Go back every month and quarter and check on how you are doing. Are you living up to your stated purposes, values, and vision? Are you able to accomplish everything you've set out to do? If not, cut back your ambitious goals so you can enjoy your life. And relax—you've earned it!

ACKNOWLEDGMENTS

THANKS TO MY FAMILY

I've been blessed with a beautiful, amazingly talented, and well-grounded wife. Lorri, thank you for your patience and support while I pursued my entrepreneurial dreams over the past 35+ years we have spent together. Thanks for giving me the freedom to move from one firm to another, set up my own firm, transfer it to another firm, and reestablish Zell Law as my ultimate focus, with you by my side as my partner and COO. Without you, your brilliance, and your guidance, I could not be half as successful as I have been and hope to be. And your input and comments on this book have proven invaluable!

To my children: Arianna, Laynie, Ethan, and Jared

Arianna, you and Andrew have shown me what it means to pursue your dreams, with integrity, perseverance, and tenacity. You two are amazing individuals and make a formidable team. Please don't move too far away; I will miss you too much.

Laynie, your journey from the depths to the heights and beyond is awe-inspiring. You have overcome more obstacles in a short period of time than most people do in a lifetime. And now, as the only female cantor in the US military and the first cantor in the US Navy, I salute you.

Ethan, you are one of the brightest and most intriguing people I know. Not only are you succeeding in pursuing a PhD in mathematics at one of the nation's best educational institutions, but you amaze me every day with your depth of knowledge in every topic imaginable. You really should think about becoming a lawyer or maybe president of the United States someday.

Finally, Jared, my youngest and brilliant son, you inspire me every day. You have overcome the greatest obstacles known to humankind. And your life is just beginning. May you continue to grow and learn and succeed in all that you do and desire to do.

My family is the reason I do what I do. I am so proud of them. Each of them inspires me to work hard and with a passion that is unbridled. Thank you all for making my life complete.

THANKS TO MY FRIENDS, COLLEAGUES, CLIENTS, MENTORS, AND TEACHERS

Fortunately, I have had the opportunity to learn from and work with so many amazing people over my career. You have all had a significant,

ACKNOWLEDGMENTS

positive impact on my life and career. Some of you have left this earth, but your spirit and energy still survive. Please forgive me if I have left anyone out, but here goes, and in no particular order of importance.

Thank you to my team at Zell Law, rev. 2: Lorri Zell, Bonnie Humphrey, Todd Spignardo, Tara McCabe, Sebastian Safaei, Caitlin Parker, Sahidah Briggs, and Alexandra Bruce. Without you, I couldn't do what I do today.

Thank you to those who helped me build and edit this book: Lorri Zell, Chuck Cascio, Dr. Steve Gladis, Rob Jolles, Kathy Sawyer, Adebambo Adio, Cathi Cohen, Katrina VanHuss, Dr. Zella Mansson, Scott Montgomery, Danny Olmes, and the team at Scribe Media.

Thank you to those from my professional life. From my early days at Arthur Andersen & Co.: John Schwieters, Barry Reisig, Gerry Ball, Rita Langsam Davis, Rich Anderson, and Tom Aiello. From my studies at William & Mary: John Lee, John Donaldson, and Glenn Coven. From my time at Coopers & Lybrand: Steve Halliday and Robert Freeman. From my time at Venable: Mike Baader, Jacques Schlenger, Steve Owen, and Bryson Cook. From Feith & Zell: Marc Zell, Mona Murphy, and Doug Feith. From PricewaterhouseCoopers: Bob Shapiro, Jim Shanahan, Dick Ruge, Joel Walters, and Mark McConaghy. From O'Connor & Hannan: Pat O'Connor, Tom Quinn, Tom Jolly, Gary Adler, Tim Jenkins, and Bill Nickerson. From FLK&S: Walter Freedman, Jay Freedman, and Thomas James. From Powell Goldstein: Mike Sanders. From Mintz Levin: Irwin Heller, Mark Wishner, and Scott Meza. From Zell Law, rev. 1 and Odin, Feldman, & Pittleman, P.C.: Catherine Schott Murray and Dorie

Weyant. From Odin, Feldman & Pittleman: Jimmy Pittleman, Dexter Odin, David Feldman, Don Goldrosen, Bruce Blanchard, Tom Quinn, Teresa Channon, and Eric Horvitz.

From my time on the Board of the Children's Charities Foundation: Phil Hochberg, Pete Teeley, and John Feinstein. From the Board of Northern Virginia Family Service: Mary Agee, Stephanie Berkowitz, Dr. Steve Gladis, Barbara Rudin, Casey Veatch, Steve Alloy, and the rest of the amazing board.

My colleagues/clients/friends/extended family: Arnold Punaro and the Punaro Family, Bobby and Sofia Castro, Eric and Barbie Castro, Paul Pagnato, David Karp, David Eisner, Deb Wetherby, Chris Hauswirth, Steve Janowsky, Dean and Kathy Thompson, Al Nashman, Lars Okeson, Larry Johnson, Ben Edson, Eric Johnson, Greg Mamay, Willy Accame, Tom McFadden, Tom James, Mike Wolk, Glenn Ballenger, Jim and Linda Flannery, the Ratner Family, Neal Simon, Marc Engel and Carin Dessauer, Matt Devost, Eli Cohen, Jim Besaw, George Perez, Gui Socarras, Pete Aquino, Phil Nolan, George Wilson, Bill Karlson, Richard Philipson, Joe Romagnoli, Dennis Belcher, Vince Griffin, Jon Shames, Josh Baker, Brian and Vicki Zell, Shanna Zell, Adam Zell, Alyssa Zell, Robin Sines, Alyse Reiser Comiter, Vimala Snow, Amanda Plonski, Scott Dankman, Ron Oklewicz, Matt Swartz, Joe Kennedy, Mike Curtin, Tim McConville, Sarah Belger, Hans Riede, Matt Dean, John Burton, Bob Margolis, Bob Kipps, John Becker, Jenn and Kris Wappaus, Lew Parker, Chris Helmrath, and Thomas Seneca.

To my clients, past and present (some of you are listed above): The examples and stories in this book are taken from my dealings with you

ACKNOWLEDGMENTS

over many years. You have all taught me so much, and I continue to learn from every one of you every day. Thank you for allowing me to work with you.

GLOSSARY

accounts receivable—Money owed to a business by its customers or debtors. A/R is reflected as a current asset on the accrual-basis balance sheet.

adjusted gross income—For federal income tax purposes, a taxpayer's adjusted gross income equals their gross income minus certain allowable deductions, including such items as educator expenses, student loan interest, healthcare insurance, and contributions to a retirement account.

advanced estate planning—Special estate planning techniques used for high-net-worth and ultra-high-net-worth individuals, some of which are described in Chapter 4.

appraisal and appraisal report—Valuation experts conduct appraisals to determine the value of a business or an asset and report their findings in a valuation or appraisal report. This is usually required to support a gift of an interest in a closely held business.

asset sale—A sale of a business's assets and selected liabilities that may be assumed by a buyer.

baby boomer—A person who was born between 1946 and 1964.

beneficiary—When referring to a trust, a person who is entitled to receive the benefits of the trust.

board of directors—The governing body with fiduciary responsibility for managing the affairs of a corporation for the benefit of the shareholders.

buy-sell agreement—An agreement among the shareholders of a corporation or owners of a business providing rules regarding the transfer or sale of stock or ownership interests, during life or upon death or disability.

C corporation—A corporation that is taxed under Subchapter C of the Internal Revenue Code and subjects the shareholders to double taxation on the earnings or sale of assets, followed by distribution of the proceeds or earnings.

capital gain—The difference between the amount realized and the income tax basis on the sale of a capital asset, such as stock or property.

Certified Financial Planner (CFP®)—An individual who is formally recognized as having expertise in the areas of financial planning, taxes, insurance, estate planning, and retirement. The designation is owned and awarded by the Certified Financial Planner Board of Standards, Inc. The CFP® designation is awarded to an individual who passes a rigorous exam and meets annual continuing education requirements.

certified public accountant (CPA)—A designation provided to licensed accounting professionals. The CPA license is provided by the Board of Accountancy for each state. The American Institute of Certified Public Accountants (AICPA) provides resources on obtaining the license. To gain the designation, individuals must pass a rigorous 4-part test and participate in continuing professional education.

Certified Valuation Analyst (CVA)—An individual with a specific certification from the National Association of Certified Valuators and Analysts (NACVA) trained to provide business evaluations.

charitable remainder trust (CRT)—A tax-exempt irrevocable trust designed to reduce an individual's taxable income and estate taxes by paying an annual annuity to the creator of the trust and leaving the remaining assets after a specified term to a charitable organization or organizations. It is subject to strict requirements imposed under the Internal Revenue Code. CRTs can be formed as charitable remainder unitrusts (CRUTs), which come in various structures, and charitable remainder annuity trusts (CRATs).

contingent note—Used in both sale transactions and gift planning, a promissory note whose principal adjusts based upon performance metrics specified in the note or a purchase agreement and is often used to cover earnout payments or indemnification obligations of a seller in a sale transaction.

cost of capital—The rate of return demanded by lenders and owners, consisting of the cost of debt and the cost of equity.

cost of debt—The rate of return demanded by lenders, typically based upon a business's commercial borrowing rate.

cost of equity—The rate of return demanded by an owner of a business, often determined using the capital asset pricing model.

disability—A physical or mental condition that limits a person's movements, senses, or activities and is usually defined under the terms of a contract or plan.

discount rate—The interest rate used to determine the present value of future cash flows in a discounted cash flow analysis.

discounted cash flow (DCF)—A valuation method that estimates the value of an investment or a business using its expected future cash flows, discounted back to the present using an appropriate discount rate.

due diligence—An investigation or a review performed to confirm facts or details of a matter under consideration. In a sale transaction, due diligence requires an examination of financial records, corporate books and records, contracts, and other items pertaining to the business before concluding a transaction with another party.

dynasty trust—An irrevocable trust designed to last for many generations and save estate and generation-skipping transfer tax.

earnout—A provision in a purchase agreement that may entitle a seller of a business to obtain additional purchase price consideration in the future if the business achieves certain financial goals, which are usually based upon achieving target revenues or profits.

EBITDA—Earnings before interest, taxes, depreciation, and amortization, usually determined in accordance with GAAP. A multiple of this measure serves as the basis for determining the value of most businesses in sale and M&A transactions.

employee stock ownership plan (ESOP)—A qualified employee benefit plan governed by ERISA and the Department of Labor that gives workers ownership in the company in the form of shares of stock and that provides significant tax benefits to the participants and the company that sponsors the plan.

Entrepreneurial Operating System®—An operating system designed to help entrepreneurs run their business as described in Traction by Gino Wickman.

equity-based incentives—Compensation incentives given to employees, managers, board members, and contractors that allow the recipient to participate in the growth in equity value of a business.

equity—Commonly referred to in the accounting sense as shareholders' equity (or owners' equity for privately held companies), it represents the amount of money that would be returned to a company's owners if all the assets were liquidated and all the company's debt was paid off in the case of liquidation. In the case of acquisition, it is the value of the proceeds received for a company minus any liabilities owed by the company not transferred with the sale.

ERISA—The Employee Retirement Income Security Act of 1974, as amended, which provides detailed rules governing qualified retirement plans and welfare benefit plans.

estate and gift tax—Transfer taxes imposed at the federal level (and in some states) at a rate of 40% on transfers of assets in excess of the allowable lifetime exemption, which is $12.06 million in 2022 and $12.92 million in 2023.

estate planning—The process of arranging who will manage your assets for your benefit if you become disabled and who will receive your assets when you die.

family office—A private wealth management advisory firm, often consisting of family members who have sold a business or inherited the proceeds from a business exit, that serves ultra-high-net-worth individuals.

fiduciary—A fiduciary is a person or an entity that acts on behalf of another person or persons, putting the beneficiaries' or clients' interests ahead of their own, with a duty to preserve assets for their benefit in good faith with legal duties of care, loyalty, and diligence.

generally accepted accounting principles (GAAP)—Financial accounting rules, standards, and procedures issued by the Financial Accounting Standards Board (FASB) in the United States and binding upon CPAs.

generation-skipping transfer tax (GSTT)—A separate federal transfer tax system imposed, in addition to estate and gift tax, on the transfer of property to a person other than a spouse who is 2 or more generations removed from the transferor.

goodwill and personal goodwill—An intangible asset that represents the portion of the purchase price in an acquisition that is higher than the sum of the net fair value of all the assets purchased and the liabilities assumed. Personal goodwill arises from the personal expertise or business relationships of an individual employee or shareholder and has value separate from the business.

grantor retained annuity trust (GRAT)—An irrevocable trust that receives assets from a grantor and pays an annual annuity to the grantor based upon the IRS's Section 7520 rate over a specified term (usually 2 to 10 years in duration). At the end of the term, any remaining assets are distributed to the trust beneficiaries or to a trust for the benefit of named individuals. It can achieve significant estate and gift tax savings when interest rates are low and assets in the GRAT are appreciating in value.

grantor trust—Either a revocable or irrevocable trust, the income of which is taxable to the grantor (i.e., creator) of the trust.

Great Recession—The economic downturn from 2007 to 2009 after the bursting of the US housing bubble and the global financial crisis.

gross income—For federal income tax purposes, gross income includes your wages, dividends, capital gains, business income, and retirement distributions, as well as other income.

Hart-Scott-Rodino Act (HSR Act)—Legislation that provides the Federal Trade Commission and the Department of Justice with information about large mergers and acquisitions before they occur.

Indication(s) of interest (IOI)—In the context of an acquisition, IOI refers to a buyer's nonbinding interest in buying a business, citing a range of potential values the buyer may be willing to pay for the business.

initial public offering (IPO)—The process of offering shares of a privately held corporation to the public in a new stock issuance for the first time.

intentionally defective grantor trust (IDGT)—An irrevocable grantor trust that taxes the income of the trust to the grantor but is designed to exclude the appreciation on the assets in the trust from the grantor's estate, thereby saving gift and estate taxes.

irrevocable trust—A trust that technically cannot be changed or revoked by the grantor unless it is amended or modified in accordance with the state law governing the trust (i.e., through a nonjudicial settlement agreement, through decanting, or with court approval).

GLOSSARY

letter of intent (LOI)—A letter agreement that contains nonbinding provisions regarding the structure, pricing, and other relevant terms of an acquisition, and binding provisions that prohibit disclosure of the terms of the buyer's offer and grants the buyer a period of exclusivity to conduct due diligence before a definitive agreement is reached to purchase the seller's business.

leveraged buyout (LBO)—The acquisition of another company using a significant amount of borrowed money to pay for the acquired company or its assets.

leveraged buyout (LBO)—The acquisition of another company using a significant amount of borrowed money to pay for the acquired company or its assets.

limited liability company (LLC)—A hybrid entity formed under state law that provides limited liability protection to its owners while providing flexibility in the way the entity may be taxed for federal or state income tax purposes.

liquidation value—The value of assets minus liabilities upon the winding up and dissolution of a company's business.

liquidation—Winding up and dissolution of a company's business.

management buyout (MBO)—A transaction where a company's management team purchases the assets and operations of the business they manage.

management succession plan (MSP)—A plan anticipating the short-term and long-term management of a closely held business in the event of the death or disability of the primary business owner.

membership interest—The ownership interest in an LLC.

merger and acquisition (M&A)—A general term that describes the consolidation or reorganization of companies or assets through various types of financial transactions, including mergers, acquisitions, consolidations, tender offers, stock purchases, asset purchases, and management acquisitions.

net promoter scoreSM (NPS®)—A measurement of customer loyalty to a company based upon responses to a single survey question on a scale of –100 to 100, with 100 being the highest rating.

noncompetition agreement—Also referred to as a noncompete agreement, an agreement or contract not to interfere or compete with a former employer or buyer (by working with a competitor).

nondisclosure agreement (NDA)—An agreement not to disclose or use the confidential information or trade secrets of a disclosing party.

ordinary income—Income from earnings, interest, rents, royalties, and other sources that may be taxed at the highest tax rates under current federal income tax law, as distinguished from dividends and long-term capital gains that may be taxed at lower federal rates.

GLOSSARY

phantom stock/equity—A nonqualified deferred compensation plan or agreement that allows participants to receive net profits from operations or an M&A transaction.

private annuity—An agreement in which an individual transfers property to a person who must pay an annuity to the transferor based on an agreed-upon schedule in exchange for the property transfer.

private equity—An alternative investment class that invests in or acquires private companies that are not listed on a public stock exchange.

probate—A court-supervised process at the state level where a deceased person's assets pass by will or intestacy to designated beneficiaries or heirs.

profit or income—The difference between a company's revenues and expenses.

promissory note—A signed document containing a written promise to pay a stated sum to a specified person or the bearer of the note at a specified date or on demand.

recapitalization—A process for restructuring a company's debt and equity mixture by exchanging one form of financing for another, such as removing or adding preferred shares from the company's capital structure.

registered investment advisor (RIA)—A firm that advises clients on securities investments and may manage their investment portfolios. RIAs are registered with either the US Securities and Exchange

Commission (SEC) and/or state securities administrators and have fiduciary obligations to their clients.

reorganization—Under Section 368 of the Internal Revenue Code, there are 7 types of reorganizations: (A) a statutory merger or consolidation; (B) an acquisition of one company's stock by another corporation, with the acquired company becoming a subsidiary of the acquiring corporation; (C) an acquisition where the acquired corporation must liquidate, with shareholders of the acquired corporation becoming shareholders in the acquiring corporation; (D) spin-offs or split-offs; (E) recapitalizations; (F) a change in identity, form, place, or organization ("F Reorganization"); and (G) a Chapter 11 asset transfer. These transactions can be tax-free if formalities are followed and cash is not exchanged in the transaction.

residency and domicile—A concept that defines where a taxpayer is required to report income and pay income tax or be subject to state estate or inheritance taxes.

revocable trust—A trust that can be revoked, amended, modified, or terminated at any time by the grantor. This is frequently used to avoid probate.

rollover equity—This results when a seller reinvests a portion of the proceeds from a sale into equity of the acquisition company that is formed to buy the seller's business.

rule against perpetuities—An arcane but still valid common law property rule that states that no interest in land is good unless it must vest, if at all, not later than 21 years after some life in being at the creation of the interest. This rule has been modified by statute in many states.

S corporation—A corporation or LLC that elects to pass income, losses, deductions, and credits through to its shareholders/members for federal income tax purposes.

security interest—An enforceable legal claim or lien on collateral that has been pledged, usually to obtain a loan or secure obligations arising under a promissory note.

self-canceling installment note (SCIN)—An installment obligation in the form of a promissory note that is extinguished automatically on the death of the lender and is typically used in family estate planning situations.

small business set-aside—Contract reserved by the federal government and administered under rules established by the Small Business Administration, which limits competition to qualifying small businesses.

special purpose acquisition company (SPAC)—Also known as a "blank check company," a shell corporation listed on a stock exchange with the purpose of acquiring a private company, making it public without going through the traditional initial public offering process.

spousal lifetime access trust (SLAT)—An irrevocable trust for the benefit of the spouse of the grantor of the trust, with the intent of excluding appreciation on assets in the trust from estate and GSTT taxation of the grantor and the spouse.

stagflation—Persistent high inflation combined with high unemployment and stagnant demand in a country's economy.

SWOT analysis—A study undertaken by an organization to identify its internal strengths and weaknesses, as well as its external opportunities and threats.

trust—An arrangement whereby a person (a trustee) holds property as its legal title holder for the good of one or more beneficiaries.

trustee—An individual person or entity given control or powers of administration of property in trust with a legal obligation to administer it solely for the purposes specified.

value gaps—These occur when the amount of money an owner needs or wants from the sale of their business will not be matched by prospective buyers.

NOTES

INTRODUCTION

1. The terms "Success(ion)" and "Business Success(ion)" have been registered for trademark protection by Zell Law with the US Patent and Trademark Office.
2. "PMA" refers to a positive mental attitude. My friend Bobby Castro claims ownership of the phrase, and if you follow him on social media, you will understand why.

CHAPTER 1

3. See Alfred Hitchcock's film *The Man Who Knew Too Much* (1956).
4. See Carol S. Dweck's trendsetting book, *Mindset: The New Psychology of Success* (New York: Random House, 2006), for more information on the distinction between "growth-minded" people and those who are in a "fixed mindset."
5. Gary Shapiro, *Ninja Innovation: The Ten Killer Strategies of the World's Most Successful Businesses* (New York: William Morrow, 2013).
6. Chris Zook and James Allen, *The Founder's Mentality: How to Overcome the Predictable Crises of Growth* (Boston: Harvard Business Review Press, 2016).
7. Liz Kislik, "How to Prepare the Next Generation to Run the Family Business," *Harvard Business Review*, September 27, 2022, https://hbr.org/2022/09/how-to-prepare-the-next-generation-to-run-the-family-business#:~:text=According%20to%20a%202021%20Family,on%20next%2Dgen%20involvement.%E2%80%9D.

8   Gino Wickman, *Traction: Get a Grip on Your Business* (Dallas: BenBella Books, 2011).
9   Shapiro, *Ninja Innovation*, 14–15.
10 Debra Jacobs, Garrett Sheridan, and Juan Pablo González, *Shockproof: How to Hardwire Your Business for Lasting Success* (Hoboken: Wiley, 2011).
11 Zook and Allen, *Founder's Mentality*.
12 Zook and Allen describe a business in "free fall" as one that has completely stopped growing, with a business model that is no longer viable (*Founder's Mentality*).
13 "Liquidation value" refers to the value of the business as it exists today, without considering its ability to continue to generate revenues or cash flow into the future. If you liquidate the business, you will receive the remaining cash, accounts receivable, inventory, furniture and equipment, and any other intangible assets such as trademarks, patents, and copyrights owned by the business. The value of these assets may be substantially less than if they were sold as part of a going concern.

CHAPTER 2

14 "Membership interest" refers to the ownership of an LLC. "Stock," on the other hand, refers to ownership in a corporation. I will use these terms interchangeably throughout the book, depending on the facts.
15 When someone has a fiduciary duty to someone else, the person with the duty must act in a way that will benefit someone else, usually financially. The person who has a fiduciary duty is called the fiduciary, and the person to whom the duty is owed is called the principal or the beneficiary. If the fiduciary were to breach the fiduciary duties, he or she would need to account for the ill-gotten profit. The beneficiaries are typically entitled to damages. "Fiduciary Duty," Legal Information Institute, accessed December 15, 2022, www.law.cornell.edu/wex/fiduciary_duty.
16 In an LLC, the members can manage the entity, or managers can manage the entity. If more than one manager is serving, the group is typically referred to as a board of managers. This can operate essentially the same as a board of directors in a corporation.
17 As a sidenote, many of my clients ask whether the transfer of the stock into a revocable trust will create tax problems. My answer is a definitive "No!" The revocable trust is ignored for income tax purposes because it is controlled by the grantor and therefore is a grantor trust. When you transfer the stock to the trust, it's treated as if you're transferring the stock to yourself. Such a trust is also an eligible shareholder for S corporation purposes.
18 See Chapter 3.

NOTES

19   According to McKinsey's 2022 "Private Markets Annual Review" report, private equity funds had over $9.8 trillion in assets under management in 2021: www.mckinsey.com/industries/private-equity-and-principal-investors/our-insights/mckinseys-private-markets-annual-review.

20   Rishi Yadav, "The Global State of Family Offices: What Family Offices Need to Do to Successfully Compete with Traditional Wealth Management Firms" (Capgemini, 2012), https://www.capgemini.com/wp-content/uploads/2017/07/The_Global_State_of_Family_Offices.pdf.

21   Yadav, "Global State of Family Offices."

22   www.familyoffice.com.

23   Will Kenton, "Leveraged Buyout (LBO) Definition: How It Works, with Example," Investopedia, November 14, 2022, https://www.investopedia.com/terms/l/leveragedbuyout.asp.

24   Non-ESOP (i.e., regular) dividends paid to stockholders are not generally deductible to the corporation.

25   A "C corporation" refers to a corporation governed by Subchapter C of the IRC of 1986. C corporations currently pay tax on their taxable income at a 21% flat rate. The shareholders typically pay tax on the dividends distributed by the corporations. This is commonly referred to as "double taxation."

26   A special benefit is available to ESOP participants if a net unrealized appreciation (NUA) election is made and certain criteria are met. If NUA is elected, the cost basis of the stock distributed is taxed immediately at the participant's ordinary income rate. The NUA amount is taxed when the stock is sold back to the corporation. NUA is subject to tax at the long-term capital gains rate—regardless of the length of time the stock was held in the plan prior to distribution.

27   Max H. Bazerman and Paresh Patel, "SPACs: What You Need to Know," *Harvard Business Review*, July–August 2021, https://hbr.org/2021/07/spacs-what-you-need-to-know.

CHAPTER 3

28   The NPS is a proprietary instrument developed by Fred Reichheld, who owns the registered NPS trademark in conjunction with Bain & Company and Satmetrix. [Frederick F. Reichheld, "The One Number You Need to Grow," *Harvard Business Review*, December 2003, https://hbr.org/2003/12/the-one-number-you-need-to-grow.]

29   Strategy Marketing Agency, "Why Is Branding Important?" accessed December 15, 2022, https://strategynewmedia.com/why-is-branding-important/#:~:text=A%20strong%20brand%20helps%20customers,connect%20with%20your%20customers%20emotionally.

30 SWOT analysis allows a business to identify its internal strengths and weaknesses, as well as its external opportunities and threats.
31 asq.org/quality-resources/fishbone; https://www.mckinsey.com/business-functions/strategy-and-corporate-finance/our-insights/enduring-ideas-the-7-s-framework
32 Marshall Hargrave, "Goodwill (Accounting): What It Is, How It Works, How To Calculate," Investopedia, last updated September 28, 2022, https://www.investopedia.com/terms/g/goodwill.asp#.
33 For instance: Martin Ice Cream v. Commissioner, 110 T.C. 18 (1998); William Norwalk et al. v. Commissioner, TC Memo 1998-279; Solomon v. Commissioner, TC Memo 2008-102; Estate of Adell v. Commissioner, TC Memo 2014-155; Bross Trucking, Inc. v. Commissioner, TC Memo 2014-107; and Kennedy v. Commissioner, TC Memo 2010-206.
34 At the publication of this book, the highest long-term capital gains rate for individuals is 20%. NIIT tax of 3.8% also may be imposed depending upon the facts of the case.
35 At the time this book was published, the highest federal individual ordinary income tax rate was 37% and was scheduled to increase to 39.6% on January 1, 2026.
36 "EBITDA" refers to earnings before interest, taxes, depreciation, and amortization.
37 Thomas Smale, "SaaS Valuations: How to Value a SaaS Business in 2022," *FE International* (blog), November 3, 2022, https://feinternational.com/blog/saas-metrics-value-saas-business/; SDE = Revenues − Cost of Goods Sold − Operating Expenses − Owners' Compensation.

CHAPTER 4

38 "Stagflation" refers to an economy that is experiencing a simultaneous increase in inflation and stagnation of economic output. [The Investopedia Team, "What Is Stagflation, What Causes It, and Why Is It Bad?" Investopedia, last updated July 31, 2022, https://www.investopedia.com/terms/s/stagflation.asp.]
39 Adam Hayes, "Dotcom Bubble," Investopedia, last updated June 25, 2019, https://www.investopedia.com/terms/d/dotcom-bubble.asp.
40 Anne Field, "What Caused the Great Recession? Understanding the Key Factors That Led to One of the Worst Economic Downturns in US History," Insider, August 8, 2022, https://www.businessinsider.com/personal-finance/what-caused-the-great-recession.
41 The Investopedia Team, "Industries That Can Thrive during Recession," Investopedia, last updated November 17, 2022, https://www.investopedia.com/articles/stocks/08/industries-thrive-on-recession.asp.
42 "The Rise of the 3D-Printed Houses," *Economist*, August 18, 2021, https://www.economist.com/science-and-technology/the-rise-of-3d-printed-houses/21803667.

NOTES

43 The maximum federal income tax rate is scheduled to increase to 39.6% on January 1, 2026. The 37% bracket applies to income of more than $628,300 in 2022 for married couples filing joint returns and $523,600 for single taxpayers. Graduated rates from 10–35% apply below those levels.

44 "Modified" adjusted gross income simply refers to your adjusted gross income with any tax-exempt interest income and certain deductions added back in. "Adjusted gross income" and "gross income" are defined in the glossary.

45 Under existing law, the NIIT does not apply to (1) income allocated to an S corporation shareholder (if the shareholder materially participates in the business of the S corporation, which is usually the case for entrepreneurs I represent), (2) gain from the sale of S corporation stock or an interest in a partnership or LLC (if the selling owner materially participates in the business being sold), or (3) gain from the sale of the assets of a partnership, LLC, or S corporation (if such gain is allocated to an owner who materially participates in the business being sold). The House of Representatives passed legislation in 2021, which failed to pass in the Senate, that would have subjected virtually all the gains and income described above to the NIIT.

46 See IRC Sections 338 and 338(h)(10).

47 These two-step transactions involve the creation of a new S corporation, into which the founder contributes his or her stock in exchange for the new company's stock. The new company (Newco) then converts into an LLC that is treated as a disregarded entity. The private equity buyer purchases the membership interest in the LLC, which is treated as an asset purchase for tax purposes. [Ankit Joshi and Oak Brook, III, "Private Equity and F Reorganizations Involving S Corporations," Tax Adviser, September 1, 2020, https://www.thetaxadviser.com/issues/2020/sep/private-equity-f-reorganizations-s-corporations.html.]

48 Some buyers are exempt from federal and state income taxes. For example, Native American–owned businesses and certain statutorily approved businesses (e.g., Mitre Corporation, LMI Corporation) are exempt from income tax. These companies may not be as concerned about writing off your goodwill as other for-profit purchasers. In addition, if the buyer has net operating losses or must carry forward losses from the past, the ability to write off the value of your assets may not be meaningful to them.

49 IRC Section 1202 contains a special exclusion for qualified small business corporations where you can exclude up to the greater of $10 million in capital gains or 10 times the basis (i.e., purchase price) of the stock if certain requirements are met. Those requirements include the following: (1) the company must be incorporated in the United States as a C corporation; (2) the company must have had gross assets of $50 million or less at all times before and immediately after the stock was purchased; and (3) the company must not be

on the list of excluded business types, which includes businesses in the fields of health, law, engineering, consulting, and other service areas.

50   An S corporation could be subject to corporate-level tax if it sells its assets within 5 years of converting from a C corporation to an S corporation and had built-in gain at the time of the conversion. See IRC Section 1374.

51   If a cash-basis S corporation sells assets or is treated as selling assets in a stock sale where a Section 338(h)(10) election is made or an F reorganization with a two-step structure is used per above, it will generate ordinary income on the difference between its accounts receivable and accounts payable and accrued expenses at the time of closing. Similarly, a partnership (or an LLC taxed as a partnership) will experience ordinary income on the sale of a partnership interest or partnership assets if "hot assets" are present at the time of the sale. See IRC Section 751.

52   See note 51.

53   This is known as "grossing up" the purchase price for the extra tax George must pay on the sale. It is calculated by dividing the extra tax by 1–17%, the differential tax rate, which in George's case would be $409,638.55 ($340,000 / (1–17%)). Buyers typically resist the seller's request to be grossed up for the extra taxes the seller must pay in a deemed asset sale, but George's counsel certainly should try for this result.

54   This is based on a 21% federal tax plus 8.84% California corporate income tax.

55   This equals $30 million in net proceeds, corporate-level tax of $8.952 million, minus $1 million in income tax basis, multiplied by 1 minus the combined federal and state tax rate of 33.3%.

56   John Cronin and Peter Faber, "Income Taxes: Mergers and Acquisitions (Portfolio 1240)," Bloomberg Tax, accessed December 15, 2022, https://pro.bloombergtax.com/portfolio/income-taxes-mergers-and-acquisitions-portfolio-1240/.

57   See IRC Section 1274.

58   See IRC Section 453A. Generally, installment sales of property by nondealers may be reported under the installment method, but two special rules apply to limit the benefits of installment reporting. The first rule requires taxpayers to pay interest on the deferred tax liability attributable to obligations arising from certain installment sales (including notes arising in the sale of a business, but this does not include sales of personal use property; i.e., this is not used in a trade or business, or farming property). The second rule provides that proceeds from a pledge of an installment obligation (arising from certain installment sales) to secure any indebtedness are treated as a payment on that obligation.

59   "About EDGAR," US Securities and Exchange Commission, accessed January 13, 2023, https://www.sec.gov/edgar/about#:~:text=EDGAR%2C%20the%20

NOTES

Electronic%20Data%20Gathering,Investment%20Company%20Act%20of%201940.

60 The lifetime exemption in 2022 was $12.06 million per person. In 2023, the exemptions increased to $12.92 million per person and $25.84 million per married couple. A married couple can enjoy a combined exemption of $24,120,000 in 2022. These amounts are currently indexed for inflation annually. After December 31, 2025, the exemptions are scheduled to drop by half. So if the exemption is $14 million at the end of 2025, half of that is $7 million.

61 $3.12 million = $4.8 million × (1 −35%).

62 $672,000 = ($4.8 million − $3.12 million) × 40%.

63 For an excellent discussion of charging orders and their enforcement, see Jay D. Adkisson, "Charging Orders: The Peculiar Mechanism," in *Asset Protection Strategies: Planning with Domestic and Offshore Entities*, vol. 1, 2nd ed., ed. Alexander A. Bove, Jr. (Chicago: ABA Book Publishing, 2019), 339–379.

64 As of the date of publication of this book, Alaska, Delaware (partial elimination), Idaho, Kentucky, New Jersey, Pennsylvania, Rhode Island, and South Dakota have eliminated the rule against perpetuities.

65 These states are Alabama (100 years for property not in trust and 360 years for property in trust), Arizona (500 years), Colorado (1,000 years), Delaware (110 years for real property held in trust), Florida (360 years), Nevada (365 years), Tennessee (360 years), Texas (300 years), Utah (1,000 years), and Washington (150 years). Other states allow certain trusts to continue without application of the rule. These states are Arizona, District of Columbia, Hawaii, Illinois, Maine, Maryland, Michigan, Missouri, Nebraska, New Hampshire, New Jersey, North Carolina, North Dakota, Ohio, Oklahoma, Virginia, and Wyoming.

66 $12 million / $2,000 per share = 6,000 shares.

67 I used Leimberg and LeClair's NumberCruncher program to determine the annuity amounts, capital gains, and ordinary income portions of each payment. The Section 7520 rate in July 2022 was 3.6%, and George's life expectancy was 20 years, based upon IRS single life expectancy tables.

68 The income tax treatment described in the text assumes that Rev. Rul. 69-74, 1969-1 C.B. 43, still applies. This treatment would be radically different if the proposed regulations issued in 2006 apply. Under Prop. Reg. §1.72-6(e) and §1.1001-1(j), George would be subject to immediate recognition of gain on the value of the 3DP interests exchanged for a private annuity. The amount received for the property would be the current fair market value of the annuity contract, determined under §7520. Because the proposed regulations were never finalized, advisors debate whether they must be followed. Some proposed regulations do carry weight like final regulations, whereas others do not.

CHAPTER 5

69 When an accountant prepares compiled financial statements and a compilation report for a client, they are simply taking the information provided by management and compiling it into a format that satisfies basic disclosure rules under GAAP. A compiled financial statement provides no assurance to the reader that the information contained in the financial statements is accurate or complete. A review is one step up from a compilation. In a review, the accountant requires some analytical testing of the information provided by management. However, a review does not get into detailed procedures for verifying the accuracy or completeness of the information. In an audit, the accountant examines and tests the internal controls of the client to ensure the controls are designed to minimize the possibility of fraud or misrepresentation. In addition, the auditor performs many procedures not performed in either a compilation or review to check the accuracy and completeness of the financial information provided by management. Auditors often suggest adjustments to the financial statements to correct accounting disclosures. Because audits take so much more time than reviews or compilations and therefore cost so much more, sellers usually do not engage accountants to audit their financial statements unless the company is in a regulated industry where audited financials are required, or a lender or an investor requires annual audits.

70 "What Is Open Source?" Opensource.com, accessed December 15, 2022, https://opensource.com/resources/what-open-source.

71 "Reverse Scaled Success Fee," Divestopedia, last updated July 1, 2015, https://www.divestopedia.com/definition/6495/reverse-scaled-success-fee.

72 "M&A Deal Points Studies," American Bar Association, accessed December 15, 2022, https://www.americanbar.org/groups/business_law/committees/ma/deal_points/.

73 The Publisher's Editorial Staff, ed., *Black's Law Dictionary*, 5th ed. (St. Paul, MN: West Publishing Co., 1979).

74 A "materiality scrape" is a buyer-friendly provision often contained in an M&A purchase agreement (e.g., a stock purchase agreement, a merger agreement, or an asset purchase agreement) that effectively eliminates or disregards (i.e., "scrapes"), for specified purposes, materiality qualifiers that are present in a representation and warranty. [Daniel R. Avery, "The 'Materiality Scrape' Provision," What's Market? (blog), Goulston & Storrs, August 2020, https://www.goulstonstorrs.com/whats-market-blog/the-materiality-scrape-provision.]

NOTES

CHAPTER 6

75 Once again, I am adapting the values discussion and portions of this section with permission from Gino Wickman's *Traction*, available on Amazon.

INDEX

A

accountings, 45, 155–156
accounts payable, 129, 249
accounts receivable, 33, 52, 129, 204, 249
accrual-basis accounting, 101–102, 204, 249
acquisitions, xxxvii–xxxviii, 61–63, 84–85, 105–106
   See also M&As (mergers and acquisitions)
adjusted earnings, 110–113, 206
adjusted gross income, 128, 181
administrators, estate, 45
administrators, plan, 76
ADR (alternative dispute resolution), 279–280
AFR (applicable federal rate), 136, 172–173, 176
agreements
   buy-sell, 30–31
   in case studies, 294–296
   employment, 243–244, 269–274
   escrow, xl, 244, 267–269, 275, 279
   in exit process, 208–210
   indemnification, 201, 209
   lease, 221–222
   loan, 274
   noncompete, 237, 244, 264–265, 273–274
   nonsolicitation, 146, 245, 265
   operating, 265, 267, 274
   option cancellation, 274
   purchase, 224–225, 228, 242–243, 247–252, 252–258, 264, 275
   security, 274
   See also NDAs (nondisclosure agreements)
Allen, James: *The Founder's Mentality*, 3
alternative dispute resolution, 279–280
analysis by paralysis, 94
annuity payments, 169–170, 194, 196
antitrust laws, xiii, 81–82
applicable federal rate, 136, 172–173, 176
appraisal reports, 23, 96, 110, 169, 234

appraisers, xxx, 23, 76–77, 96–97, 106–110, 159, 162–163, 234
asset purchases, xxxii, 130, 132, 240, 243, 261
asset sales, 51–53, 129, 132–133, 277–278
assets, unrecorded, 205
Associated Press, 114
attorneys, xxxvii–xxxix, 47–49, 154, 208–210, 227–228, 247–248
auction process, xvii, xxxviii–xxxix, 232–233, 236–237, 246, 262, 291–293
authorization, business, 203–204

B

baby boomers, 6, 17
back seller financing, 66
bank accounts, joint, 44–45, 49–50
Bankers Healthcare Group, xiii
Becker, John, 143
beneficiaries, 10, 11–12, 47–48, 156, 158, 168, 183–184
benefits, work, 149–153, 201–202, 214–215, 253–254, 278
Berke, Kai-Leé, 120
Biden, Joe, 93
Bloomberg State Tax Portfolio 1240, 134–135
boards of advisors, 11–12, 14, 121
boards of directors, xvi, xxvi, 8–13, 14, 17, 50–51, 103, 121, 200–202, 272
boards of managers, 8–13, 48–49, 50–51, 103
Bob (George's lawyer), 285–288
bonuses
  change-in-control, xxxiv, 146–147, 152, 194–195, 244
  equity, xxvi, 50
  performance, 37–38, 48, 149, 152
  retention, 148–149, 152–153, 194–195, 244
"bottom fishers," 122, 126

branding, 100–101
brokers, 263
  See also business brokers
The Bucket List (movie), and bucket lists, 301
Buffett, Warren, 114
business brokers, xxxvii–xxxix, 33, 54, 96, 161, 229, 231–233, 235, 246–247
business judgment, 281–282
Business Success(ion) plan, *8*, 70
  about, 15–18
  in case studies, 39, 48–49, 285–296
  children and, 70–72
  cycles in, 6
  design of, 7–8
  Free Fall Framework in, 32–34
  impediments to, 141–142
  Legacy Framework in, 24–31
  Rocket Ship Framework in, 18–24
  types of, 34–36
business worth, xxix–xxxi, *88*
  to others, external, 104–117
  to others in owner space, 95–104, 116
  to owner, 89–95
buyer claims, 278–279
buyers, 52–53, 144
  See also family offices, as buyers; PE (private equity) firms: as buyers; strategic buyers

C

C corporations, 74–75, 129–130, 132–133, 191, 212, 223, 277
Capgemini, 60
capital gain, 52, 105–106, 127, 129–132, 136–137, 176–177, 182, 212
Carter Chambers (fictional character), 301
cash flow, xxvii, xxviii, xxx–xxxi, 24–25, 63, 91–92, 106–110, *107*, 114–115, 116–117

INDEX

cash-basis accounting, 101–102, 204, 250
cash-only sales, 127–133
Castro, Bobby, xiii, 17–18
Castro, Eric, xiii–xiv
cause, in employment termination, 145, 148–149, 244, 266, 269–272, 295
certified financial planners, xxix, 304
certified public accountants
　See CPAs (certified public accountants)
Certified Valuation Analysts, 96
CFOs (chief financial officers), 26–27
CFPs (certified financial planners), xxix, 304
charisma, 65–66, 67, 69, 70, 142
charitable planning, 179–186
charitable remainder trusts
　See CRATs (charitable remainder annuity trusts); CRTs (charitable remainder trusts); CRUTs (charitable remainder unitrusts); FLIP-CRUT (flip charitable remainder unitrust)
chief financial officers, 26–27
chiefs of operations, 27
Chris Long Foundation, 304–305
closing, 146, 150–151, 239–244, 251–252
collaboration, of exit team, 234–235
communication, contingency, 236
companies, analysis of, 108–109
companies, publicly traded, 75, 78, 165
compensation, for services, 10, 12
compensation income, 213
Congress, 164, 187
Consumer Electronics Association, 3
A Contract to Unite America (Simon), 308
contracts, xxxvi, 175, 229, 242, 280, 281–282
COO (chiefs of operations), 27
cost of debt, 63, 107

covenants, 264–267, 280–281
COVID-19 pandemic, 58, 81–82, 93, 123, 144
CPAs (certified public accountants), xxxvii–xxxviii, 9, 47, 90, 121, 228
CRATs (charitable remainder annuity trusts), 183, 184–185
CRTs (charitable remainder trusts), 180–186, *180*
CRUTs (charitable remainder unitrusts), 183–185
customers, 100, 223–224

D

Day, Doris, 2
DealRoom, 283
Dean, Matthew, 89
death, 44–51, 67
debt, in financing, 62–63
Department of Justice, 81
Department of State, xvi
depreciation, 52, 102, 129, 136
derivatives, 185
Devost, Matt, 126
disclosure and leaks, 236
disclosure schedules, 256–257
discounts, 106–108, *107*, 165
DLOM (discount for lack of marketability), 165
DOJ (Department of Justice), 81
dot-com bust (2000s), 123
double-Lehman formula, 230–231
Drive (Pink), 99
Du Bois, W.E.B., 299
due diligence, xxxv
　in business worth, 93
　on buyers, 83
　in case studies, 293–295
　employees and, 121–122, 150–151
　in exit process, 232, 241–242, 244–245, 246–247, 256, 264
　forms for, 103

347

due diligence *(continued)*
  preparation for, 200–201, 210, 219–220, 226
  in SPACs, 79

E
earnings before interest, taxes, depreciation, and amortization
  See EBITDA (earnings before interest, taxes, depreciation, and amortization)
earnouts, xxxiii, 115–116, 137–141, 143, 148, 240, 279–282, 284, 293
EBITDA (earnings before interest, taxes, depreciation, and amortization), xxxi, xxxiii, 109, 111–114, 117, 140, 150, 163, 206, 280
economic fluctuations, 6, 122–126
Economist, 124–125
EDGAR filings, 147
Edson, Ben, 1
Edward Cole (fictional character), 301
Eisner, David, 51
Employee Retirement Income Security Act of 1974
  See ERISA (Employee Retirement Income Security Act of 1974)
employee stock ownership plans, xxviii, 72–77, 85, 234
employees, xxxiv–xxxv
  benefits for, 22–23
  continuing, 13, 29–31, 38, 282, 312
  contractors compared with, 214–216
  in exit process, 194–195, 222–223, 243–244, 257, 269–273, 288
  key employees, 48, 106, 146–147, 269
  local, 99
  records about, 102–103
  during sales negotiations, 121–122, 143–153
  trust and, 25–27

End Game Framework
  See Free Fall Framework
engagement letters, xvii, 161, 286–287
environmental issues, in diligence preparation, 222
EOS (Entrepreneurial Operating System), xxiv, 15, 20–21, 36
equity
  cost of, 107–108
  employee-held, 145
  incentives based on, 22–23
  offers of, 97
  proof of ownership of, 205, 206–208
  rollover, xxvii, 53, 57–59, 194–196, 241, 265–267, 277
  stock as, 22, 103, 213
equity sales
  See M&As (mergers and acquisitions)
ERISA (Employee Retirement Income Security Act of 1974), 76, 210
ESOPs (employee stock ownership plans), xxviii, 72–77, 85, 234
estate planning, xxiv, 44–49, 154–158, *155*, 169–170, 228
estate planning, advanced, xxxvi
  business appraisers for, 234
  in Business Success(ion) plan, 22–23
  timing of, 160–162
  transfer amount of, 166–169
  valuation gaps in, 162–165
exclusivity period, 244–245
executors, 34, 154, 155–156
exit plan
  about, xxiii–xxv, 4–6
  long-term, 7, 8, 13, 15–17
  short-term, 15–16, 17, 35
exit process
  actions needed for, 276–279, 282–284
  agreements for, 295–296
  auction in, 291–293
  due diligence for, 294–295
  overview, 297

INDEX

post-closing follow-up, 296
potential problems, 279–282
preparation for, 285–291
exit strategies
  case studies, 44–49, 84
  employees as buyers, 72–77
  family as buyers, 62–71
  outsiders as buyers, 51–62, 77–84

F

F reorganization, 53
Faber, Peter, 134–135
families, in exit strategies
  advanced estate planning for, 158–169
  basic estate planning for, 154–158
  case studies, 191–197
  charitable planning for, 179–186
  holding companies for, 186–189
  overview, 197
  various plans for, 169–179, 189–191
family, in post-exit life, 305
family foundations, 182
family holding companies, xxxv, 186–189
family limited partnerships, 186, 187
Family Office Exchange, 61
family offices, as buyers, 52, 60–62
family-owned businesses, 6, 13–14, 17, 66–72
Federal Trade Commission, 81–82
fiduciaries, 11–12, 47
financial planners, xxix, xxxviii, 21–22, 90, 235, 304
financial statements, xxxviii, 102, 108, 204–206, 211–218, 225–226, 228, 289–291, 294
Fishbone, 104
FLIP-CRUT (flip charitable remainder unitrust), 184–185
FLPs (family limited partnerships), 186, 187

footnote disclosures, xxxvii, 102, 205–206
forecasts, in determining value, 108
forms
  for employment authorization, 102
  for publicly traded companies, 78
  for taxes, 102–103, 159, 212–213
foundations, 303–305
founders, xvi, 2–3, 31, 59, 69–70, 141–142, 146–147, 160, 162, 163
The Founder's Mentality (Zook and Allen), 3
401(k) plans, 151
frameworks, xxiii–xxiv, 17–18, 34–36
  See also Free Fall Framework; Legacy Framework; Rocket Ship Framework
fraud, 257–258, 259–260
Free Fall Framework, xxiv, 18, 32–34, 35, 36
Freeman, Morgan, 301
FTC (Federal Trade Commission), 81–82

G

GAAP (generally accepted accounting principles), xxvii, 101–102, 204–206, 249–250
generation-skipping transfer tax, 164, 169
George (entrepreneur)
  about, 37–40
  adjusted earnings and, 110–113
  in Business Success(ion) plan, 285–296
  business worth and, 91–92
  cash-only sales and, 132–133
  earnouts and, 139–140
  estate planning and, 44–49
  exit strategy and, 191–197
  needs of, 84
  post-exit life of, 311–312
  during recessions, 124–125
  state taxes and, 134

gift tax appraisals, 110
goals, 310–311
good reason, in employment
    termination, 141, 145, 148–149,
    244, 266, 269–270, 272–273, 295
goodwill, xxx, 52, 104–106, 129, 240
GRATs (grantor retained annuity
    trusts), xxxv, 169–170, *170*, 190
Great Recession (2007-2009), 123
GST tax changes, 170
Gust, Gerard: *Secrets to Succession*, 69

H

Hannah (entrepreneur)
    about, 37–40
    adjusted earnings and, 111
    in Business Success(ion) plan,
        285–286, 288, 289, 290–292,
        293–294, 296
    estate planning and, 46–48
    exit strategy and, 191–192, 194–195
    during recessions, 124–125
Hart–Scott–Rodino Antitrust
    Improvements Act (1976), 81–82
holdbacks, 278–279
House of Representatives, 170
HR (human resources), 98, 99, 102–103,
    152, 290–291
HSR (Hart–Scott–Rodino Antitrust
    Improvements Act of 1976),
    81–82
human resources
    See HR (human resources)
hyperinflation, 125

I

Ian (George's son), 38, 191–197
IDGT (Intentionally Defective
    Grantor Trusts), xxxv, 171–174,
    174, 190, 197
implied covenants of good faith and
    fair dealing, 280–281

income, 24, 90, 128, 136, 176, 179, 181,
    184–185, 205, 212–213
    See also ordinary income
incumbent framework
    See Legacy Framework
indemnification baskets, 258–259
indemnification caps, 257–258
indemnification limitations, xl, 275
indemnification obligations, 257
indications of interest
    See IOIs (indications of interest)
inflation, 94, 184–185
initial public offerings, xxviii–xxix,
    77–80, 86
insurance broker, 263
insurgent framework
    See Rocket Ship Framework
intellectual property, 114, 219–221
Intentionally Defective Grantor Trusts
    See IDGT (Intentionally Defective
    Grantor Trusts)
interest income, 136, 176
internal processes and systems, 98–99
Internal Revenue Code
    See IRC (Internal Revenue Code)
Internal Revenue Service
    See IRS (Internal Revenue Service)
internet businesses, 113–115
Internet Tax Freedom Act, 217
investment bankers, xvi–xvii, 162,
    229–233
IOIs (indications of interest), xxxix,
    161, 229, 237–238
IP (intellectual property), 114, 219–221
IPOs (initial public offerings), xxviii–
    xxix, 77–80, 86
IRC (Internal Revenue Code), 53, 72,
    97, 129, 187, 213–214
IRS (Internal Revenue Service)
    cash sales and, 136
    ESOPs and, xxviii, 85
    estate taxes and, 159

INDEX

payroll taxes and, 215–216
private annuities and, 178
tax rulings of, 129, 213, 223
transfer timing and, 160–162
trusts and, 169, 173, 176, 179, 181, 185
valuation discounts and, 164
ITFA (Internet Tax Freedom Act), 217

J

Jason Stevens (fictional character), 300–301
Jessica (George's daughter), 38, 191–197
Johnson, Larry, 153
JTWROS (joint tenants with right of survivorship), 49–50
junk bonds, 63

K

Kipps, Bob, 95
Kiyosaki, Robert, 119

L

lawsuits
 See legal matters
LBOs (leveraged buyouts), 62–63
Legacy Framework, xxiv, 18, 24–31, 34–35, 36
legal matters, 145, 199–204, 208–211, 217–219, 225–226, 279–280
Lehman formula, 230–231
letters of intent
 See LOIs (letters of intent)
leveraged buyouts, 62–63
leveraged ESOPs, 72–74
liabilities, unrecorded, 205
life insurance, 30–31, 71–72, 186
Lifestyle
 See Legacy Framework
limited liability companies
 See LLCs (limited liability companies)
liquidation, 33, 130

litigation
 See legal matters
living probate, 46, 157
LLCs (limited liability companies), *187*
 benefits of, 31
 boards in, 11
 in case studies, 38, 192, 197
 in exit process, 202–203, 212–214, 221–222, 223
 family holding companies as, 186–189
 in sales, 52, 127
lockups, of shares, 78
LOIs (letters of intent), xxxix
 in advanced estate planning, 161–162
 advisors on, 228, 229, 233
 binding provisions of, 244–247
 in case studies, 292–293
 nonbinding provisions of, 238–244, 247
 purchase price and, 249–250
Long, Chris, 304–305

M

M&As (mergers and acquisitions), xxvi, *199*, *200*
 about, 51–53
 attorneys in, 227–228
 buyer types in, 54–62
 caution in, 80–86
 cycles of, 6, 113
management buyouts, xxvii, 62–66, 85
management succession plans
 See MSPs (management succession plans)
management teams, 71, 98
Manchin, Joe, 93
marketing, 97, 100
MBOs (management buyouts), xxvii, 62–66, 85
McKinsey 7S, 104

351

membership interests, xxviii, 38, 45–47, 129, 192, 194–196, 202, 206–207
mergers, 261
  See also M&As (mergers and acquisitions)
mergers and acquisitions
  See M&As (mergers and acquisitions)
MSPs (management succession plans), xxiv–xxv, xxvi, 8
  about, 7–15
  in family-owned businesses, 67–68, 71
  frameworks for, 35–36
  in Free Fall Framework, 32, 34
  in Legacy Framework, 26–29
  in Rocket Ship Framework, 23–24
  trusts and, 48–49, 50–51, 157
  variations in, 16–17
  multiples of earnings, xxxi, 59, 112–114, 117

N

NDAs (nondisclosure agreements), 120–122, 146, 209, 219, 224, 235–237, 245, 246, 274, 291
needs, 90–91, 94
net income CRUT, 184
net investment income tax, 128
net promoter score, 100
net-income-with-makeup CRUT, 184–185
Nicholson, Jack, 301
NI-CRUT (net income CRUT), 184
NIIT (net investment income tax), 128
NIM-CRUT (net-income-with-makeup CRUT), 184–185
ninja innovation, 2–3, 18–19
Ninja Innovation (Shapiro), 3
nondisclosure agreements
  See NDAs (nondisclosure agreements)
nonfundamental representations and warranties, 253–254, 277

NPS (net promoter score), 100
NVFS (Northern Virginia Family Service), 304

O

"open source" concept, 219–221
ordinary income, 52–53, 105, 128–131
ownership matters, in diligence preparation, 206–208, 219–222

P

Parker, Lewis, 301–302
partnerships, 180, 212–213
passive income, 212
PE (private equity) firms
  about, 55–56
  as buyers, xvii, xxvi, 52, 55–59, 120, 129, 141
  in exit process, 241, 246
  family offices compared to, 61–62
perpetuities, 189
personal relationships, in diligence preparation, 222–226
personal representatives
  See executors
Pike, Albert, 306
Pink, Daniel: *Drive*, 99
plan, post-exit, 306–313
power of attorney, 47–48, 154, 157
premerger notifications, 81–82
private annuities, 32, 178–179
private equity firms
  See PE (private equity) firms
probate, 28, 45–46, 47, 154–157
profits, 52, 97, 100, 125, 141
promissory notes, 30, 66, 73–74, 135–137, 171–173, 176, 239–240, 250–251, 274, 284
provisions, xxxix
  binding, 244–247
  in business agreements, 209
  nexus, 218

INDEX

nonbinding, 239–244
noncompete, 209
nondisclosure, 12
self-cancellation, 174–175
public company data, 109
publicly traded companies
  See companies, publicly traded
purchase price, 239, 249–252
purpose, in post-exit life, 299–306
PwC, 6

Q
Quality of Earnings assessments, 206, 226, 241–242, 297
QuickBooks, 101

R
R&W insurance, 260–264
Randy (investment banker), 286–294
real estate, 187–188, 221–222
recapitalizations, 191–192
recessions, 123–125
Red Stevens (fictional character), 300–301
registered investment advisors
  See RIAs (registered investment advisors)
reorganization transactions, 80–86
reports, quarterly, 78
Representation and Warranty insurance, 260–264
representations and warranties, xl, 247–248, 252–258, 260–261, 262, 267, 275, 292–293, 295
residency and domicile, xxxii–xxxiii, 133–135, 143
revenues, 52, 100, 105, 113–115, 138–141, 204–205, 256, 281
RIA representations and warranties, 254–256
RIAs (registered investment advisors), 61, 65, 211, 227, 255

Rocket Ship Framework, xxiv, 18–24, 34, 36, 86
rule against perpetuities, 189

S
S corporations, 52–53, 74–75, 103, 131, 137, 180, 212
SaaS (software as a service) companies, 113–114
salaries, 37–38, 149–150
sale of business, 17, 24–25, 29, 30
  See also M&As (mergers and acquisitions)
savings and loan crisis (1980s–1990s), 123
SCINs (self-canceling installment notes), 32, 173–176
SDE (seller discretionary earnings), 113–114
SEC (Securities and Exchange Commission), 77–78, 147
Secrets to Succession (Gust), 69
Section 409A, 97, 213–214
Securities and Exchange Commission, 77–78, 147
security interest, 64, 250–251
self-canceling installment notes, 32, 173–176
sell vs. hold, 91–92
seller discretionary earnings, 113–114
Senate, 93, 170
severance payments, 149–150, 269–270, 275, 295
Shapiro, Gary: *Ninja Innovation*, 3
shareholders, 11–12, 72–74, 103, 268–269
shockproof quality, 19
Simon, Neal: *A Contract to Unite America*, 308
Sinema, Kyrsten, 93
single-Lehman formula, 230
SLATs (spousal lifetime access trusts), xxxv, 166–167, 190, *190*

Smale, Thomas, 113
Small Business Administration, xv
small business set-asides, xvii
SMART goals, 310–311
software as a service companies, 113–114
South Dakota v. Wayfair, Inc., 217–218
SPACs (Special Purpose Acquisition Companies), xxviii–xxix, 78–80, 86
spousal lifetime access trust, 166–167, 190, *190*
stagflation, 123
Stall-Out framework
   See Legacy Framework
stock, 22, 77–78, 81–86, 103, 127, 180–181, 191, 213, 268–269
   See also ESOPs (employee stock ownership plans)
stock sales, 52–53, 128–132
   See also M&As (mergers and acquisitions)
Stovall, Jim, 303
   The Ultimate Gift, 300
strategic buyers, 52, 53–55
strengths, weaknesses, opportunities, and threats, 103–104
structure, of transaction, xxxii, 127, 128–130, 240–241
succession plan, business
   See Business Success(ion) plan
suppliers, xxxvi, 101, 224–225
Swindoll, Charles R., 199
SWOT (strengths, weaknesses, opportunities, and threats), 103–104

T

Tax Court, 169
Tax Cuts and Jobs Act (2017), 131
taxes
   in C corporation sales, 130
   in diligence preparation, 211–218
   estate, 22, 32–33, 45, 159–160, 169
   fluctuations in, 93–94
   gift, 45, 50, 160, 234
   income, 52–53, 106, 127, 180–182, 212–214
   ordinary income, 52–53, 75–76, 106, 128–131, 193–194
   payroll, 214–216
   promissory notes and, 135–137
   sales, 216–218
   state, 131–135
   on stock, 81
   use, 216–218
TCJA (Tax Cuts and Jobs Act of 2017), 131
team, for exit process, 227–235, *227*, 285–291
Ted Hamilton (fictional character), 300
termination, of employees, 145, 269–273
3DP (printing business)
   about, 37–40
   adjusted earnings for, 110–113
   in cash sale, 132–133
   earnouts and, 139–140
   estate planning for, 45–49
   owner exit from, 191–197
   post-exit, 311–312
   during recessions, 124–125
   in sell vs. hold decision, 91
   and state income tax, 134
   team handling sale, 285–296
Traction (Wickman), xxiv, 99
trade secrets, 114
transactions, xxvi–xxvii, xxxiv, xxxviii, 80–86, 158–164, 200–203, 228–237, 265, 276
transfers, of business, 110, 156–160, 162–164, 166–169, 171, 178–179, 185–188

INDEX

Treasury Department, 164, 187
Trump administration, 93, 164
trust protectors, 167–168, 171
trustees, xxv–xxvi
    for ESOPs, 74, 76–77, 234
    in estate planning, 156–158, 167–169
    for MSPs, 8–9, 10, 11–12
    successor, 46–49, 50
    types of, 158
trusts, 10, 11–12, 110, *157*, 167–169, 191–197
    See also CRATs (charitable remainder annuity trusts); CRTs (charitable remainder trusts); CRUTs (charitable remainder unitrusts); FLPs (family limited partnerships); GRATs (grantor retained annuity trusts); IDGT (Intentionally Defective Grantor Trusts); SLATs (spousal lifetime access trusts)
trusts, charitable, xxxv, 179
trusts, dynasty, 162, 164, 187–188, *187*, 189–190, *190*
trusts, irrevocable, 162, 163–164
trusts, non-grantor, 176–178
trusts, revocable, xxiv–xxvi, 8, 28, 34, 46–47, 50, 156–158

U

UBTI (unrelated business taxable income), 185
The Ultimate Gift (Stovall), 300
underwriters, 77–78, 263
the unexpected, xxiv–xxv, 2, 7–8, 23–24, 44, 125
unleveraged ESOPs, 72–74
unrelated business taxable income, 185
US Family Business Survey, 6
US Supreme Court, 217–218
US v. Cartwright, 89

V

valuation discounts, 164, 186–188
valuations, xxx
    IRS and, 161, 214
    methods of, 96–97, 106–112
    types of, 104–106, 234
    variables affecting, 113–117
value gaps, 4, 54, 97–104, 162–163
values, personal, 307
vendors, xxxvii, 224–225
veterans, xv
vision, post-exit, 306–311
volunteering, xli–xlii, 304, 306
"vulture" capitalists, 122

W

wants, and needs, xxix, 91, 95
Waterboys.org Initiative, 305
Wickman, Gino: *Traction*, xxiv, 99
Wong, Tien, 43
working capital, 226, 239, 249–250, 267, 293

Z

zeroed-out GRATs, 169–170
Zook, Chris: *The Founder's Mentality*, 3

Made in the USA
Monee, IL
21 July 2024